INTIMATE MEMORIES

By
Geoff Bowden

The Badger Press, Westbury, Wiltshire
2006

INTIMATE MEMORIES

THE HISTORY
OF
THE INTIMATE THEATRE
PALMERS GREEN

By
Geoff Bowden

The Badger Press, Westbury, Wiltshire
2006

Dedicated to the memory of
Sir John Clements and Ronald Kerr

Published in Westbury, Wiltshire by
The Badger Press

Copyright © 2006 Geoff Bowden

Typesetting and layout by David Reed

ISBN-10 0-9526076-3-8
ISBN-13 978-0-9526076-3-2

Printed and bound in Great Britain by Antony Rowe Ltd., Chippenham, Wiltshire.

ACKNOWLEDGEMENTS

I would like to thank the following for their invaluable help in my research:

Graham and Kate in the Local History and Archives Section of Enfield Libraries, Jeff in the Archives Section of the London Borough of Haringey, Richard Mangan of the Mander and Mitchenson Theatre Collection, the staff of the London Metropolitan Archives, the staff of the Theatre Museum Study Room, the staff of the BBC Written Archives Centre and the ITV production staff connected with the television series *The Last Detective*.

Esther Aspland, Michael Attenborough, Edna Baker, Muriel Barker, Simon Barry, Colin Bean, Mike Best, R. A. Bolitho, Phyllis Broome, Edna Buckmaster, Rita Burridge, Tony Burns, Fred Campbell, Betty Corbridge, Nicholas Courtney, Kevin Davies, Ken Davis, Stuart Delvin, Stanley Dicker, Charles and Fiona Dyer, Colin Fenn, Cyril Foley, David Forder, Elaine Garwood, Pamela Gatward, Michael Gibbon, Geoffrey Gillam, Ron Gray, Daphne Hanson, Michael Harding, John Hart Dyke, Owen Holder, Roy and Debbie Hudd, Cathy Huffer, Janet Iorns, Linda James, Michael Knowles, George La Grue, Anna Lethieullier, Irene Lewis, K.A. Lock, David McGillivray, Beryl Marlow, Avis Milner, Patrick Newley, Dave Osborne, David Paramor, Leslie Parnell, Nicholas Parsons, Kay Patrick, Crompton Payne, John Peach, Sally Pearson, Gilda and Jimmy Perry, Marianne Price, Richard Purver, John Rouhan, Keith Salberg, David Sculpher, Gerald Smith, Marianne Stone, Ian Stretch, Ellen Trigger, Annie Tucker, Joy Turrell, Richard Wheel, Leonard White, June Whitfield, Stephen Wischhusen, Aubrey Woods.

Thanks also to the BBC Written Archives Department for allowing me to quote from various BBC memos and correspondence.

I would also like to express my gratitude to the Society For Theatre Research for offering me the Kathleen Barker Award, which helped with research costs. Also Data Connection and Father Roger Taylor of St. Monica's Church for financial help with publishing costs.

My grateful thanks to Nick Charlesworth at Badger Press for all his help and advice in producing this book and finally my heart-felt thanks to David Reed who is responsible for the layout of this volume and without whom this book would never have seen the light of day!

**Aerial view of The Intimate Theatre 9th May 1945
Photographed from St. John's Church tower, Bourne Hill N13**

**The Intimate Theatre in its later days
when amateur productions were the main attraction**

CONTENTS

PREFACE

When I first moved to Palmers Green in 1975 I was delighted that my flat was just a few minutes walk away from an actual theatre – the Intimate. Being interested in amateur operatics I quickly joined a local musical theatre company who, at that time, staged their productions at the Intimate. For the next twelve years, until the company moved to pastures new, I appeared in many shows at the theatre and attended even more.

Leaping forward to just a few years ago, my mind suddenly returned to those Intimate years and I thought it would be interesting to visit the local library and read about the venue's history. Imagine my surprise (or rather shock) when I discovered that hardly anything had been written about the building apart from the odd paragraph or two in various local history books. I really thought the dear old Intimate deserved better than that so I decided there and then to research its history.

What an enjoyable few years it has been piecing together the various strands of the theatre's past. Many names have helped me along the way and these I gratefully acknowledge on another page.

I do hope you will enjoy reading about Palmers Green's own little playhouse as much as I have enjoyed writing it.

Geoff Bowden

THE INTIMATE THEATRE 2006

The Intimate Theatre, or St. Monica's Church Hall as it was originally known, lies next to St. Monica's Roman Catholic Church on Green Lanes in Palmers Green. Large gates lead patrons through from the thoroughfare to a small car park before arriving at the front doors

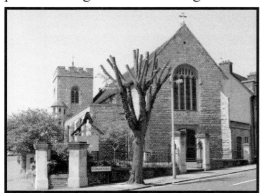

St. Monica's Church, Green Lanes

of the theatre itself. A large billboard used to stand just to the right inside the gates announcing that week's attraction.

Just above the doors a new sign announces that this is the Intimate Theatre and a little way above that on the wall is a motto in Latin *Deus Per Omnia (God Is With Everyone).*

On entering the theatre one finds the box office on the left hand side, slightly enlarged since those early days whilst the right hand wall is where the photographs of the artists would have been displayed. Ahead lies the entrance to the stalls and to the right a staircase leads to the circle. The old cloakroom, by the side of the stairs has now become part of the gentlemen's toilet.

The main body of the auditorium has benefited recently from a new coat of paint with a vivid red ceiling and blue walls and now has removable seating in the stalls area as the venue these days is used for church events of all types plus occasional theatre performances. The circle, however, still possesses the original tip-up style of seating, behind which the

The newly decorated circle

lighting and sound room can be found. On the stairs and around the walls can still be found the old gas mantles, which are still used today.

To the left of the stage, looking from the audience, is a door leading through to two dressing rooms. One of these would have been used as the manager's office back in the early days of the theatre. To the right of the stage is a pass door leading to backstage and right of that is the entrance to the café/bar area with a small kitchen beyond. Above the stage is a crest with the inscription *Ne Cede Malis (Yield Not To Adversity)*.

The Intimate Theatre stage

The stage itself is small, being 27 feet wide and 14 feet high with practically no wing space. Actors have to climb a few steps to reach the stage area and they are then virtually in view

One of the dressing rooms

The back of the theatre, showing the stage door and the 'rat-run'

The 'rat-run'

The motto situated above the stage

of the audience. Until a few years ago, to cross backstage from stage left to stage right involved going outside the theatre via the stage door, walking through a kind of makeshift tunnel and then entering the theatre by another door located on stage right. In the last few years actors no longer have to take their chance with the weather as the two back doors have been extended so that the 'rat run', as it was affectionately called, is now completely under cover within the theatre building.

A dressing room can be found on stage left just by the stage door and nearby stairs lead down to further dressing rooms in the basement. When it was a thriving venue in the 1930s and 1940s the theatre statistics listed four dressing rooms plus one chorus room providing accommodation for a grand total of eighteen actors overall. Slight improvements over the years mean that more space is now available and certainly when the amateur operatic societies were using the theatre in later years it was not unusual to find forty or more artists on stage, albeit looking slightly squashed! The scene store and workshop so necessary for weekly rep is also located in the basement underneath the stage itself.

Overall the theatre looks little different to how it would have looked when John Clements first opened it as a playhouse back in 1935 and still retains that elusive atmosphere so lacking in many modern theatre structures.

Author, Geoff Bowden at the theatre entrance - June 2006

4

JOHN CLEMENTS
AND THE EARLY YEARS

Local playgoers and theatre lovers had cause to celebrate when they read the *Palmers Green and Southgate Gazette* for 6th December 1935, for there on page 9 was the announcement:

Repertory Theatre For Southgate
Ambitious Scheme at St. Monica's Hall

Plans to establish a permanent repertory theatre in Southgate are now almost completed.

The Gazette is able to announce that after Christmas, St. Monica's Hall, attached to St. Monica's Church, Palmers Green, will become the headquarters of a new group of West End players to be known as The Intimate Theatre Company.

Debut Soon

John Clements

The new company will make its debut on Boxing Night when the well-known play *The Dover Road* by A. A. Milne will be presented. Further performances will take place every night, with the exception of New Year's Eve, and it is hoped to establish the theatre as a permanent concern on the 13th or 14th of January.

Behind this ambitious scheme, which promises to give a district, mainly dependent upon cinemas for its entertainment, a progressive theatre, is a young man, Mr. John Clements. Mr. Clements, who will be the producer, has successfully appeared many times on the West End stage, and has also done a good deal of film work.

Until then, residents in search of entertainment could see the latest film releases at such venues as the Queen's Hall Cinema in Green Lanes, which had opened in 1912, or the Palmadium, also in Green Lanes, which had been a cinema since 1921. If 'live' entertainment was their fancy then a short tram ride from Palmers Green would take them to the Wood Green Empire or the Finsbury Park Empire, but both of these theatres were basically variety houses; there was no local theatre offering more challenging fare. The arrival of the

Intimate Theatre looked set to change all that as it promised quality drama on their doorstep. St. Monica's Roman Catholic Church, on Green Lanes in Palmers Green, was built in 1914 and the adjoining Church Hall, built at a cost of between £20,000 and £25,000, was opened by Cardinal Bourne in December 1931. The hall was fitted with modern equipment for the presentation of stage plays by local amateur drama groups, and also possessed a sprung floor for dancing for the various community activities it housed. The building also had a small balcony fitted with permanent seats.

In 1935 John Clements was an ambitious 25-year-old actor with many West End appearances and film roles to his credit. He had made his first stage appearance at the Lyric, Hammersmith in 1930 as *Lucas Carey* in *Out Of The Blue,* followed by roles in *She Stoops To Conquer* and *The Beaux Stratagem* and had subsequently played in Sir Ben Greet's Shakespearian productions. Stardom came in record time and soon he was in demand for film roles. Gaumont British Film Studios approached him to play in *The Divine Spark* and then Alexander Korda asked him to appear in *The Ticket Of Leave* and H. G. Wells' *Things To Come.* Clements, however, was missing his stage work and he had a long-held dream of running his own theatre. St. Monica's Hall seemed to this young actor an ideal venue to make his dream a reality. He quickly entered into negotiations with the Church authorities to lease the building, persuading them, according to the magazine *Theatre World* (January 1939), ' that "theatre" and "sin" did not necessarily go hand in hand and that really Church and Stage were closely allied' and on 26th December 1935 St Monica's Hall became the Intimate Theatre.

In an interview with the *Palmers Green and Southgate Gazette* for 6th December 1935, John Clements outlined his plans to convert the hall into an up-to-date cosy theatre on intimate lines with better seating accommodation on the ground floor and various other alterations. He also outlined his plans for a theatre supporters' club, which, for a small annual subscription, would enable members to buy their tickets cheaply.

Preparations for any new venture rarely run smoothly and the transformation of this venue was no exception. Fog delayed the delivery of the new tip-up seating for the stalls on Christmas Eve and when they finally arrived at the Intimate the workmen who were to have installed them refused to carry out the task as it was now Christmas Day! Fearing that the Boxing Day opening was in jeopardy, the actors, in true theatrical fashion, rolled up their sleeves and fitted the screwed down wooden seating themselves!

On Boxing Night 1935 the Intimate Theatre opened its doors for the first performance by the Intimate Theatre Company. The opening production was A. A. Milne's play *The Dover Road* and it ran until Saturday 4th January 1936 with evening performances commencing at 8 p.m. and a Saturday matinee at 2.30 p.m. John Clements later recalled (in the programme for *Heroes Don't Care*, January 1937) that he and several others had 'worked straight through from early on Christmas morning until the curtain rose on Boxing Night, with no sleep at all, putting up seats, scenery, curtains, lights and dress rehearsing in between times – everybody fighting time for all they were worth to get the curtain up for the opening performance – and doing it to a half-empty house!'

THE INTIMATE THEATRE
Lessees—THE INTIMATE THEATRE Co,. Ltd.

GREEN LANES, N. 13.

The Intimate Theatre Company

PRESENTS

'THE DOVER ROAD'

A COMEDY IN THREE ACTS
BY
A. A. MILNE

THE PLAYERS :

(In the order of their appearance)

Dominic	...	...	KEITH PYOTT
The Maidservant	...	..	DORIN MOUNTFORD
The Manservant	...		PETER SLADE
Leonard	...	...	MAURICE GRIFFITH
Anne	...	...	SHEILA RAYNOR
Mr. Latimer	...	...	JOHN CLEMENTS
Eustasia	...	...	MEGAN LATIMER
Nicholas	...	...	ERIC PHILLIPS

Produced by   · -   JOHN CLEMENTS

The Action of the Play takes place in the Reception Room of Mr. Latimer's House, a little way off the Dover Road

Act 1. Evening

Act 2 Next Morning

Act 3. Some days later. Evening

Setting by   -   -   MAURICE GRIFFITH
Electric Equipment by The North Met, Co.
Champagne used in Act 1 is Bulmer's famous " Pomagne,'
Cider de Luxe.   Wigs by Gustave.
Cigarettes by Abdulla.
Programme Cover designed by George Grayston.

Managing Director	.....	... JOHN CLEMENTS
General Manager		.... CARL F, WRIGHT
Business Manager	....	..... ADRIAN THOMAS
Secretary	..	.... DOREEN DIXON
Stage Manager	...	.-. ARTHUR R. WEBB
Assistant Stage Managers	...	⌈DORIN MOUNTFORD ⌊PETER SLADE
Electrician	.....	... A. STRETCH

Box Office open Daily 10.30 a.m. to 9.0 p.m.

Phone : PAL. 3798.

The Dover Road by A. A. Milne
which was the Intimate Theatre's opening production
Thursday 26th December 1935

The Times on 28th December 1935 reported that 'a promising start' had been made by John Clements and his company and pointed out that 'the venture is the first attempt made in North London to bring the theatre within easy reach of a population which in recent years has grown enormously.'

The local *Palmers Green and Southgate Gazette* (27th December 1935) carried the headline

The Intimate Theatre Bows To Palmers Green With Excellent Performance of *The Dover Road*

The reviewer was much taken by the new look St. Monica's Hall:

It will not be difficult for us to get accustomed to the new name for, as the audience on Boxing Night saw, the building is now essentially a theatre – and a nice cosy theatre at that. Chief among the alterations, which have been made since the Company took possession, has been the putting down of comfortable tip-up chairs on the ground floor. Altogether a very successful attempt has been made to achieve a friendly intimate atmosphere and it is now obvious that the Company's choice of venue is a really excellent one.

7

The local critic was also full of praise for the actual production:

> The Intimate Theatre Company has come as a first-class Christmas present
> to local enthusiasts for the drama and I hope it is a gift which will be fully
> appreciated.

> Of one thing I am certain. If the company maintain the standard of performance
> they showed on Boxing Night we shall have only that black-hearted demon
> Public Apathy to blame if the near future does not see the company firmly
> established....the production of John Clements was smooth and facile...the
> acting maintained a high standard throughout, the whole show being put over
> with stimulating confidence and directness. The biggest bouquet goes to Mr.
> Clements who gained a considerable personal success in the delightful part of
> Mr. Latimer.

'THE DOVER ROAD'

will be played every Evening at 8 o'clock
from December 26th until January 4th.
Matinee Saturday, January 4th, at 2.30.
(No Performance on New Year's Eve).

The INTIMATE THEATRE COMPANY

begins its policy of a different
. . production every week. . .

On Monday, January 13th

with

'HAY FEVER'

by NOEL COWARD

Nightly at 8 o'clock.   Matinees Saturdays at 2.30.

Jan. 20th. - - 'THE GREEN PACK'
by EDGAR WALLACE
Jan. 27th. - - 'SIXTEEN'
by PHILLIP & AIMEE STUART

1936: Weekly rep. begins in Palmers Green

After this encouraging start there was a week's break before the company began their policy of staging a different play every week. On Monday 13th January 1936 the curtain went up on Noel Coward's *Hay Fever* and weekly rep suddenly became a reality in Palmers Green. Tickets were priced at 3/6, 2/6, 1/10 and 1/-. The box office was open from 10.30 a.m. until 9 p.m. and performances were nightly at 8 p.m (soon to change to 8.15 p.m.). with a Saturday matinee at 2.30 pm. From 1st February any seat could be purchased for the Saturday afternoon performance for 1/-. The theatre's seating capacity was 458. This was divided as such:

Stalls: 268
Pit Stalls: 90
Dress Circle: 100

The theatre was also licensed for 45 standing patrons in the stalls.

That the Company wished to encourage a wider audience than just Palmers Green and surrounding areas was made quite clear in the programme for *Hay Fever* when it stated: 'If you are coming from the West End the Piccadilly Line underground will bring you to Wood Green and from there a 29 tram or 238 bus passes the door of the theatre.'

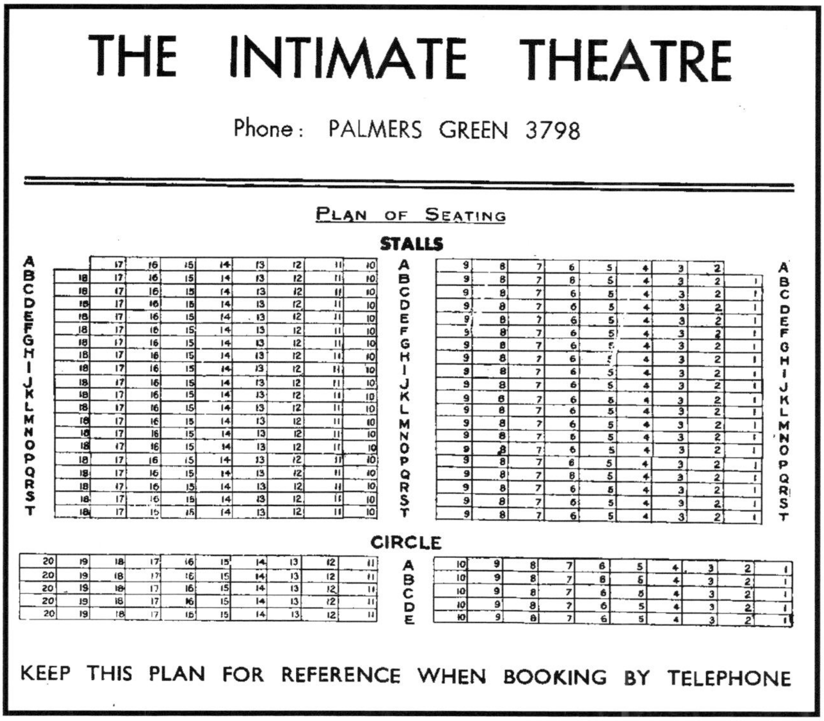

THE INTIMATE THEATRE

Phone: PALMERS GREEN 3798

PLAN OF SEATING

STALLS

CIRCLE

KEEP THIS PLAN FOR REFERENCE WHEN BOOKING BY TELEPHONE

Theatre seating plan from the 1930's

The new enterprise found a staunch supporter in the local weekly *Palmers Green and Southgate Gazette,* whose leader column on Friday 17th January 1936 was devoted to the Intimate Theatre:

What We Think
Our Own Intimate Theatre

Southgate Borough has wakened up suddenly to find itself the possessor of a first-rate professional repertory theatre.

The question is not without its humorous aspect, for, without wishing to be unkind to Southgate, it must be pointed out that this theatre has come along without anyone in the district having to lift a finger to launch it.

Had it not been for a certain young actor by name John Clements, who lives far away from here, it seems certain that Southgate would still be without a theatre – and not particularly troubled about the matter, either.

We have frequently heard people express surprise that a Borough of 60,000 odd people should be entirely dependent upon the movies for its evening entertainment, but there is no record of any real attempt on the part of any enthusiast or band of enthusiasts to put matters right, apart from the one-night-weekly visits of the Greater London Players.

Even the amateurs have not in the past made much of a brave show. There are exceptional cases, as always, but there is good reason to think that the average dramatic society in this district is really much more concerned with giving its members a chance to appear on the stage than with making any useful contribution to dramatic art.

Most of them rely purely upon friends to support – they are honest enough to admit that without these friends they could not carry on.

And now Southgate has its own repertory theatre and a cast of West End players – given them for absolutely nothing. If the Intimate Theatre succeeds, they will enjoy its amenities; if it fails – well, it won't be their headache.

May we therefore suggest that the most Southgate play-goers can do in these circumstances is to support the new venture and to try to further its interests. Many of them have wanted a theatre in Southgate, and now it has been presented to them they must do their share.

The Intimate Theatre does not ask for, and does not want, a lot of fulsome praise from the *Gazette* or any other newspaper. But it does ask for the support of many who read the *Gazette* and that is why we commend its cause to you. Don't just wait around to see if everything goes well; support the theatre from the beginning and give its players a fair chance to show what they can do.

No one wants to disparage the cinema, which is very well represented in this district. The cinema serves its purpose – and, on the whole, serves it well – but at the same time we fail to see any reason why the theatre and the cinema should compete or squabble in such a district as Southgate, where there must be a large number of people who appreciate the essential difference between the two mediums of entertainment, and all sufficiently intelligent to appreciate the best of both.

The Intimate Theatre should not be considered as competition for the movies. Instead it should be realised that it offers a pleasant alternative for those whose desires are not completely satisfied by the screen.

To John Clements and his company of players, all praise is due. They have taken on a very big job, and we can only express the hope that their efforts will prove fruitful.

Elsewhere in that issue of the paper was the bold headline:

Theatrical History Made In Palmers Green
The Intimate Theatre Opens Its Doors
With Pleasant Presentation of
Hay Fever
Now It's Up To You!

North London theatrical history was made on Monday, when the Intimate Theatre, Green Lanes, Palmers Green, opened its doors for the first time as a permanent professional repertory theatre.

In future this theatre will present a different play each week soliciting your support – and your shillings and half-crowns – just as do the clutter of movie-houses upon which local entertainment seekers have been entirely dependent in the past.

Yes, it is a bold venture. Indeed, I doubt if anyone could safely predict at this stage what measure of success will be gained by the brave company of players who have launched our first living theatre.

Worthy Of Support

As usual, the question lies with the public – and everyone knows what a curious animal is the public.

They may pack the Intimate Theatre to the doors; they may put on their confounded, pig-headed apathy act – but most of them, I'm sure, will let a few loyal enthusiasts do all the hard work in establishing the theatre on a firm basis, and then go along and say 'How nice it is to have a real theatre.'

Monday was certainly a first night of considerable distinction. The audience – a fairly large one – started off in rather frigid mood, but the gay, inconsequential nonsense of Noel Coward's *Hay Fever,* put over by the players with real ability and spirit soon broke down the general reserve and by the time Act 2 arrived a good time was being had by all.

Of the company's first performance on Boxing Night I said – can I quote myself?- 'It struck a promising note for the future.'

Confident Note

So it did, and Monday's performance struck that same note once again, though this time it was louder and more confident. It showed clearly that here we are dealing with a company of players who know their job, collected under the banner of a producer who is determined to have only the best.

How can they possibly flop if only the public in this district will shake off its theatrical coma sufficiently to book a seat for the next Intimate Theatre show?

The play itself was given a glowing review with John Clements again singled out for praise, both for his 'snappy, well-maintained production' and for his portrayal of *Simon Bliss* as 'a pleasantly uncouth and sometimes ardent young man…His love-making scene with *Myra Arundel* (played by Dorin Mountford) was one of the funniest in the play.' The critic was also much taken with Gladys Spencer in the leading role of *Judith Bliss:* 'I have seen *Hay Fever* several times but have never seen a more satisfying, deliciously funny Judith Bliss than that which Gladys Spencer gave us. She put across a performance notable not only for it's extraordinary vitality, sense of contrast and of comedy, but gave a new, exciting spontaneity to situations, which for some of us were not new. There was never a moment when she failed to make Judith a supremely interesting and often uproariously funny person with an over-developed sense of the dramatic.'

At the end of the opening night's performance the paper reported that the local M.P. Beverley Baxter made a brief speech in which he particularly referred to the quality of speech on the stage. He promised to bring some of his fellow-Members of Parliament to hear how the English language should be spoken!

Despite the success of the opening night and the local press's wholehearted support, Clements' sound policy of providing good plays, well produced, did not initially bring in an audience. For the first few months business was bad, very bad, and the company's financial position was extremely precarious, especially when people who had promised capital suddenly backed-out fearing the whole venture to be a flop. In fact, it was not until the company's eighth presentation, Noel Coward's comedy *Private Lives* that any money was made.

THE INTIMATE THEATRE

Lessees—THE INTIMATE THEATRE Co., Ltd.

GREEN LANES, N. 13.

" Private Lives "

BY

NOEL COWARD.

THE PLAYERS :

(in order of their appearance)

Sibyl Chase	....	SHEILA RAYNOR
Elyot Chase	—	JOHN CLEMENTS
Victor Prynne	......	EDWARD WHEATLEIGH
Amanda Prynne	....	MEGAN LATIMER
Louise	......	DORIN MOUNTFORD

Produced by - - - JOHN CLEMENTS

Private Lives **February 1936**

Although John Clements has played every conceivable type of role since he went on the stage, the one comedy part that he has always wanted to portray, ever since he first the first original London production, has been Elyot in " Private Lives, " and this is the first time he has had an opportunity of doing so. His career has been amazingly varied, covering all three fields of dramatic art - the stage, the screen, and the radio.

His first big part in the West End was in "Caviare" at the Little Theatre, and he followed it with a series of leading roles, mainly in costume productions - notably the dissolute brother in "The Venetian" at the Little and Apollo. Lucien Bonaparte in "Napoleon" at the Embassy, and Laertes in the special celebration performance of "Hamlet" on Shakespeare's birthday at the Arts Theatre. He played Mr. Darling in "Peter Pan" at the Palladium in 1931, and more recently the juvenile lead in "If Only Father" at the Savoy. His latest screen performances include The Enemy Airman In "Things to Come," Florimo in "The Divine Spark," and the star role in "Ticket of Leave" which was written specially for him – and his broadcasting experience includes the leading part in "Som Day," and Edgar in "Wuthering Heights,"

Not content with acting only he is also of course an experienced producer and has always had one great ambition - and at last he has achieved it - here it is -

" THE INTIMATE THEATRE "

John Clements' biography and photograph from the *Private Lives* programme February 1936

Gradually audiences increased as word spread of the high standard of production and leading members of the company, such as Gladys Spencer, Sheila Rayner and Keith Pyott, soon became firm favourites with the regular theatregoers, a fact noticed by John Clements in one of his programme notes (*Marry At Leisure* - September 1936):

Only a few months ago 'a theatre' appeared in Palmers Green. No one knew anything about it, or about anyone connected with it. "The Intimate Theatre? What's that? Never heard of it." We heard that on all sides. Perhaps, at moments, it all seemed hopeless without launching an extensive advertising campaign and that was not possible. But it did not seem hopeless for long. And now in this short time, and not because of extensive advertising, but because you came to see us, told your friends to come, and came again and again and told us we were welcome, I think we can claim that the Intimate Theatre has become an established landmark and a vital factor in this district.

You have changed it from 'a' theatre into 'your' theatre, and everywhere we go we, who are part of it, and who such a short time ago were strangers, are met with the same friendliness and are made to feel we belong.

Local resident Edna Baker recalls attending several of the company's productions and believes that John Clements was way ahead of his time in his direction and lighting of the various plays. Certainly he established an excellent reputation for his repertory company and drew playgoers from all over London. He also gave himself a punishable workload directing more than forty plays in the first year alone as well as playing roles in at least thirty-four of them!

If this wasn't enough to keep him fully occupied for every moment in the day, John Clements was still making films and on 22nd June 1936 even found time to get married to Inga Ahlgren, from Sweden, at St. John's Church, situated just a few minutes from the Intimate Theatre. A quiet champagne breakfast was held on the stage of the Intimate following the ceremony but the following day it was business as usual with John travelling to Denham Film Studios to start work on Alexander Korda's new picture *Rembrandt* starring Charles Laughton.

Another local resident, George La Grue remembers John Clements as extremely popular with the local population, becoming a true community figure, giving talks and after-dinner speeches to various local organisations. On one occasion, George recalls, Clements agreed to perform the opening ceremony for a new youth club in Wood Green and, in spite of all the pressures and demands on his time as theatre manager, producer, actor and film star, spent the whole evening at the club playing table tennis and darts with the youngsters there.

The Chief Electrician at the Intimate in those early days was local man Alec Stretch. Alec lived in Bush Hill Park and having trained as an electrician then joined his father's firm Stretch Electric. His son Ian recalls that 'my father's real love was cinema and theatre. I have no knowledge of how he became involved with the Intimate but I know that he always looked back fondly on his time there and was particularly proud of one production in which he was required to simulate a major fire of London on the stage!'

By May 1936 the theatre was flourishing but never one to take things for granted, Clements realised that the summer, with its attendant distractions, could see a downturn in the fortunes of the company. He, therefore, decided to introduce a reduced pricing structure for that period of the year with stalls at 2/6, 1/6 and 1/- and circle seats at 2/-. He had tried a similar scheme earlier in the year for Saturday matinees when he charged just one

Brian Hayes

price (1/-) for any seat in the house. This had boosted matinee audiences and his summer reductions also found favour – the Intimate was now firmly established. *The Star* reported that 'John Clements has built up a company as keen as any repertory in the Kingdom' and went on to point out that 'Gladys Spencer, Brian Hayes, Graham Stuart and Robert Eddison (all regular actors in the Intimate company) are names that already mean more to Wood Green, Enfield, Finsbury Park and Tottenham than any in the West End.' *The Times* for the 30th June 1936 added 'After six months of plays covering a wide range of subjects and authors the band of players attached to the Intimate Theatre, Palmers Green, have attracted an audience which can be relied upon to support their efforts.' The paper also praised John Clements and singled out Maurice Griffith for the high standard of the settings.

In August 1936 the theatre closed for three weeks so that essential alterations could be made including the installation of a safety curtain and improved stage lighting. *The Times* reported that these alterations were being made because of the success of the Intimate Company and the paper revealed that Clements had agreed to take the lease for three years and was contemplating setting up a similar experiment in another part of London.

John Clements' wife Inga took to the Intimate's boards in July 1936 when she played a small part in A. A. Milne's play *Mr Pim Passes By* but she really came into her own in October of that year, during the run of Agatha Christie's thriller *Love From A Stranger,* when Gladys Spencer collapsed and Inga read the part from the script in order for the drama to continue.

John Clements' filming commitments caused problems in November when his car broke down en route from the film studios to the theatre and he was forced to miss both of Saturday's performances of *Hay Fever.*

The Intimate's reputation for presenting first

**From *The Two Mrs. Carrolls*
programme, August 1936**

class plays in a first class manner continued to grow and local playgoers were delighted to see playwright Terence Rattigan and actors such as Frank Lawton and Edna Best in the audience during the year. Mary Ellis, the Metropolitan opera singer and West End star of Ivor Novello's musical extravaganza *Glamorous Night*, attended the theatre to watch a performance of Somerset Maugham's *The Letter* in December. Miss Ellis praised Gladys Spencer's performance as a 'really magnificent piece of acting.'

On Boxing Day 1936, the first anniversary of the opening of the Intimate showed just how much the company had achieved in just twelve months when John Clements was greeted by thunderous applause from two packed houses. The Intimate was now well and truly on the drama map, although not everyone knew of its existence as was made clear in one of the printed programmes when Gladys Spencer revealed she had received a letter addressed to the Indefinite Theatre whilst actor Brian Hayes received a parcel marked for the Imitation Theatre!

The printed programmes produced each week around this period make interesting reading as they reveal just how much the theatre, the staff and the cast wished to be regarded as friends of the locality. There is a chattiness about the articles that is quite beguiling and it is obvious that there was a determination from the outset to ingratiate themselves with the local population. John Clements supplied occasional articles on all aspects of theatre work and there was a regular *Intimate Chat* page that kept playgoers up-to-date with the work commitments of the theatre's actors when they were absent from the Intimate, and welcomed new actors to the fold. There was also a column entitled *Intimate Confessions* in which questions were put to one of the actors in the company. Charles Lloyd Pack, father of Roger, of *Only Fools And Horses* and *The Vicar Of Dibley* fame, supplied some delightfully eccentric answers when it came to his turn under the questioner's spotlight. When asked to list three people he would like to meet he named Adolf Hitler, The Duke Of Windsor and Ginger Rogers. His pet aversion turned out to be 'people who sneeze' and his greatest ambition was 'to evade false teeth!'

The programme's adverts make nostalgic reading.

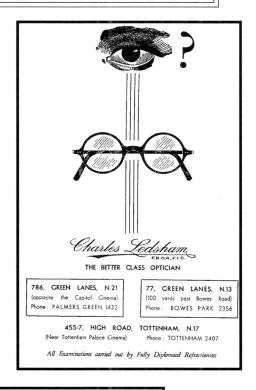

One may not regard the Palmers Green area as an obvious tourist resort but that did not deter one advertiser

And I wonder how many ladies in the audience took advantage of this corset:

A.E. Lacey and Sons of 5, Alderman's Hill, the oldest established stationers in the district asked the plaintive question in their advert 'May we deliver your early morning paper?' And amongst the notepaper, fountain pens and fancy goods for sale there were also flags for the Coronation.

The 1937 Coronation in May was celebrated at the Intimate with a production of Gordon Daviot's play *Richard Of Bordeaux* with John Clements and Sheila Rayner heading the cast. On Coronation Day itself, a special matinee was staged at 2.30 p.m. and in the evening the theatre opened its doors at 7 p.m. Ticket holders for the evening performance were invited to listen to the Empire Broadcast and the King's Speech which would be relayed in the theatre. The play itself would not commence until 8.30 p.m., thus enabling patrons 'who prefer to listen to the broadcast in their own homes to reach the theatre in good time for the performance.'

THE INTIMATE THEATRE

PALMERS GREEN, N.13

"Richard of Bordeaux"

By GORDON DAVIOT

THE PLAYERS

Fair Page Maudelyn	BRIAN HAYES
Dark Page	CHARLES READING
Richard I	JOHN CLEMENTS
Anne of Bohemia, his Queen	SHEILA RAYNOR
Duke of Gloucester, Thomas of Woodstock ...	EARLE GREY
Duke of Lancaster, John of Gaunt ...	W. E. HOLLOWAY
Sir Simon Burley, the King's tutor ...	GRAY SHAW
Duke of York	GEORGE CORMACK
Michael de la Pole, Chancellor	KEITH PYOTT
Earl of Arundel	GRAHAM STUART
Thomas Arundel, Archbishop, of Canterbury	REYNER BARTON
Robert de Vere, Earl of Oxford	ROBERT EDDISON
Mary Bohun, Countess of Derby ...	DORIN MOUNTFORD
Agnes Launcekron	INGA LILLEMOR
Henry, Earl of Derby (Bolingbroke, Son of Lancaster)	BRUNO BARNABE
Thomas Mowbray, Earl of Nottingham ...	JACK BROWN
Sir John Montague	KEITH PYOTT
Edward, Earl of Rutland	CHARLES READING
Doctor	ROBERT EDDISON
A Man in the Street	ROBERT EDDISON
Second Man	GRAY SHAW
Third Man	GRAHAM STUART
Woman with Loaves	SHEILA RAYNOR
Woman with Vegetables	DORIN MOUNTFORD
First Page	PHILLIDA MARLEY
Second Page	DIANA MARLEY
Lord Derby's Page	CLIVE BAXTER

Produced by JOHN CLEMENTS

Richard Of Bordeaux Coronation week 1937

Later that month the Intimate staged its first new play. Up until then plays had been presented which had all met with success at some time on the London stage, but John Clements was determined to present Palmers Green with the occasional premiere and on 24th May 1937 he achieved a triple goal by producing and starring in his own play *Young Society* with a cast of sixteen players! If Clements harboured any dreams of the play transferring to the West End, these were quickly shattered by the critics with *The Times* calling it 'loosely-knit and trivial' and W.A. Darlington in *The Daily Telegraph* concluding that it was 'too slight for the West End.'

Still it was a world premiere and in August Clements tried again. This time he wasn't the author! The play was called *Yes And No* by the celebrated playwright Kenneth Horne (not to be confused with the comedy actor and star of BBC radio's *Beyond Our Ken* and *Round The Horne*) and it was billed as 'prior to the West End'. Diana Churchill joined the company to head the cast that included Intimate favourites Robert Eddison, Gladys Spencer, Sheila Rayner and Brian Hayes.

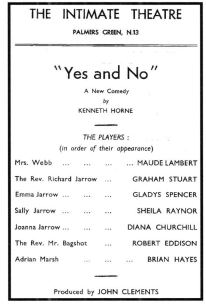

THE INTIMATE THEATRE

PALMERS GREEN, N.13

"Yes and No"

A New Comedy
by
KENNETH HORNE

THE PLAYERS :
(in order of their appearance)

Mrs. Webb	... MAUDE LAMBERT
The Rev. Richard Jarrow ...	GRAHAM STUART
Emma Jarrow	GLADYS SPENCER
Sally Jarrow	SHEILA RAYNOR
Joanna Jarrow	DIANA CHURCHILL
The Rev. Mr. Bagshot ...	ROBERT EDDISON
Adrian Marsh	BRIAN HAYES

Produced by JOHN CLEMENTS

Gladys Spencer, Diana Churchill and Sheila Raynor in a scene from Kenneth Horne's comedy *Yes and No*, which had its premiere at the Intimate August 1937

This time the critics were favourable in their reviews with *The Times* commenting that the play 'makes a bold bid for novelty. Happily it always achieves more than that'. *The Star* was even more enthusiastic: 'This really funny, well-acted play could be taken lock, stock and barrel and dumped down in the West End', whilst pointing out that 'John Clements has built up a company as keen as any repertory in the kingdom'. *The Sunday Times* added: 'The piece enjoyed the advantages of expert production and resourceful playing' and rejoiced that the Intimate 'was filled with an alert, receptive and thoroughly theatre-minded audience'. Glowing reviews like these plus local audience reaction ensured that the play transferred to the West End in October of that year where it opened at the Ambassadors Theatre with Miss Churchill and Mr. Eddison recreating their original roles and adding another feather to the Intimate's cap.

During the Intimate's run of *Yes And No* John Clements' punishing workload finally caught up with him when he collapsed on the Tuesday evening resulting in an enforced three weeks rest. Playgoers were secretly concerned that his film successes would result in Clements leaving the Intimate. A competition entry from Mr. Arthur Tidey of 2, Hoppers Road, around the play title *Yes And No* brought this fear out into the open:

> *Yes And No*
> Are we pleased with John Clements' film success?
> Decidedly 'Yes'
> If it means from the Intimate Theatre he'll go?
> Emphatically 'No'.

John Clements' reply, however, must have set many minds at rest:

> My dear Mr. Tidey I'm proud of your verse
> Though the fact that it's verse is a bit of a curse
> For I feel I must try, though I haven't much time
> To write you an answer in some sort of rhyme
> And I fear as a poet I couldn't be worse.
>
> However I'll try for I want you to know
> That nothing on Earth would induce me to go
> I'm more proud of the Intimate Theatre's success
> Than the praise I've received from a generous press
> And I'm not going to leave it – emphatically 'No'.
>
> I may film a bit more and play here a bit less
> Than I have in the past that I freely confess
> But play here I will – and I'll play here a lot
> Whether Denham or Hollywood like it or not
> And I mean what I say Sir – decidedly 'Yes!'

John Ruddock, John Clements, Alwyn Whatsley and Charles Lloyd Pack
in *Death Takes A Holiday* February 1938

Gladys Spencer, Sheila Raynor, Margaret Radcliffe, Freda Bamford and Jane Thornburn
in *Little Women* May 1938

Towards the end of the year whilst the Finsbury Park Empire boasted comedian Sandy Powell with his 1937 Road Show plus special attraction Betty Kirby-Green, who described how, with Flying Officer Clouston, they broke four records on their flight to the Cape and back, the Intimate was staging an ambitious two week run of *Hamlet* starring and produced by John Clements. *The Times* remarked that this production 'recalls the courage and enterprise shown by Mr. John Clements and his company when they founded the theatre nearly two years ago', and they found Mr. Clements' interpretation of the prince had 'imposing power'. A member of the audience at that production was the poet Stevie Smith, who lived with her Aunt Madge (referred to as 'The Lion of Hull' or 'The Lion Aunt') in Avondale Road. In a letter to Denis Johnston, dated 8th December 1937 (published in *Me Again: The Uncollected Writings Of Stevie Smith,* Virago 1981) she says:

> '... it is getting very late and I am afraid I shall never get home and tonight I am taking the Lion to see *Hamlet* done by our rep theatre. She has been reading this grand old play and she says: It is very sad. There are a lot of well-known sayings in it; there are a lot of people killed. Yes of course she has read it before but as a young girl. I think she has forgotten, but staunchly she reads it through in the most repulsive sort of family bible edition of Shakespeare dated about 1860.'

Stevie was obviously no stranger to the Intimate Theatre although she was certainly not uncritical of the company as is proved by her letter in October of that year:

> 'Nina and Harriet and I went to *Moon In the Yellow River* and I am very glad I did not wait for Bottle Green (Stevie's name for Palmers Green) to put it on and almost certainly risk its mangling by indifferent casting.'

Maintaining his policy of adventurous programme planning, Clements presented three more brand new plays during the next eighteen months: *Only Yesterday* by Adrian Brunel, *Quiet Is Best* by Allan King and Alwyn Whatsley's *The Trespassers.* Each of them received a review in *The Times* and if they did not exactly set the theatrical world alight, the reviews from national newspapers certainly helped to keep the Intimate Theatre's name in the public eye.

During 1938 John Clements was absent for a while due to filming commitments. The film in question, Alexander Korda's version of A.E.W. Mason's novel *The Four Feathers,* was, arguably, Clements' best film and certainly it is still regarded today as the best screen version of this oft-filmed story. Clements had recently signed a two-year contract with London Films, which involved him making two pictures a year. Naturally enough this curtailed his theatrical work although he still managed to be connected with twenty-five productions at the Intimate during the twelve months!

"PRODUCED BY ——"

I have been asked to explain in detail the meaning of these two words, and it occurs to me that there are possibly many of you who have no more than a vague idea of what they mean, or at any rate as far as this kind of theatre is concerned.

The work of the producer varies, of course, a great deal—what it entails depending on the type of play, the company, the stage on which he works, the time at his disposal, and so on. But in the case of this theatre, where a play is produced with one week's rehearsal, here is at any rate a rough idea of the producer's work.

First of all he must read the play carefully, if he does not already know it well, and decide how, in general, he wants it to be played. He then selects his cast. The next step is to tell the Scenic-artist whereabouts on the stage he wants doors, windows, fireplaces, etc.—and the artist then designs his scenes to suit these requirements. Next he tells the Stage Manager what furniture he needs, where it is " set," and so on. Now he is ready for the first rehearsal. The Stage Manager " sets " substitute furniture according to the producer's plan, and the company are shown how the stage is arranged.

At the first rehearsal the play is read straight through and the producer tells the players what movements he wants as they go along. These directions are written down as they occur and are learnt by the players as they learn their parts. For example, if you examine an actor's script you would find the following kind of thing written in the margin :—X.L., X.R., SIT, X Table—which mean " cross to left," " cross to right," " cross to table," etc. Thus, suppose an artist has a line such as " won't you come in ? "—and by it's side the mark X.L. he learns the move " X.L." jointly with the line " won't you come in ? "

" Business " is always an important factor in a production—this means the various little things the characters do such as lighting cigarettes, pouring out tea, etc., all of which though they appear " haphazard " are in reality carefully planned and " timed." If they were not, they would be a distraction—instead of an aid to effect. " Business " is often an extremely complicated problem and needs very accurate handling.

Now comes the later rehearsals—when the players have learnt their parts and their moves. It is now the producer's job to study the artists' interpretations of their roles, to suggest an altered intonation here, a change of gesture there, more speed to this scene, more intensity to that scene, and so on, thereby moulding the individual performances together to bring the play as a whole to life.

And now we come to the dress rehearsal. The scene is up, the furniture in place, all " props " (e.g. tea trays, glasses, bottles, suitcases, letters) are in their pre-arranged positions—either on the stage (where necessary in a drawer or cupboard), or " off stage " ready for the artists to use as required. (This the Stage Manager arranges.)

Now for the lighting. The producer goes into conference with the electrician and tells him the effects he wants, what colouring, etc., where he wants the lights to fade, or to " come up," or go out as the case may be, and each effect is tried out and " plotted " before the rehearsal begins. Now come the effects rehearsal—thunderstorms, rain noises, telephone bells, sounds of cars, bands playing, etc. These the Stage Manager submits for the producer's approval, and this having been given the full dress rehearsal begins. During this the producer takes notes of any alterations or last-minute " tidyings up " he wishes to make—and when these have been dealt with the show is ready for the opening performance, by which time the producer has discovered several grey hairs, lost several pounds, and wonders what on earth ever induced him to go on or near a stage ! Should the play get a good reception he goes home feeling that the theatre is the only profession in the world and sits up half the night reading another play. Should the play get a bad reception he—well we won't go into that !

JOHN CLEMENTS

**John Clements explains the duties of a Producer (nowadays called the Director)
in the programme for *Black Limelight* June 1938.**

"Jane Eyre"

Sheila Raynor

1938 also marked the one hundredth performances at the Intimate of two stalwarts of the repertory company, Sheila Rayner and Gladys Spencer. Sheila, married to another rep company regular, Keith Pyott, celebrated her achievement in May by assuming the title role in *Jane Eyre,* while Gladys reached her anniversary in September in the play *The Brontes Of Haworth Parsonage.*

Stevie Smith was still supporting her local theatre as can be seen in her letter to Denis Johnston, dated 30th May 1938:

> 'The Gate Theatre has been an absolute wash out this season, nothing worth looking at, such a pity; but that splendid old girl who played the great grandmother, was it, in *Tobacco Road* came out to Palmers Green the other day and played another splendid old girl in *Nine Till Six*.'

By January 1939 the fame of the Intimate Theatre had spread to such an extent that the noted drama magazine *Theatre World* devoted an article to the venue, written by George Fearon. Fearon was suitably impressed by the theatre's friendly atmosphere and gives a delightful description of the venue at intermission:

> To have given this one-time church hall a grandiose title would have been a tactical error. It only seats 458 people. *The Grand Theatre* would have misled the public, but now that it has become firmly established it might easily

Intimate Chat

SHEILA RAYNOR . . . 100 . . . NOT OUT !

Congratulations to our ever popular Sheila Raynor who plays in her 100th production for us this week. That 100 has included many brilliant performances, " Mary Rose," Lillian in " Eden End," Stasia in " The Passing of the Third Floor Back," Lalage in " The Outsider " and Fanny in " Autumn Crocus " to mention just a few that stand out so clearly in one's memory although they mean going a long way back. More recently her lovely performance in " Berkeley Square," Grazia in " Death Takes a Holiday " and that grand comedy performance Tweeny in " The Admirable Crichton " and last but by no means least her Ophelia in " Hamlet."

May we see her reach her 200, and still be " not out ! "

*   *   *

The John Clements' competition brought in a large number of entries, and no fewer than three competitors were successful in placing the six performances in the winning order. They were Miss Rose Byrne of Edmonton, Miss Margaret Dexter of Southgate and Mr. N. A. Stiles of Tottenham.

Hamlet was an easy winner. There was great rivalry for third place, Sirki in " Death Takes a Holiday " beating Stanhope in " Journey's End " by one mark only.

The winning order was as follows :—

1. Hamlet.

2. Richard of Bordeaux.

3. Sirki in " Death takes a Holiday."

4. Stanhope in " Journey's End."

5. Uncle Dick in " Yellow Sands."

6. Elyot in " Private Lives."

The method of calculating the result is as follows. Every single entry is taken into account and marks are given to each character according to its place in the entry. Six marks for a first place, five marks for a second and so on—the winner being the character who gets the greatest number of marks from the added results of all the entries.

The *Intimate Chat* page from the programme for *Jane Eyre* May 1938

25

be renamed *The Grand Intimate Theatre.* It is a grand place with a personality all of its own. It doesn't give the impression of trying to be what it is not. There is no snob element in the audience; rather one gets the impression in the interval that the 400 people are playing a game of happy families or general post.

No sooner does the curtain come down for the interval, than trolleys loaded with coffee and biscuits are wheeled along the gangways. The scrum round these is reminiscent of the rugger field, only the men are handling cups with a certain amount of trepidation. Unspilled they are passed down the gangways to thirsty ladies. Someone in the cheaper part of the stalls suddenly notices a friend in the front row.

There is a waving of hands, an excited rush and little miss back row is busily engaged in an earnest conversation about the local sales with her front row friend. The curtain rises – the clatter of coffee cups suddenly ceases, the hubbub stops as though by magic – all attention is focussed on the stage. Nobody – except myself – seems to have noticed that the trespasser has not returned to her proper seat.

I really believe that if she had been spotted she would not have been asked to return. She has found an intimate and in joining forces with her was carrying out the tradition of the theatre.

Fearon had been in the audience for the Intimate's production of J.B.Priestley's *I Have Been Here Before* in October 1938 and was full of praise for the company:

The play did not appeal very much to me – but the acting did. The play was acted with skill by all, plus one outstanding performance. I refer to John Ruddock's *Dr. Gortler.* An excellent piece of character work, the like of which is all too infrequently seen on the English stage. That exquisite performance made the play worth while.

It might be questioned how a theatre with such a small seating capacity can be an economic proposition; careful management and uniformly good business have assured that it is. The artists all receive a flat rate – "take it or leave it"; they nearly all take it.

A popular playwright of this period, H.F. Maltby, found himself eternally grateful to the Intimate in June 1939 when he managed to achieve a long held dream. The theatre was staging his play *The Rotters,* which Maltby had written in 1915. Back then he had intended to play the leading role in the first staging of the play but was thwarted by being posted to the Front. Now almost twenty-five years later he was to achieve that goal when the original actor was taken ill and Maltby, who was producing, took his place at three days notice.

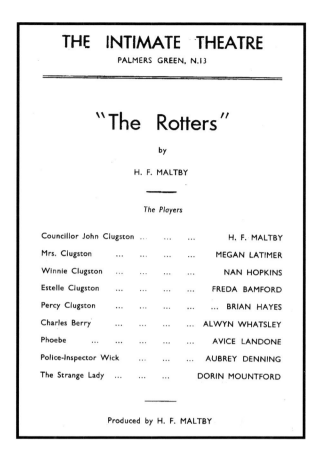

THE INTIMATE THEATRE
PALMERS GREEN, N.13

"The Rotters"

by

H. F. MALTBY

The Players

Councillor John Clugston	H. F. MALTBY
Mrs. Clugston	MEGAN LATIMER
Winnie Clugston	NAN HOPKINS
Estelle Clugston	FREDA BAMFORD
Percy Clugston	... BRIAN HAYES
Charles Berry	ALWYN WHATSLEY
Phoebe	AVICE LANDONE
Police-Inspector Wick	AUBREY DENNING
The Strange Lady	DORIN MOUNTFORD

Produced by H. F. MALTBY

H. F. Maltby

A month later came another notable first for the Intimate when the theatre's production of *The Cathedral* by Hugh Walpole was broadcast on the Regional Programme of BBC Radio on Saturday 15th July. Not only was this the first transmission from the theatre but it was also the first time *The Cathedral* had been heard on radio.

In just three and a half years the Intimate Theatre, thanks to John Clements and his company, had become a theatre of some repute.

ACTORS APPEARING AT THE INTIMATE 1935-1940

John Clements' resident company included husband and wife team Sheila Raynor and Keith Pyott, Gladys Spencer, Betty Potter, Jane Grahame and Brian Hayes.

Gladys Spencer, leading lady of so many productions at the Intimate during these years was actually born in Paris and began her career on the French stage. Whilst on her honeymoon in England, the actor Godfrey Tearle persuaded her to appear in a production here and she decided to stay. Prior to joining John Clements' company she had appeared in a film, *The Wish Bone,* with the music hall comedienne Nellie Wallace.

Sheila and Keith lived in Stonard Road in Palmers Green and both later appeared in films as well as continuing with stage work. Keith featured in many post war films including *Quartet, The Colditz Story, Chimes At Midnight, Village Of The Damned* and *The Devil Rides Out.* Sheila appeared in *The Mask Of Cain, Room At The Top* and *The Violent Playground.* She appeared as Carol White's mother in the film *Dulcima* and also had small roles in *A Clockwork Orange* and *Madonna and Child* (part of the *Terence Davies Trilogy*). She died in 1998 at 89 years of age.

Brian Hayes' sister was the celebrated character actress Patricia Hayes, who appeared at the Intimate in *Mrs. Moonlight* (July 1937), *Black Coffee* (Sept 1937), *A Hundred Years Old* (Oct 1937), *Night Must Fall* (Dec 1937), *A Cuckoo In the Nest* (Jan 1938) and *Nine Till Six* (Apr 1938). Patricia later enjoyed a successful career as foil to comics such as Benny Hill and Tony Hancock, as well as numerous other television, stage and film roles. Her finest hour was probably her award winning television performance as *Edna, The Inebriate Woman* in 1971.

Glynis Johns' father Mervyn Johns was another well-known face in those early years appearing in such plays as *Tons Of Money* (July 1936), *The Green Bay Tree* (July 1936), *Full House* (Aug 1936) and *Marry At Leisure* (Sept 1936). As well as stage work, Mervyn made over sixty films including *Dead Of Night, The Day Of The Triffids, The Halfway House* and *Scrooge* where he played *Bob Cratchit* to Alistair Sim's *Scrooge.*

The celebrated Shakespearian actor Robert Eddison made early career appearances in *After October* (Apr 1937), *Good Morning Bill* (May 1937), *Aren't We All?* (Jun 1937), *Bird In Hand* (Aug 1937) and *Only Yesterday* (Feb 1938).

Richard Haydn, perhaps best known to the general public as *Max* in the film of *The Sound Of Music,* acted in *The Letter* (Nov 1936), *Payment Deferred* (Feb 1937), *A Bill Of Divorcement* (June 1937) and *Aren't We All?* (June 1937).

Eileen Way, who later found a regular niche in supporting roles on television and film, was a Palmers Green favourite in those early years appearing in many productions including *Full House* (Aug 1936), *London Wall* (Mar 1937), *Rookery Nook* (Mar 1937), *Just Married* (Dec 1937) and *Busman's Holiday* (Jun 1938). Reviewing *After October* Apr 1937), the *Gazette* critic wrote: ' Watch out for a delightful performance from Eileen Way. She's the Intimate Theatre's best scene-stealer just now!'

Avice Landon (or Landone), the distinguished stage, film and television actress, made numerous appearances in 1939 and 1940 including *Winter Sunshine* (May 1939), *Home Chat* (Jul 1939), *Plunder* (Dec 1939) and *Full House* (Sep 1940), the final play of John Clements' management. In July 1940 Avice married Bruno Barnabe, a fellow member of the Intimate Company. Avice won the Clarence Derwent Award for her role of *Sylvia Bennett* in *Not In the Book* at the Criterion in 1958 and later scored a personal success as the secretary *Monica Reed* in the West End revival of Coward's *Present Laughter* in 1965. She also teamed up with Peggy Mount to star in two series of ITV's comedy *Winning Widows* in the early 1960s and was also one of the regular cast in the BBC series of A.P.Herbert's *Misleading Cases.*

Peggy Thorpe Bates and her husband Brian Oulton made several appearances with the company shortly before the theatre closed in 1940, appearing in *Peg O' My Heart* (Jun 1940), *The Man In Possession* (Jul 1940), *Saloon Bar* (Jul 1940) and *The Two Mrs. Carrolls* (Jul 1940). Brian actually directed the last two plays of John Clements' reign at Palmers Green in September 1940: *Lot's Wife* and Ivor Novello's *Full House.*
Peggy, daughter of the musical comedy star Thorpe Bates, will be remembered by many as *Hilda Rumpole* – 'She-Who-Must-Be Obeyed' in the popular television series *Rumpole Of The Bailey.*

Douglas Emery made many appearances as an actor during this time including *The Case of The Frightened Lady* (Oct 1937), *The Queen's Husband* (Mar 1938), *Black Limelight* (Jun 1938), *Thark* (Jun 1938) and *Love On The Dole* (Oct 1938). Emery would return to the Intimate as resident director in the 1960s.

Frith Banbury the noted director made several appearances as an actor during this period including *Hamlet* (Nov 1937), *Berkeley Square* (Feb 1938) and *Flat To Let* (Mar 1938).

Charles Lloyd Pack, as mentioned earlier, was a frequent visitor during these pre-war years. His many appearances included *Black Coffee* (Sep 1937), *Whistling In The Dark* (Aug 1938), *Anna Christie* (Feb 1939), *The Cathedral* (Jun 1939) and *The Last Of Mrs. Cheyney* (Aug 1939). He was later a stalwart of British films, usually playing characters of a meek or flustered variety, such as the frightened and blackmailed hairdresser in the groundbreaking film *Victim.*

One-Off Appearances

Annabel Maule in *Jane Eyre* (May 1938). Annabel, later moved to Kenya to become, firstly, Artistic Director and then Managing Director of the Donovan Maule Theatre, her parents' theatre and was awarded the MBE.

James Hayter in *French Without Tears* (Sep 1939). James was later incredibly busy on stage, television and in film in a variety of parts but perhaps is best remembered for playing *Mr Pickwick* in the film *The Pickwick Papers*. He replaced Stanley Holloway as *Doolittle* in the original London production of *My Fair Lady* and his fruity voice could also be heard on the *Mr. Kipling's* cake adverts.

Leonard Sachs in *Lady Precious Stream* (Sep 1937). Sachs is probably best known today as the Chairman of the long running BBC series *The Good Old Days*.

Stringer Davis in *Nina* (Jul 1939). Davis was married to Margaret Rutherford and appeared as her foil *Mr. Stringer* in her Agatha Christie *Miss Marple* films.

Eric Portman in *She Stoops To Conquer* (Nov 1939). Portman became a much-admired actor on stage, and film. In 1942 he was voted one of the top ten money making film stars in Britain and later years saw him in *A Canterbury Tale, The Colditz Story, We Dive At Dawn, The Whisperers* and a memorable *Jess Oakroyd* in the 1956 remake of *The Good Companions*. He was equally busy on stage and in 1957 he received a Tony Award nomination for his role in Rattigan's *Separate Tables*.

Sydney Tafler in *Twelfth Night* (May 1940). Tafler later became a well-known face on the British film scene usually cast as a villain or Cockney 'spiv'type of character and also joined Sid James for the successful television comedy series *Citizen James*.

There were also fleeting visits by Renee Asherson in *Housemaster* (Apr 1939), Ambrosine Phillpotts in *The High Road* (Aug 1937), Thorley Walters in *Mademoiselle* (Nov 1937), Elspeth March in *Traitor's Gate* (Apr 1939) and Diana Churchill in *Yes And No* (Aug 1937). Churchill's second husband, incidentally, was Mervyn Johns, mentioned above.

Eric Portman

Richard Haydn

Renee Asherson

Brian Oulton

James Hayter

THE FORTIES

In September 1939 war was declared and all theatres initially closed, only to reopen shortly afterwards. The Intimate had the distinction of being the first London theatre to reopen, with a production of Terence Rattigan's *French Without Tears,* and for the first four days of its run was the only theatre open in the London area. The reopening was not without its problems as *Intimate Chat* (*Yes, My Darling Daughter* - September 1939) recalled:

> Mind you, it was not easy to reopen at eighteen hours notice (two members of the company having been called up) but everybody put their backs into it and the curtain rose at 7.15 p.m. on Monday evening.

As the curtain had to be down by 10 p.m., performances had to begin at the earlier time of 7.15 p.m. and an extra matinee on Thursdays was introduced. It was obvious that the conditions imposed by war would affect the theatre but the company was determined that disruption would be kept to a minimum, even in the event of an air raid:

NOTICE

In the event of an Air Raid Warning being sounded during the performance the fact will be announced from the stage.

Patrons who live within five minutes' walking distance of the theatre, can, of course, return home if they wish – others are strongly recommended to remain in their seats.

THE PERFORMANCE WILL CONTINUE.

The company instigated The Intimate Theatre Tobacco Fund. A box was attached to the box office in the foyer and patrons were asked to make cash donations so that cigarettes could be purchased for the armed forces. In November it was announced that £5. 2s.10d had been collected and the first batch of cigarettes would be sent the following week to the British Expeditionary Force so as to reach them in time for Christmas.

One of the actresses in the company, Megan Latimer, was an unfortunate victim of the blackout when she walked into a lamppost and received a very nasty black eye. Her only comment was that she promised to take more water with her drink in future!

Megan Latimer

Despite the war conditions it was business as usual at the Intimate. The occasional new play turned up amongst revivals of past West End successes. In January 1940 William Templeton's play *Signature Tune* was premiered and in June of that year Kenneth Horne's new comedy *Wasn't It Odd?* received its first production.

The first week of August saw a revival of *Richard Of Bordeaux* to mark John Clements' one-hundredth appearance on the Intimate stage. The programme took this opportunity to pay tribute to Mr. Clements.

JOHN CLEMENTS
An Appreciation

John Clements

This popular and long-awaited revival of *Richard Of Bordeaux* marks a very special occasion – John Clements' 100th Intimate Theatre performance.

Looking back over these hundred performances it is very difficult to pick out a few and say "these were the best" – there have been so many – but some of the ones that I remember most vividly are his *Hamlet,* his *Elyot* in *Private Lives, Ragatzky* in *The Outsider, Stanhope* in *Journey's End, Peter* in *Berkeley Square, Sirki* in *Death Takes A Holiday, Steiner* in *Autumn Crocus, Uncle Dick* in *Yellow Sands,* and last, but by no means least, his *Richard Of Bordeaux.* I have probably omitted to mention your own particular favourite, and am quite prepared for a shoal of indignant letters on that account!

As for his work as a producer I can only say that his uncanny gift of bringing a play to life, and his brilliant handling of lighting and all stage "effects" have contributed as much to this theatre's great popularity as his fine acting.

This article might well have been headed "Success Story" or "Four Years Hard Labour", because the success of the Intimate Theatre is a personal triumph for J.C. and one that he has only achieved by unremitting hard work coupled with a flair for getting the best out of his company by unfailing consideration and brilliant leadership.

Whatever other successes J.C. may achieve in his career (and there will undoubtedly be many), I am certain that none will give him more satisfaction than the success of the Intimate Theatre. I am equally sure I am voicing the hope of all of us, artistes, staff and audience when I say: "Long may John Clements and his Intimate Theatre continue on their successful way."

As it turned out this tribute was extremely timely as six weeks later the Intimate, along with other theatres, would be closed and John Clements' association with the theatre would be over.

Wartime conditions were now worsening and audience numbers at the theatre had fallen off alarmingly. On Monday 9th September 1940 the theatre staged Ivor Novello's play *Full House.* The incongruity of the title was not lost on the reviewer for *The Palmers Green and Southgate Gazette* (13th September 1940):

> There is an accidental irony in the title of the play for the audiences at the Intimate have been almost the entire reverse of full houses. This, it need hardly be said, has not been due to any falling off in the quality of the fare provided or even to lack of interest by theatregoers, but to a combination of wartime circumstances over which neither company nor public have any control....Regrettably, however, a position has been reached at which the management have decided to close the theatre temporarily, and this was announced by Mr. John Clements from the stage on Monday night.. In stating that the present play would be the last for the time being, he hoped that it would only be necessary to close down for a short time.

An advert in the same issue of the newspaper announced:

INTIMATE THEATRE
As from Monday September 16th
Temporarily closed. Re-opening shortly.

The theatre, in fact, remained closed for the remainder of 1940 and much of 1941. During this time John Clements toured with ENSA but he managed to make a local appearance on Sunday 30th March 1941 at the Odeon Cinema in The Bourne for the Spitfire Star Variety Entertainment. This was a variety gala in aid of the Spitfire Fund, 'helping to speed the day when Southgate's own Spitfire will take the air.' On the bill were Leslie A. Hutchinson, better known as the cabaret entertainer 'Hutch', Michael Redgrave, Judy Campbell, Joe Loss, Jeanne De Casalis, Harry Welchman, Billy Merson and John Clements, who, according to the local press 'told stories and sang with the aid of a ukulele'

When *The Palmers Green and Southgate Gazette*, in their issue for 8th August 1941, announced the Intimate Theatre's re-opening, it was tinged with sadness as local playgoers discovered that John Clements would not be returning to lead the company.

JOHN CLEMENTS SAYS GOODBYE
Intimate Theatre Wrench

John Clements and his company have parted from the Intimate Theatre, Palmers Green, which they founded and to which they gave superb 'life'. We give below John Clements' letter to us and take opportunity to wish him and his friends, wherever they may be, Good Fortune. Here is the letter:

John Clements

"May I make use of your columns to write what is, to me at all events, a very sad letter?

It is with great regret that I and the Intimate Theatre company have to say goodbye to all our many friends in this district.

Since we closed the Intimate Theatre last September I have done my utmost to make it possible to reopen it. But for a variety of reasons, among them the fact that in present circumstances I should no longer be able to devote any time to it, personally, we have been forced to abandon all hope of doing so.
I cannot begin to tell you what a wrench it was to me when I handed over my keys of the Intimate a few days ago.

I and that small group of people who have worked so hard with me from the beginning have been very proud of that theatre – proud of being the founders of it, proud of the standard of its shows, proud of the reputation it acquired, of its happy, congenial atmosphere, of its excellent company, and by no means least, of its audience.

I have told that audience on numerous occasions in the past how very much we all appreciated their enthusiastic support of the work we did. And I tell them again, for the last time, that we always think of them with very great gratitude and sincere affection.

And now the Intimate Theatre has passed into other hands. I wish them the greatest success and I hope that the old Intimate audience will flock to their accustomed places in the theatre and give them an encouraging welcome."

Clements, of course, went on to have a very distinguished career in the theatre playing such roles as *Elyot Chase* in a revival of Noel Coward's *Private Lives, Petruchio* in Shakespeare's *The Taming Of The Shrew, Jack Tanner* in Shaw's *Man And Superman, Professor Higgins* in *Pygmalion* and the title role in *Macbeth*. With his second wife, the actress Kay Hammond, he became noted for his revivals of seventeenth and eighteenth century comedies, often directing the productions himself and he also had a successful career in films, appearing in such blockbusters as *Ghandi* and *Oh, What A Lovely War*. Clements was appointed Advisor on Drama to Associated Rediffusion Ltd. and presented a number of plays for this television company. In 1955 he joined the board of directors of the Saville Theatre, the management of which came under his personal control and he presented such plays as *The Wild Duck, The Rivals* and *The Way Of The World*. He was a member of the Old Vic Company in the early 1960's and in 1965 was appointed Director of Chichester Festival Theatre where, until 1973, he presented the yearly season of plays. Clements even tackled a West End musical when he appeared as the domineering father, *Edward Moulton-Barrett* in *Robert And Elizabeth* with June Bronhill and Keith Michell at the Lyric Theatre in 1964. He was awarded the CBE in 1956 and was knighted in 1968. He died at the age of 78 in 1988.

Frederick Marlow

On Monday 18th August 1941 the Intimate Theatre reopened its doors under the management banner of G. M. Productions. This company was run by Frederick Marlow and he would remain lessee of the venue until his death in 1964. Fred was born in Edmonton and worked at the old Edmonton Empire when just 14 years of age. Five years later he was appointed manager before working for Moss Empires and then setting up in business as a variety agent. His decision to become lessee of the Intimate was a courageous one. To take over the running of a theatre at any time is a risky venture but to take over in wartime showed great nerve and faith in the local population. However, as *The Palmers Green and Southgate Gazette* noted on 8th August 1941 'there is no theatre in or around London with a more loyal clientele than this cosy and aptly named centre of dramatic art' and Fred's publicised aim to provide much-needed relaxation for the war-weary people of the district endeared him to playgoers at the outset.

Not every face at the theatre was new for Fred had the sense to bring back to Palmers Green two of the leading actresses from John Clements' company, Sheila Raynor and Gladys Spencer, both popular favourites with local audiences. The resident director was now Ronald Kerr and the new scenic artist was Stanley Premm. The opening production was *French For Love* by Marguerite Steen and Derek Patmore and John Clements and his wife attended the opening night as a gesture of 'good luck'.

If audiences welcomed the re-opening of their theatre as a place where, for a few short hours at least, all present problems and fears could be put aside, they sadly could not be forgotten entirely as inside the auditorium there were still reminders of the world situation such as the ARP notice printed in the programme:

> **RED LIGHT** on left of stage denotes that an alert has been sounded
> **GREEN LIGHT** on right of stage denotes the All Clear has been sounded

The programme also helpfully stated:

> Patrons are reminded that the nearest Air Raid Shelter is immediately opposite the theatre.

The actor Leslie Parnell, at that time a resident of Winchmore Hill and who later appeared in several productions with the repertory company, remembers an air raid warning whilst in the audience with his mother. He recalls taking cover in an air raid shelter at the bottom of Eaton Park Road, a few roads from the Intimate, on the way home. A few years later Leslie made his professional stage debut as an actor at the Intimate in a production of George Bernard Shaw's *St. Joan*.

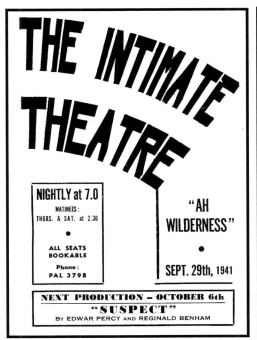

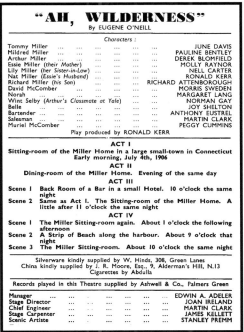

Over the years the Intimate Theatre proved to be an excellent training ground for actors and actresses making their way in the profession. Local resident Ethel Aspland remembers that when the theatre decided to stage Eugene O'Neill's drama *Ah, Wilderness* in September 1941 the management contacted The Royal Academy For Dramatic Art for a student to

Richard Attenborough

take the role of a fifteen-year-old boy. That student turned out to be Richard Attenborough, now Lord Attenborough, making his professional debut and Ethel recalls that he gave an excellent performance, receiving terrific applause at the curtain call. Ethel's memory of the play and Attenborough's reception is borne out by the *Palmers Green and Southgate Gazette* (3rd Oct. 1941) critic:

> The Intimate is fortunate in its young actors and actresses, a well-trained set of people who are gaining valuable experience in the company of several first-rate exponents of the theatrical art and under a producer who is competent and painstaking. *Richard* is played by Richard Attenborough, whom the audience took to their hearts at once. With good reason, for he contributed a crystal clear, sound performance.

Richard Attenborough returned to the Intimate that December in James Hilton's *Goodbye Mr. Chips,* when Ronald Kerr played *Mr. Chipping,* and stayed on for the following week's drama *Cottage To Let.* Sadly, that was Attenborough's last appearance at the Intimate. Two years later he scored a great success as the gangster *Pinky* in Graham Greene's *Brighton Rock,* a part he later filmed, and in 1952 he, with his wife Sheila Sim, played the leading roles in a new play by Agatha Christie called *The Mousetrap.* His successes in plays and films both as an actor and director continue to this day, as indeed does Agatha Christie's play! By a strange coincidence Sheila Sim also appeared several times at the Intimate shortly after Richard's appearances there, becoming a regular member of the company during 1942 and 1943 playing roles in Ivor Novello's *Fresh Fields* and *Full House,* Noel Coward's *Hay Fever,* Goldsmith's *She Stoops To Conquer* and Shaw's *Arms And The Man,* as well as *Devonshire Cream, Quality Street, The Brontes Of Haworth Parsonage, After October, The First Mrs. Fraser, Quiet Wedding, Spring Meeting, If Four Walls Told, Murder On The Second Floor, Other People's Houses, Yellow Sands* and *Aren't Men Beasts.* Sheila returned to the theatre for one more appearance in May 1946 when she played the title role in a two-week production of Shaw's *St. Joan.*

In 1942 Mary Stone, fresh from RADA where fellow students included Terence Morgan, Alan Badel and Pete Murray, joined the theatre's staff as assistant stage manager and actress. She had been taught at RADA by Ronald Kerr, the resident director at the Intimate, and it was he who had persuaded her to take the job at Palmers Green. Mary later changed her name to Marianne Stone and moved away from the stage into films where she became Britain's most prolific supporting actress of the post war period. Her first film was *Brighton Rock* in 1947 and she went on to play small roles in an incredible number of movies from *The Pickwick Papers* to the Beatles film *A Hard Day's Night,* from *A Night To Remember* to *Lolita* plus several forays into British comedy including nine *Carry On* films.

Mary remained at the Intimate for three years playing a multitude of roles as well as carrying out the duties of an ASM for the princely sum of £3 per week. Usually the roles given to assistant stage managers were of 'the maid' variety but every now and then a meatier part would turn up such as *Bessie* in *The Corn Is Green, Jessica* in *The Merchant Of Venice* and *Cecily Cardew* in *The Importance Of Being Earnest.*

Marianne Stone

"THE CORN IS GREEN"
By EMLYN WILLIAMS

The Characters in order of their appearance :

John Goronwy Jones	G. R. SCHJELDERUP
Miss Ronberry	MARJORIE MANNERS
Idwal Morris	DOUGLAS HURN
Sarah Pugh	CATHEINE MAYHEW
The Squire...	ERNEST HAINES
Bessie Watty	MARY STONE
Mrs. Watty	HELEN MISENER
Miss Moffat	UNA VENNING
Robbart Robbatch	BRIAN FORBES
Glyn Thomas	DENNIS BEDFORD
Will Hughes	DAVID KENTISH
Morgan Evans	NOEL SAMUEL
Old Tom	MARTIN CLARK

Play produced by RONALD KERR

The action of the play takes place in the Living-room of a House in Glansarno, a small village in a remote Welsh countryside. The time is the latter part of the last century and covers a period of three years

ACT i
Scene I	An afternoon in June
Scene 2	A night in August. Two years later

ACT II
Scene I	An early evening in August. Two years later
Scene 2	A morning in November. Three months later

ACT III
An afternoon in July. Seven months later

The Corn Is Green **May 1943**

Mary recalls: ' I was immediately impressed with the actual building. The theatre had such a lovely frontage with a proper box office on the left as you entered and glossy photographs of the actors on the right hand wall. There was not a resident company as such although some of the actors became regulars. I remember Antony Eustrel, who later went to Hollywood and made several films there, and Sheila Rayner, who with her husband Keith Pyott, lived in Stonard Road, right next to the theatre. I particularly admired Joslin Parlane, a blonde actress in her early thirties, who played huge roles at that time. Ernest Haines was the character actor and Marjorie Wilde, the character actress. Visiting actors included Una Venning, who had been understudy to Gladys Cooper and who bore a striking resemblance to that actress, and Julian Dallas and Richard Stapley, both of whom went to Hollywood. Ronald Kerr, who had taught me at RADA, directed and achieved miracles in the time given. Stanley Premm was a wonderful scenic artist and the technical staff consisted of Martin Clark, the Chief Engineer, and James Kellett, the Stage Carpenter, both of whom lived round the corner in Stonard Road. The furniture for the productions was supplied by a firm called *Old Times* based in Victoria. They would deliver the items and props either on Sunday or early Monday morning. On Saturday evenings after the final performance, the stage crew would strike the set and wrap up all the properties so that they would be returned when the furnishings arrived for the next play. Actors were expected to supply all present day costumes themselves, such as cocktail dresses, evening gowns, lounge suits and dress suits, so it is not surprising that they welcomed the odd period play when costumes would be hired, usually from *Bermans* or *Nathans* whilst wigs were obtained from *Gustave's* in Covent Garden. The theatre was open all year and although there were frequent air raids I cannot remember any serious disruptions.'

A typical week for the actors at that time was as follows:

Tuesday:
Read through of next week's play in the morning and rehearsals in the afternoon.

Wednesday:
Rehearse Act 1 all day.

Thursday:
Rehearse Act 2 in the morning.
Matinee in afternoon.

Friday:
Rehearse Acts 2 and 3.

Saturday:
Rehearse all morning.
Matinee in afternoon.

Sunday:
Usually Day Off but this was not always the case especially for the backstage staff!

Monday:
Dress rehearsal all day, often until a few minutes before the curtain went up!

The actors were usually told of the casting of a play a week before rehearsals commenced so for the regulars in the company that meant appearing in a play every evening whilst rehearsing next week's during the day plus beginning to learn lines for the play in two weeks time. Appearing in weekly rep was certainly hard work!

Mary has fond memories of the Intimate not least because it was at the theatre she first met her late husband, the film critic, broadcaster and writer, Peter Noble. Peter was, at that time, a reporter on *The Wood Green Observer* and reviewed the plays at the Intimate. Mary noticed that she always received glowing notices from this critic and so, intrigued, she resorted to peeping through the front stage curtains on opening night to see what this person looked like! Later Richard Attenborough introduced them to each other at the Arts Theatre Club and in 1947 they married and were together for fifty-four years until Peter's death.

ST. JAMES'S THEATRE
KING STREET, S.W.I

Under the direction of GILBERT MILLER and PRINCE LITTLER
Licensed by the Lord Chamberlain to ... PRINCE LITTLER

In association with the Arts Council of Great Britain

ASSOCIATED ARTISTS LTD.,

under the Direction of

JOHN CLEMENTS

presents

The First of A Season of Plays in Repertory

" THE KINGMAKER "

by

MARGARET LUCE

EVENINGS at 6.45 p.m.
MATINEES : Tuesday and Thursday at 2.30 p.m.

The Second Play of The Season
which will be played alternately with
" THE KINGMAKER "
will be
" MARRIAGE A LA MODE "
by
JOHN DRYDEN

Mary left the Intimate in 1945 and joined John Clements' company in 1946 for a year, touring for six months and appearing for the other six months in a season at the St James' Theatre where they staged two plays *The King Maker* by Margaret Loos and *Marriage A La Mode* by Dryden. After her marriage Mary turned to the cinema and never looked back, appearing in over 224 feature films!

Throughout the rest of the war years it was business as usual for the Intimate with the doors open for business fifty-two weeks of the year. The management was determined that nothing would prevent the curtain going up each evening. In June 1944, around the time of the 'D Day' landings, the theatre programme stated:

Should any news of particular interest be received during a performance, it will be announced from the stage during the intervals.

In the theatre foyer and café boxes had been placed for donations to the theatre's Trawler Fund and wool was available at the box office, free of charge, for patrons who wished to knit for the Trawlers.

One of the leading actors in the Intimate company at this time was Antony Eustrel. Though not young nor conventionally good-looking he certainly attracted his fair share of female

"WUTHERING HEIGHTS"

By EMILY BRONTE
Adapted by JOHN DAVIDSON

Characters in order of appearance :

Catherine Earnshaw	JOY SHELTON
Heathcliff	ANTONY EUSTREL
Joseph	MARTIN CLARK
Ellen Dean	JANET BURNELL
Edgar Linton	DAVID CROSSE
Isabella Linton	MAVIS WALKER
Hindley Earnshaw	DERMOT CATHIE
Hareton Earnshaw	PETER MURRAY
Catherine Linton	MARY STONE

Play produced by RONALD KERR

The scene throughout is the Living-room at Wuthering Heights, on the Yorkshire moors

ACT I
Late afternoon on a weekday in Summer, 1781

ACT II

Scene 1	Three years later, 1784
Scene 2	A night a year later

ACT III
Twenty years later

Wuthering Heights June 1943

admirers and when he made his regular plea to the audience to contribute to the Trawler Fund, he always received a gratifying response. Avis Milner, a teenager at the time recalls:

'Being a big fan of Antony Eustrel's and wishing to meet him, I decided to collect for the Trawler Fund, door-to-door, with a made up cocoa tin. I had a super response and duly took my tin to the stage door. At the time Mr. Eustrel was playing *Heathcliff* in *Wuthering Heights* and came off-stage to see me. He was delighted with my effort and we both counted the contents of the heavy cocoa tin. There I was in the star's dressing room with "my hero"! I am afraid I cannot remember how much was collected but I do remember receiving a kiss from *Heathcliff*!'

In October 1944 the theatre reported that £52/9/9d had been collected for 'our three trawlers'. No doubt due in no small way to Mr. Eustrel's popularity!

Local author Alan Dumayne remembers frequenting the Intimate around this period as he recalled in his excellent book *Once Upon A Time In Palmers Green:*

'My own memories of the theatre go back to the wartime years. A chum of mine used to do a paper round for *Guys*, the newsagents, on Winchmore Hill Green. His wages included two free tickets every week for the Intimate Theatre, which the shop received as reimbursement for advertising the theatre's productions.

He would often invite me to accompany him – always on Monday evening, with seats in the circle. I marvelled then, as I still do in retrospect, at the repertory company, who would put on these fine plays week in, week out, with an entirely new production to delight everyone every Monday. Members of the cast would be learning next week's words whilst performing this week's play, yet the standard was very high indeed. David Garth, who has since worked in many different spheres on television, was a particular favourite of mine.'

Although the war was still continuing audiences had greatly improved. In fact, a production of Noel Coward's *This Happy Breed* proved so popular in January 1945 that the management staged it again three weeks later to satisfy the many patrons who were unable to obtain seats during the first run. Spurred on by audience reaction to that play, the theatre management decided to experiment with the occasional two week run. In March they returned to Coward with a fortnight's run of his comedy *Blithe Spirit* and later in the spring presented *The Barretts Of Wimpole Street* by Rudolf Besier. These were obviously proving successful as the autumn schedule included two-week runs of *Pink String And Sealing Wax, Flare Path, Ten Little Niggers* and *Uncle Harry.* They must also have been popular with the actors as it gave them a little welcome respite from the weekly slog of learning lines!

Pink String And Sealing Wax was also notable for introducing a young actress who would eventually carve an amazingly successful career in comedy working with virtually every major British comedian. Not for nothing does Roy Hudd call her 'the comic's tart' as she has worked with Frankie Howerd, Benny Hill, Arthur Askey, Terry Scott, Julian Clary, Tony Hancock, Jimmy Edwards, Ronnie Barker, Jennifer Saunders and, naturally enough, Roy himself. Her name is, of course, June Whitfield. June returned to the Intimate in January 1946 to appear in the Agatha Christie thriller *Love From A Stranger* and made her final appearance at the venue in *Shadow And Substance* in June 1947. It was on one matinee day, during her time at the Intimate, that June committed the cardinal sin of actors:

June Whitfield

'The management switched the matinee time from five thirty to two thirty but, for some reason, I had a memory lapse and, at curtain-up time, I was to be found gaily having tea with a girl friend at the Arts Theatre. My friend asked me what I was up to and I replied: "Well, I'm doing this play at the …oh my God!" I suddenly remembered I should be at the matinee!'

June jumped into her car and drove at breakneck speed across London and arrived at the Intimate to hear the producer announce to the audience that, 'Miss Whitfield has now recovered from her indisposition and will resume her role in the second act. June was mortified for days but the company was very kind to her and said that it could have happened to anyone, but as June remarked:

'Unfortunately it happened to me but I think I was forgiven!'

June remembers her brief time at the Intimate with affection, and recalls that the theatre certainly lived up to its name as backstage 'it was very Intimate indeed with only three dressing rooms, a tiny proscenium and no wing space whatsoever, which made scene changes virtually impossible.' She also remembers that the Intimate had a reputation for staging 'a mixed repertoire of adventurous and commercial plays, well-supported by the locals.'

In those immediate post-war years the theatre retained that mixed repertoire policy. As well as the obvious crowd-pleasing comedies and thrillers, Ibsen's *A Doll's House* took to the Intimate stage in December 1945 with the celebrated actor Michael Hordern in the cast, Shakespeare's *Othello* was staged for two weeks in February 1946 and Shaw's *Saint Joan,* with Sheila Sim in the title role, filled the theatre for a fortnight in May 1946. The occasional staging of a brand new play also took place. In September 1945 *Skylight* was premiered at the theatre. The author, Peter Dyer, was a local resident and a regular patron of the Intimate. He had recently been invalided out of the Fleet Air Arm and had written the play whilst home on leave. Peter later appeared on the Intimate stage as a member of the repertory company.

Seat prices had not increased that much since the opening of the theatre in 1935 as a flyer for January 1946 reveals:

Orchestra Stalls and Circle: 3/6d
Centre Stalls: 3/-
Back Stalls: 1/9d
Saturday Evenings and Holidays: 3/- - 4/6d
Saturday Matinees: All seats 2/6d
Standing Room: 1/9d

1946 proved to be a memorable year for a young Southgate resident, David Sculpher, for that was the year he decided to join the Intimate's backstage staff as an assistant stage manager. David's parents, who lived in Conway Road, had owned a large theatrical costumiers shop in City Road before and during the war. 'As a young boy, I regarded the five floors of armour, costumes, wigs and make-up as an Aladdin's cave', remembers David, 'but sadly the shop was burnt down in the Blitz. My parents decided they could not replace the shop as only a few costumes were saved from the ruined premises. Instead they chose to free-lance, supplying wigs and make-up for all the large amateur operatic societies. They were also members of a very good amateur dramatic company so it is not surprising to learn that I, too, was mad about theatre, so much so that at fourteen years of age my mother took me out of school as she felt I wasn't learning anything of use! In desperation my mother approached a stage manager called Alan Berry and asked him

All Rights Reserved June 1948

Easy Virtue August 1948

The Barking Dog April 1949

Gaslight **June 1949**

***Little Lambs Eat Ivy* August 1949**

***Point To Point* August 1949**

what she should do with me! Alan suggested I apply for a job at the Intimate Theatre. Strangely enough, at that time I had not heard of the Intimate but I went along for an interview and got a job as ASM. They did not seem to care who they took on as long as the slave worked for free! At some theatres you even had to pay a premium to work as an ASM. Luckily the Intimate did not do that but they did not pay me either!'

For the first twelve months David worked for no pay whatsoever, eventually receiving ten shillings a week when he entered his second year. He stayed at the Intimate for four years and by the time he left he had been promoted to the post of Master Carpenter and was earning the princely sum of £4.

David remembers his first working day vividly: 'It was a Saturday and the theatre was staging two performances of the play *The Lady From Edinburgh* with Marjorie Wilde, a very funny and accomplished actress. I spent the entire day under the stage in the props room, having been told to tidy this very messy store. Well, I set about my task with great enthusiasm and eventually had the entire room in excellent shape. I think the management were amazed that I had completed it so quickly. I was then told that the real work would begin after the second performance when the set would have to be dismantled and that I would be working virtually all night. I thought this was wonderful. Being allowed to work all night for nothing! What an idiot I was!

'The usual routine for the stage staff on Saturday evenings after the second performance was as follows. The props and general stage dressing from the set were placed in the auditorium near the exit ready for the guys from the *Old Times* store to pick up on Monday. The scenery was lowered through a hole into the workshop under the stage and the flats for next week's production were brought out. Two carpenters then placed the scenery in position helped by the rest of the backstage crew. When that was all completed we were allowed to go home so most Sunday mornings at about 3 am. I could be found cycling back to Southgate!

'On Mondays I arrived early as we had to touch up the scenery with paint (where it had been knocked carrying it out of the workroom) before adding the various props and stage dressing that arrived from *Old Times* that morning. The items from *Old Times* were very impressive and mostly antique. I know they cost a lot of money if damaged! They made a big difference to the sets as there was only so much that could be achieved with standard flats. All this had to be done before 2 pm when the dress rehearsal began. These dress rehearsals were quite lengthy affairs as the lighting had to be sorted out as well.

'On Tuesdays the whole cycle started again! Whilst the actors sat in a circle in the bar with next week's scripts, the set for next week's play was being sorted out in the workshop. I was lucky enough to work at the Intimate with a marvellous scenic designer called Stanley

Premm, who, in his younger days, had been a scenic painter for the Vienna State Opera. Stanley had long white hair and must have been, at that time, in his eighties. There was not enough height in the workshop to place the set upright so Stanley had to paint the flats on their sides. He worked with a six inch brush and six buckets of different coloured paint. By dabbing away very quickly he produced these incredible scenes. I had never seen anything like it. I learned so much from him that came in useful in my later career and I have never forgotten him. I guess he was like an old Rolf Harris!

'We very rarely made new flats, being content instead to just repair the old ones. Consequently the ones we used were very weighty as there was so much paint on them. If you looked sideways at the flats you could see all the different coloured paints that had been used over the weeks. Every so often we had to take them outside the theatre to hose them down and scrape the paint off until eventually we got down to the canvas.

'Actors liked working at the Intimate as it was so close to London. They could invite agents to see them work. We often produced plays that had recently finished runs in the West End and because of our location we could often persuade the original West End stars of those plays to appear in it again for a further week at Palmers Green. I remember meeting Richard Attenborough and Sheila Sim who often visited the theatre to see plays as they were friends of the director Ronnie Kerr. We had incredible audiences at that time with the auditorium virtually full every night. Fred Marlow would watch the play every Monday evening sitting in the same seat on the aisle so that he could stretch out his stiff leg'.

Looking back now at the weekly workload David is astounded. 'I don't know how we did it for fifty two weeks a year. It was hard work but I guess I was at the right age and of course I was terribly keen and enthusiastic. I remember we even had to work on Sundays if there was a complicated set that week. However, I was thankful for all the experience and discipline of those years. I remember also that you were allowed, and encouraged, to try things out if you had any ideas. I can honestly say that my Intimate Theatre experience stood me in good stead for everything I subsequently tackled in my career.'

David also remembers two mishaps that happened to him during his time at Palmers Green. 'I often had to clean the grid, containing pulleys and ropes, above the stage and on one occasion I thought it would be fun to slide down one of these ropes onto the stage. Of course as soon as I clambered onto the rope my weight was propelling me quickly down to the stage level and I foolishly tried to cling on to the rope with my hands, thus scraping and burning them quite badly. My fellow ASM rushed over to me and before I could stop her put iodine on my hands. I was in agony! That was the last time I played *Tarzan!*

'The other silly thing I did involved magnesium flash powder. We used a teaspoonful of this powder for any explosions required in plays but I decided one day that I would like to see what kind of explosion would occur if I used the entire contents of the tin. I planned to use a newspaper as a fuse so that I would be well away from the powder by the time it exploded. Unfortunately I had not realised that magnesium explodes on heat so as soon as I lit the paper the powder went off. I was told that the flash could be seen for miles. Not that I cared as I was too concerned about my burnt hands. There was a possibility that I would not be able to use my hands again but luckily after a week I was well enough to go back to work. Even more amazing is that the theatre took me back!'

In 1950 David was called up to do his military service and on returning to civilian life worked in various other repertory theatres. He did return to the Intimate for a few months in the late 1950s when the theatre was desperate for an electrician before moving on to Sadler's Wells Opera, the Royal Shakespeare Company, the Royal Opera House, Covent Garden and various West End productions as a décor designer. Like so many others who began their careers at the Intimate, he remembers those early years with warmth and affection. 'I felt sorry for those actors who graduated from drama school and never experienced the grounding that weekly rep gave', said David, ' I can honestly say that the basic training I received at the Intimate was still serving me well at the end of my career'.

The Gioconda Smile **October 1949**

ACTORS APPEARING AT THE INTIMATE 1941 – 1945
(Not Already Mentioned In The Text)

Regular members of the company during this period included Joslin Parlane, Ernest Haines, Marjorie Wilde, Una Venning and Mary Stone.

David Garth made the first of many appearances at the theatre in *Suspect* in February 1945. Over the next couple of years he became a 'regular' at the venue, appearing in the very first play to be televised from the theatre (*George And Margaret,* Nov 1946) as can be seen in the chapter devoted to the televised productions. Garth, who was born in Calcutta, made his first professional appearances at Sheffield Rep before moving to Palmers Green. He later carved a very successful career in television, appearing for six years as *Dr. Armstrong* in *General Hospital* as well as many other plays and series.

Antony Eustrel, mentioned earlier, proved to be the heartthrob of the war years at the Intimate. Born in 1903, he played many leading roles at Palmers Green in such plays as *The Barretts Of Wimpole Street* (Sept 1941), *Jane Eyre* (Oct 1941), *Time And The Conways* (Jan 1942) and *Gaslight* (Jan 1942). Antony appeared in various Shakespearean roles at the Memorial Theatre, Stratford-upon-Avon in 1944 and 1945 and then joined Donald Wolfit's Company at the Winter Garden Theatre. He appeared in several British films before moving to Hollywood where, according to *The Encyclopaedia of British Film*, he played 'professional Brits in a variety of genres, including a butler in *Goodbye Charlie* (1964). He died in 1979.

The film director and actor Brian Forbes made several appearances during this period with featured roles in *The Corn Is Green* (May 1943), *The Maitlands* (Jan 1944), *The Second Mrs. Tanqueray* (Nov 1944), *Love Isn't Everything* (Nov 1944) and *Mrs. Inspector Jones* (Dec 1950). Forbes later added screenwriting to his list of talents, being responsible for such films as *The Angry Silence*, *The League Of Gentlemen* and *Only Two Can Play*. As a film actor he appeared in many films including *An Inspector Calls, The Wooden Horse* and *The Guns Of Navarone* and as a film director he produced *Whistle Down the Wind*, *Séance On A Wet Afternoon*, *The Whisperers*, *The Wrong Box*, *The L-Shaped Room*, *The Slipper And The Rose* and many others.

The comic actress and author Irene Handl could be found at the Intimate in 1941 appearing in the popular comedy *George And Margaret* (Nov 1941). Irene had scored a great personal success as the maid *Beer* in the original London production at Wyndham's Theatre in 1937 so it was rather a coup for the Intimate that she joined the resident company for this staging. She returned two years later for the farce *Rookery Nook* (Aug 1943) and then made a guest appearance much later in her career when she starred for a week as *Lily Piper* in Jack Popplewell's *Busybody* (Aug 1965), a part she had played with great success at the Duke Of York's Theatre the year before.

Anna Wing, later to find television fame as the matriarch *Lou Beale* in the early years of BBC's soap opera *Eastenders,* appeared in a string of plays in 1944 including *Busman's Holiday* (May 1944), *The Truth About Blayds* (June 1944), *Eliza Comes To Stay* (June 1944) and *Candida* (July 1944).

The disc jockey Pete Murray, then known a little more formally as Peter Murray, made a couple of appearances, his first being in *Wuthering Heights* (June 1943). He returned briefly two years later for A.A.Milne's play *Sarah Simple* (Oct 1945).

Patrick MacNee appeared at the Intimate in *Hay Fever* (Feb 1942), *Distinguished Gathering* (Oct 1944) and *Wuthering Heights* (June 1947) long before he found fame as the suave *John Steed* in the cult television series *The Avengers* playing opposite Honor Blackman, Diana Rigg, Linda Thorson and Joanna Lumley.

The portly actor Sebastian Cabot could be found at Palmers Green in several productions during this period including *Charley's Aunt* (Dec 1943), *The Maitlands* (Jan 1944), *The Second Mrs. Tanqueray* (Nov 1944) and *Love Isn't Everything* (Nov 1944). Cabot made many film appearances in supporting roles before achieving success in America, mainly on television, playing pompous but loveable buffoons.

Peggy Cummins joined Richard Attenborough in *Ah, Wilderness* (Sep 1941) and returned for *Quiet Wedding* (May 1952) and *Sixteen* (Jun 1942) before going on to star in many British films including *The Captain's Table, Dentist In The Chair, Hell Drivers* and *Meet Mr. Lucifer.*

Character actress Marie Ault, who had appeared with success in silent films in the twenties, most notably in Alfred Hitchcock's *The Lodger* and the trilogy of *Rat* films starring Ivor Novello (*The Rat; The Triumph Of The Rat* and *The Return Of The Rat*), delighted local playgoers in 1941 and 1942 with roles in such plays as *Jane Eyre* (Oct 1941), *Dear Brutus* (Nov 1941), *Ladies In Retirement* (Dec 1941) and *A Murder Has Been Arranged* (Feb 1942).

Joy Shelton made many appearances at the theatre during this period in such dramas as *The Barretts Of Wimpole Street* (Sept 1941), *Suspect* (Oct 1941) and *The Doctor's Dilemma* (Jun 1943). Joy married the actor Sydney Tafler in 1944, the year Tafler returned to the Intimate for *Rope* (Mar 1944) and *The Queen Was In The Parlour* (Apr 1944) and that month Joy joined Sydney for a production of *The Ghost Train.*

The character actress Barbara Lott, later seen regularly on television as Ronnie Corbett's domineering mother in the comedy series *Sorry!,* was another visitor to Palmers Green at this time where she could be seen in *Acacia Avenue* (Feb 1945), *Jane Steps Out* (Apr 1945) and *Ten Little Niggers* (Oct 1945).

Helen Cherry, the actress wife of Trevor Howard, trod the boards in Palmers Green in 1942 in *Dusty Ermine* (Aug 1942), returning the following year in *Children To Bless You* (Feb 1943) and *Jupiter Laughs* (May 1943).

One-Off Appearances

Maria Charles featured in the play *The Man From Toronto* (Apr 1945). Maria later played *Dulcie* in the original London cast of Sandy Wilson's musical *The Boy Friend.*

Yvonne Mitchell joined the company to play the title role in Shaw's *Major Barbara* (Oct 1941). A noted stage, television and film actress, Yvonne was also author of several plays and novels. Her finest hour in the cinema was probably playing the title role in Ted Willis's *Woman In A Dressing Gown.* Yvonne returned to the Intimate briefly in 1968 when she appeared in the play *Out Of Order.*

Husky-voiced Joan Greenwood appeared in *Dr. Brent's Household* (Jan 1944).

Sir Michael Hordern could be seen briefly at Palmers Green, long before he was knighted, when he appeared in Ibsen's *A Doll's House* (Dec 1945).Hordern had a very distinguished stage career appearing frequently with the Old Vic company and the Royal Shakespeare Company and was a notable *Prospero* and *Lear.* He also made nearly one hundred films and appeared regularly in television drama.

Debonair Jeremy Hawk was in the cast of *Ladies In Retirement* (Dec 1941). He was later to be found regularly on television both as a compere of quiz shows and as a straight man to comics such as Benny Hill. He was at one time married to the actress and revue performer Joan Heal and their daughter is the actress Belinda Lang.

Pete Murray

Irene Handl

Yvonne Mitchell

THE PLAYGOERS' SOCIETY

In the programme for *The Dominant Sex* in December 1941 it was suggested that a Playgoers Society be formed which would meet at regular intervals throughout the year 'to read and discuss unusual plays' and to play host to visiting guest speakers. This suggestion obviously struck a chord with the Intimate audiences and there was an excellent response to the idea.

On Sunday 31st May 1942 the first meeting of the Society took place with the Mayor of Enfield presiding and Dame Irene Vanbrugh as the guest speaker. The membership stood at over three hundred and it was decided to hold the meetings monthly on Sunday afternoons.

Guest speakers over the years included author and theatre historian W. MacQueen Pope, theatre director Val Gielgud, brother of Sir John, actors Naunton Wayne, Robert Atkins, Lyn Harding, Esmond Knight, musical comedy star and local resident Stephanie Voss and Dame Sybil Thorndike. On Sunday 29th October 1950 the Playgoers were delighted to welcome the Hollywood film star Tyrone Power, who gave an informal talk at a meeting chaired by the British film and stage star Jack Hawkins. Both actors had recently filmed *The Black Rose* in England and Tyrone Power was, at that time, appearing at the London Coliseum, to great acclaim, in the play *Mister Roberts*. The actor Leslie Parnell remembers attending that Playgoers Club meeting and chatting to Tyrone Power afterwards. ' He showed me a cutting from an American paper', recalls Leslie, ' detailing his antics on a

Tyrone Power

yacht in the Pacific with a teenage girl. He was indignant, saying the studios handed out this sort of rubbish to keep his name in the public eye and to boost his macho image but, as he said, how could he be on a yacht in the Pacific when he was doing eight performances a week in the West End!'

Jack Hawkins

A popular event at Society meetings was the occasional *Brains Trust*, where several guests under the guidance of a Chairman discussed various theatre topics. On 30th October 1960 *A Brains Trust* saw the welcome return of Richard Attenborough and Sheila Sim as two of the panel, joined by actor Laidman Browne, the then resident director of the Intimate rep company Jimmy Grant Anderson plus the company's leading lady Margaret Gibson. In the chair was another regular member of the acting company Raymond Dyer. During the course of that meeting the members recounted their most embarrassing moments on stage and then talk turned to forgotten props. This gave Jimmy Grant Anderson the opportunity to tell a wonderful anecdote about the celebrated actor Sir Seymour Hicks.

Hicks was alone on the stage and the play called for him to take out his revolver and shoot himself. His hand went to his pocket. No revolver. He crossed to a cupboard for anything

Marie Burke

that might look like a poison bottle, but the cupboard was bare. He looked round to the table for a knife. No knife.

So he stepped straight down to the footlights, wagged his head from side to side and exclaimed: "Good gracious. I have broken my neck!"

The following April's *Brains Trust* saw Jimmy Grant Anderson once more on the panel, joined by comedian Gillie Potter and actresses Irene Handl, Carol Marsh and Marie Burke whilst November's edition featured Dulcie Gray, John Arnatt, Bernard Kay, Sylvia Francis and playwright Arthur Lovegrove, all kept in order by Intimate regular John Barron. A year later, in November 1962, saw Fenella Fielding, Judy Campbell and comedy actor Graham Stark gracing the Intimate stage for the afternoon.

By 1960 the aims of the Playgoers Society were listed as

> to support the Intimate Theatre in every possible way, and to promote a knowledge of and interest in the theatre in general.

> A varied programme is arranged, consisting of interesting and informative talks given by well-known personalities in the world of theatre. Visits and social evenings are also arranged and every effort is made to vary the monthly programmes, in order to cover as wide a field as possible during each year.

The membership fee at that time was 10/- per person per annum; 25/- for three members of the same family; 30/- for four members of the same family and 5/- for young persons under the age of twenty-one.

The society was obviously flourishing around this time and the following year reported a 50% increase in membership. Sadly, this growth was not reflected in the Intimate's fortunes as the chairman of the society, Dr. Clunie Harvey made clear to the members at a meeting in September 1961. He pointed out that the society was not doing enough to help the theatre and that attendance at the venue had been falling since August 1960.

In 1964 the Society launched *The Theatre Fund* with the object of increasing the entertainment amenities for the benefit of actors and audiences. Within weeks £100 had been raised.

After struggling on in the vain hope that the theatre would miraculously return to its glory days, the Playgoers Society finally called it a day in 1973, four years after professional rep had ceased to exist at the Intimate. The local *Gazette* reported its demise on 9th March.

Judy Campbell

CURTAINS FOR INTIMATE PLAYGOERS

Hope has been abandoned that the Intimate Theatre, Palmers Green will again be used by a repertory company.

The 25 year old Intimate Playgoers Society, formed to support local rep are holding their final meeting at the theatre on Sunday 18th March to wind up their affairs.

After a few difficult years, repertory theatre finally died at the Intimate with the reversion of the theatre to its original use as a parish hall for next-door St. Monica's Roman Catholic Church in 1970.

In a letter to members, chairman of the Playgoers Society, Mr. Ernest Faregrave has written: "No doubt you will be surprised to hear from me after so long an interval. But when the professional theatre closed down and our meetings were no longer possible, your committee hesitated to call for a meeting to terminate our activities while there was the remotest chance of a future for the society. However we feel that such action can no longer be delayed."

Members are asked to consider the resolutions: that the society be dissolved and that the outstanding balance of about £80 or £90 on the society's books be equally divided between the local societies for Research Into Muscular Dystrophy and Multiple Sclerosis.

Mr. Faregrave believes that the wrong choice of production for local people's tastes was the main reason for the Intimate rep's commercial failure. He said: "When the old rep company was wound up in 1968 one or two people tried to make a go of it.

Howard Kent made a brief splash with Richard Todd and Dilys Laye in *Man With A Load Of Mischief* but on the whole the type of production was not what local people wanted. People in Palmers Green liked a good Agatha Christie – not the sound of a lavatory flushing off-stage. It's sad because the Intimate Theatre was the opening gambit for many well-known actors and playwrights, but at least the theatre is being well-used by amateur drama groups."

The Playgoers last meeting is to be chaired by the former Mayor of Southgate, Mr. Harry Farbey and it is to be hoped a number of special guests will attend. They include Aubrey Woods, son of the late Mr. Harold Woods, a former secretary of the society, Mrs. W. Clunie Harvey, wife of Dr. Harvey, former Medical Officer of Health for Southgate and a former chairman of the Playgoers Society and Mr. Bill Budd, former manager of the Intimate Theatre.

RONALD KERR

Ronald Kerr

If the late 1930s are chiefly remembered for the excellence of John Clements' productions, which put the Intimate well and truly on the theatrical map of London, then the late '40s were almost a similar golden age with a wide variety of drama on offer and audiences flocking to the Palmers Green venue. Television had not yet made much of an impact on the general public so theatre was indeed thriving. This was due in no small measure to the resident director of that period, Ronald Kerr. His workload was almost on a par with that of John Clements. From 18th August 1941 when the theatre re-opened until 1st November 1947 when he left the Intimate, Kerr directed virtually every production, which amounted to over two hundred and eighty plays! He also occasionally took leading roles in the productions playing *Charles Condomine* in Coward's *Blithe Spirit, Mr. Rochester* in *Jane Eyre, Shylock* in *The Merchant Of Venice,* the title roles in *Abraham Lincoln* and *Othello* as well as featured roles in *The Two Mrs. Carrolls* and *The Marquise.*

Ronald Kerr was born in 1905 and made his first London stage appearance in *The Farmer's Wife* in 1924 and then joined Sybil Thorndike's Company, appearing in London, Paris and South Africa. In 1928 he added stage directing to his talents working at Daly's, The Royalty and The Garrick theatres as well as the Q, People's Palace and Embassy theatres. He had taught at the Royal Academy of Dramatic Art prior to working at the theatre and was highly regarded by the actors in the company. Obviously the time restraints of rehearsing and staging a play in a week, whilst presenting another play in the evenings, restricted the depth and finesse that could be brought to a production. Nevertheless Kerr achieved minor miracles in the time at his disposal. June Whitfield enjoyed working with him and thought him 'a gifted and resourceful director'; David Garth claimed that Kerr had a profound effect on his thinking as an actor whilst Leslie Parnell remembers him as 'a fine actor and producer, although he could have an acid tongue at times.'

The actor and comedian Nicholas Parsons made some early career appearances at the Intimate and still speaks with affection about Ronald Kerr:

'Nobody could get more out of a play in a week than Ronald. If you were willing to learn and take direction he was a superb teacher. He had an amazing ability to give you enough to get a rounded portrayal, which was rare in weekly rep.'

Nicholas Parsons

Nicholas pointed out that as Kerr had worked at RADA, he had that gift to impart knowledge and direction. He acknowledges that Kerr greatly influenced his career and development as an actor:

'It was what I learnt from Ronnie that helped me later to be a successful straight man.'

Nicholas Parsons first appeared at the Intimate in *The Hasty Heart* in January 1947 playing the American *Yank*. The play proved so popular that it returned to Palmers Green the following month with Nicholas Parsons once again in the cast. Ronald Kerr remembered his portrayal and when Kerr was later in charge of Bromley's New Theatre, he invited Nicholas to join the company. As Nicholas pointed out: 'It was the start of one of the most interesting phases of my professional life.' Nicholas did return to the Intimate Theatre for a few more appearances in 1950 and 1951 in such dramas as *Mr. Gillie* (Sept 1950), *The School For Scandal* (Oct 1950), *Mrs. Warren's Profession* (Jan 1951) and *Charley's Aunt* (Sept 1951) when the local critic described him as the tallest aunt he had ever seen!

Although Kerr left Palmers Green to set up a rep company at Bromley in November 1947 that wasn't the end of his association with the Intimate. Kerr's connections with the New Theatre at Bromley came to a sudden end because of a homosexual incident. Although common in the theatre world, homosexuality was still against the law at that time and though details of this incident are very sketchy, Kerr found himself ostracised by other theatres. Nicholas Parsons remembers that Kerr managed to find work at a theatre in Hayes before Fred Marlow invited him back to the Intimate. Nicholas recalls that Fred was extremely kind to Kerr, telling him that what he did in his private life was his own business and that he wanted him back at the theatre because he was an excellent director.

On 22nd May 1950 when the curtain went up on Emlyn Williams' play *The Light Of Heart* the programme once again boasted Ronald Kerr as producer. He went on to produce another forty plays including *The Heiress* and *Harvey* in which he played leading roles as well as the title role in a production of *Macbeth*. It was during this second stint as the company producer that Kerr was instrumental in linking the Intimate with the Palace Theatre in Maidstone, running the two in conjunction and transferring each play there after a week's run at the Intimate. As Nicholas Parsons pointed out: 'This proved to be very popular with the actors as it meant that they enjoyed the luxury of performing the same play for two weeks'.

However, Kerr's second period as Intimate director of productions came to a tragic end when he committed suicide in the early hours of March 20th 1951, just seventeen days after his last performance as *Macbeth* and just ten days after his last production at the Intimate.

On the afternoon of 19th March 1951 Ronald Kerr was arrested for 'importuning male persons for an immoral purpose' and charged to appear at Marlborough Street Magistrates Court on the following day. In the proceedings of the Marlborough Street Magistrates Courts for 1951 there is the following entry for 19th March 1951:

> 21.   Name of defendant: Ronald Stuart Harvey Kerr. (Producer) (46)
>   Date of Offence: 19th March 1951
>   Charged: 3.30 p.m.
>   Bailed: 4.05 p.m.
>
> Nature Of Offence: Being a male person, did persistently importune male persons for an immoral purpose at 3, King's Ford, Grosvenor Hill, Providence Court, W.1. S.I. Vagrancy Act 1898.

As was mentioned above, homosexuality was illegal at that time and Kerr had been in trouble with the law before over this and the combination of those two facts was enough to drive him to utter despair. Despite the pleadings of friends Kerr committed suicide in the early hours of 20th March. He was forty-six years of age. The inquest into Kerr's death was reported at length in *The Palmers Green and Southgate Gazette* for 30th March.

Ronald Kerr's Last Hours Of Distress
Phone Message: 'This Is Goodbye'

The last hours of Ronald Kerr, actor-producer at the Intimate Theatre, Palmers Green, when his friends fought to persuade him against taking his own life, was described at Saturday's Bromley (Kent) inquest on his death. He was found gassed in the lounge of his home early on March 20th. The North West

Kent Coroner (Mr. S.O.Matthews) recorded a verdict of suicide while the balance of mind was disturbed.

Evidence told of telephone messages to friends in which Mr. Kerr said 'This is goodbye. I am going to take my life' after he had been charged to appear at Marlborough Street Magistrates Court and of his drinking rum to gain courage. It showed that he had returned home after the telephone messages and was persuaded to go to bed. Early next morning he was found dead by his friend Mr. Alan Gourley, former stage director at the New Theatre, Bromley. Mr. Gourley, an artist, who lived with Kerr, told the Coroner he had known him since 1931.

On March 19th Kerr telephoned him from London some time after 5.30 p.m. and told him he was due to appear at the court on a charge the following morning.

"He seemed very self-possessed and calm but obviously very concerned. He said he had written three letters – to myself, his mother and the manager of the Intimate Theatre. He also said he had been to solicitors and made a will.

"I tried to find out where he was and pleaded with him to let me come up to him, but he said 'You will persuade me to change my mind and I cannot have that'.

"Then", went on Mr. Gourley, " Kerr said 'You must not worry about it. I am doing this in complete possession of my senses. I am doing it all on a basis of reason. I am now going to take my life. This is goodbye.' He then rang off.

"We could do nothing about it", said Mr. Gourley. But later that evening Kerr arrived home "in a terrible state". His clothes were wet; there was mud on his coat.

"He said he had been drinking rum. He wanted courage to take his life on the railway line", said Mr. Gourley.

"We (Gourley and friend) tried to reason with him. Later that night he went out of the side door and we chased after him. Then again later he went out again. I found him in the drive. There followed a distressing scene – he was begging me to ask Mrs. Clipston and her daughter to go home and then he would come back. He accused me of acting like a policeman.

"They did go home and he came in, but later I found him in the locked bathroom and I had to force the door. But after that he became completely calm. He listened to me and said he would face up to his responsibilities.

"I slept with him in the same bed that night just to be near him. His last words were, 'You will phone Fred Marlow in the morning for me. I will not be in a fit state to speak to him.'"

Mr. Gourley said he awoke at about three in the morning to find Kerr gone. He found him downstairs in the lounge, his face towards the gas fire jet and a raincoat over his head. The three letters were found nearby.

Mrs. S. Clipston of Hayes, Kent, told of a telephone call she had received from Mr. Kerr similar to the one to Mr. Gourley.

She went to his home and saw him when he returned later that evening. He said he had been 'on the line somewhere'. She believed the court case was the cause of his attitude.

The Coroner: "He had had some trouble of this kind before. I wonder whether he could not go on any longer with it. Perhaps he thought he had failed himself?" Mrs. Clipston: "No, I think it was just this particular case. He could not face the court."

Mr. Vivian Bartley, a solicitor, said that on March 19th in the afternoon, Kerr, who was a complete stranger, called at his office and made a will. As he was going out he said: 'I hope people will not think I am of unsound mind because this will probably be disputed.'

Commented the Coroner: "It may be that when he went to the solicitor's office he was in a fit state to make a will and his mind was not so much disturbed as if he left to take his life immediately. It was after that he telephoned. When he took his life, I am quite sure that his mind was disturbed. That is quite clear from his actions on arriving home. He was a prominent person in his profession and I have no doubt that he felt that the charge he had to meet was a serious one and he was extremely distressed about it."

The Gazette also paid tribute to Kerr's work at the Intimate:

He showed that he had a deep understanding of drama and the stage and also loved his work. He also made his mark in many acting roles with special aptitude for costume or period plays. He will be long remembered for *Mr. Barrett* in *The Barretts Of Wimpole Street* and the title role in *Othello*. Only two weeks ago, Mr. Kerr had scored a great success as *Macbeth*....He was at one time a teacher at the Royal Academy of Dramatic Art and many well-known actors and actresses of today owe much to the thorough grounding he gave them in the technique of the stage.

The Bromley and Kentish Times for 23rd March 1951 also paid tribute to Ronald Kerr and pointed out that

> He reopened the Intimate Theatre, Palmers Green during the last war and in six years built it up to be one of the foremost repertory theatres in London. Among now famous stars who had their first chance there, under his direction, were Richard Attenborough, Sheila Sim, Joy Shelton and Joyce Redman.

Kerr was undoubtedly a major figure in the story of the Intimate and his tragic death brought another chapter of the venue's history to a close.

FRED MARLOW (For G.M. PRODUCTIONS) presents

"THE MERCHANT OF VENICE"

By WILLIAM SHAKESPEARE

The Duke of Venice	KEITH SHEPHERD
The Prince of Morocco	MICHAEL BIRD
The Prince of Arragon	EDMUND GREY
Antonio	ANTONY EUSTREL
Bassanio	DEREK BIRCH
Salario	ANTONY VERNEY
Gratiano	JOHN JOWITT
Solanio	DAVID MAUDE
Lorenzo	GORDON GANTRY
Shylock	RONALD KERR
Tubal	MARTIN CLARK
Launcelot Gobbo	MICHAEL CONRY
Old Gobbo	KEITH SHEPHERD
Clerk of the Court	EDMUND GREY
Portia	IRIS BAKER
Nerissa	JOSLIN PARLANE
Jessica	MARY STONE

Servants to Portia, and other Attendants

The Entire Production under the direction of RONALD KERR

PART ONE

Scene 1	Venice
Scene 2	Belmont

INTERMISSION

PART TWO

Scene 1	Venice
Scene 2	Belmont

INTERMISSION

PART THREE

Scene 1	Venice
Scene 2	Belmont

The Merchant Of Venice December 1943
Directed by and starring Ronald Kerr

THE TELEVISION YEARS

December 1946 marked a significant point in the Intimate's history. On Monday 2nd December *George And Margaret* by Gerald Savory became the first complete play to be televised live from a theatre by the British Broadcasting Corporation. *The Palmers Green And Southgate Gazette* for Friday 6th December was under no doubt of the importance of the event and devoted a goodly part of its front page to the news.

WORLD PREMIERE IN HISTORY OF TELEVISION
INTIMATE THEATRE FAME
EXPERIMENT PLEASES
"The Most Perfect Yet"

A world premiere in the history of television, the transmission of the whole of Gerald Savory's delightful comedy, *George And Margaret,* from the Intimate Theatre on Monday evening, was a tremendous success.

The cast and staff of the theatre worked in complete harmony with the television experts and technicians and the result was perfect reception on the screen and a thrilling experience for those fortunate enough to be present at the transmitting end of the event.

BBC 'high-ups' make no secret of the fact that they are delighted with the outcome of the experiment. One of them described it as "the most perfect yet".

Early on Monday residents and passers-by noticed a new feature on the Palmers Green skyline, a tall mast topped by an aerial had reared itself from one of the covey of dark green BBC television vans that had taken up occupation of the precincts of the Intimate Theatre on Sunday.

All day long things were going on in and about the theatre. Cables of extraordinary thickness and complexity were being laid, apparatus was being set up, tests made, rehearsals staged, and, because the electricity mains were insufficient to carry the amount of "juice" necessary, one of the BBC's special generators was brought into action.

EFFICIENCY WITHOUT FUSS

Throughout the amazingly complicated preparatory work and during the vitally important period of the actual television, activities were carried on with a cool and calm efficiency, a complete absence of fuss that speaks volumes in praise of the organisation of the BBC and the competence of its members. The BBC is so often the subject of kicks that the few humble and well-earned ha'pence represented by these words of appreciation are surely overdue.

It was an excited and rather tense audience that filled the theatre well before time for the curtain raising. Up in the circle was installed part of the mechanism of the wonderful trick of television; in the centre three massive cameras, of weird design to the untechnical eye, and at either end a group of huge floodlights.

Each piece of apparatus had its attendant genie, the cameramen wearing headphones through which a constant stream of direction reached them from one of the vans outside. Down in this van a further group of technicians was receiving the television on a screen and carrying out certain processes, one known simply as "mixing".

The sound went direct by land line to be broadcast, but the vision, transmitted through the aerial, was picked up at Swain's Lane, Finchley, boosted and sent on again to Alexandra Palace for further boosting before being transmitted to the receiving sets of the general public.

The moment came when the floodlights were switched on and an expectant hush fell on the audience. Ronald Kerr, a fine actor himself and the Intimate's producer of so many enjoyable plays, stepped from behind the curtain. He spoke with feeling of the tribute paid to "this little theatre" in being chosen to make television history.

"A lot depends tonight on you and your reaction to the play," he told the audience, "but I am not going to do what I believe is done sometimes – that is, I am not going to ask you to laugh, because hollow laughter would be worse than none. This great battery of lights makes you visible to each other and you may find this embarrassing, but do not let it deter you, if you are really enjoying yourselves, from laughing like anything."

Mr. Kerr said that members of the cast were worked up to a pitch of nervous tension in view of the exacting ordeal that lay before them, but when a few minutes later the curtain rose – to a murmur of appreciation for the charming setting – nothing of this was apparent in the demeanour of the players.

Whatever their inward emotions may have been, they gave the impression of superb confidence, and their presentation of Gerald Savory's delightful comedy *George And Margaret,* was if anything even more enjoyable than when I saw it a week previously. All members of the cast were on their toes, giving of their best, and there was not a single hitch throughout the polished and finely acted performance.

Frederick Marlow presented the play and members of the cast were Ernest Haines, Marjorie Wilde, Ann Castle, David Garth, Owen Holder, Joyce Cummings, John Whiting and Dorothy Dewhurst.

A tribute must be paid to others at the Intimate who did not appear in the limelight, but who most certainly have earned a share in the honour of the event. They are: Peter Loftus (manager), Alan Warren (stage manager), Gloria Harris (assistant stage manager), Stanley Premm (scenic artist), Eric Nye (stage carpenter) and J.W.Lines (electrician).

Mr. Gerald Savory was prevented from attending by his absence in America, but his mother, actress Grace Lane, was present in the audience and thoroughly enjoyed the Intimate production of her son's play.

The BBC aerial at the Intimate - December 1946

The BBC and Fred Marlow had met in November to discuss the arrangements and the theatre management made the decision to run the play for two weeks so that the BBC could televise it on the second Monday of the run, giving the actors a week of performances before facing the cameras. The car park was closed to the general public as the BBC needed it for their Outside Broadcast vans and the *Gazette* carried a wonderful photograph of the BBC aerial outside the Intimate. This aerial, looking like a gigantic fire escape, enabled the picture to be transmitted to Swains Lane in Finchley whilst the sound was sent to Alexandra Palace by landline.

As well as the car park the theatre had to remove the whole of the front row of the Dress Circle seating so that the TV cameras and lighting could be installed, whilst the second row was also out of action as it was reserved for the actual cameramen and technicians. The BBC reimbursed the theatre for these forty seats so that the Intimate did not lose out financially from 'lost' ticket sales although playgoers sitting in the remaining three rows in the circle must have had a very interrupted view of the stage. The BBC also wanted access to wasteland adjoining the theatre off Stonard Road to store a generator and asked for permission to remove fencing if necessary. The Corporation stipulated that they would pay for any extra electricity used.

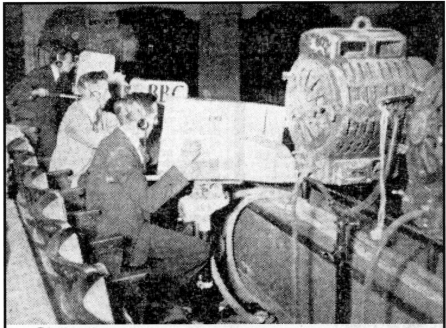

In the circle of the theatre these weird objects were installed. They are the television cameras, or technically the Emitrons. Extra lamps were also installed to supplement the normal lighting on the stage and to reduce shadow. All three operators, one covering the long view, the second the medium view, the other for close-ups, were in action throughout the play. The picture of each camera was taken through heavy cables (seen on the right of the picture) to the B.B.C. van outside the theatre where a producer selected the best picture for transmission to Swains Lane, Finchley, from whence it was re-broadcast to Alexandra Palace for rediffusion to the public.

BBC cameramen in the circle as photographed by
The Palmers Green and Southgate Gazette 6th December 1946

A full list of the BBC's requirements was given in a letter to Fred Marlow, dated 4th November:

Dear Mr. Marlow,

Further to our conversation today, I now enclose a contract for the broadcast of George And Margaret in our television service on Monday, December 2nd 1946.

I give below a list of the facilities we shall require:-

1.   *a) Permission to use the car park for our O.B. vans*

       b) That you inform us if you are able to obtain permission from the owner of the waste-land adjoining the theatre off Stonard Road to park a generator there; also

       c) Permission to remove fencing, if necessary, in which event it is understood that we will replace immediately after the broadcast.

2.   *A full dress rehearsal with the Cast, from 2.00 – 5.30 pm on the day of transmission.*

3.   *Access to the theatre all day on Sunday and Monday, December 1st and 2nd.*

4.   *The use of your Stage Carpenter, Electrician and one Stage Hand on Sunday 1st December from 9 am; to be paid for by us at normal union rates, for fitting up lighting, etc.*

5.   *The use of the same staff for December 2nd, times, etc to be decided later.*

6.   *The removal of the whole front row of the Dress Circle seating for Camera and Lighting positions; the cost of this labour to be defrayed by us.*

7.   *Admission to theatre performance for Projection Staff during the week prior to the television broadcast, requirements for which will be notified to the Manager of the Theatre as soon as these are known.*

It is understood that we will bear the cost of any extra electric current, which we may use.

The price of the forty Dress Circle seats mentioned in paragraph 6 above is included in the figure quoted in the contract.

I shall be glad if you will let me have your signed acceptance as soon as possible.

Yours sincerely,

Holland Bennett
Television Booking Manager

The BBC used three cameras for the transmission: the first operator covered the long view, the second operator the medium view and the third concentrated on close-ups, Extra lamps were installed to supplement the normal lighting on the stage and to reduce shadow and a dress rehearsal was held in the afternoon so that the cameramen could acquaint themselves with the play before the evening transmission.

The cast of *George and Margaret* - December 1946
Back: Ernest Haines
Middle: David Garth, BBC cameraman, Joyce Cummings, Owen Holder, Dorothy Dewhurst
Front: Ann Castle, John Whiting

Members of the cast of that historic production included Owen Holder and John Whiting. Owen recalls: 'At that time I wanted to be a playwright and John was determined to be an actor. As it turned out I remained an actor and John, of course, became an excellent playwright!' John Whiting was the author of such plays as *A Penny For A Song, Marching Song* and *The Devils,* which was later filmed by Ken Russell. Whiting died in 1963 and two years later the Arts Council established The John Whiting Award for dramatists in commemoration of the playwright and his contribution to post-war British theatre.

Whilst at the Intimate Theatre Owen Holder fell in love with a fellow cast member of *George And Margaret,* the actress Joyce Cummings. 'When we married', said Owen, 'I was still at the Intimate and after the ceremony I had to return to the theatre for the afternoon rehearsal! My wife was in another repertory theatre appearing in the play *Quiet Wedding* so she was a bride twice in one day!'

Another member of the *George And Margaret* cast was David Garth and it is interesting to note that he made a welcome return to the theatre many years later in a production of *Gaslight* in 1983. Ernest Haines, the Intimate's hard working character actor notched up his 145th production at Palmers Green with his appearance in this play.

The BBC paid a facilities fee to the Intimate of £59, which included actors' fees and loss of seating plus £30 for stage labour. The schedule for that historic evening consisted of:

7.15 – 7.16 pm	Introductory Caption
7.16 – 7.58 pm	Act 1
7.58 pm.	Interval Caption and Next Act
8.08 pm	Bar Bell
8.08 – 8.50 pm	Act 2
8.50 pm	Interval Caption and Next Act
9.00 pm	Bar Bell
9.00 – 9.45 pm	Act 3
9.45 pm	End Caption

The Director for this television outside broadcast was Campbell Logan, a notable name at the BBC at that time. The evening seemed to have been a success, so much so that the BBC was willing to repeat the adventure as Logan hinted in a letter to Fred Marlow on the day after the broadcast: …'From all accounts, in spite of the mishap to our close-up camera, the show appears to have gone down very well. I hope very much that you will think it worth while repeating the experiment at a future date..' Logan went on to praise the Intimate's technical staff, without whose tremendous work 'the show could not possibly have gone on' and concluded by saying 'I felt that the cast rose magnificently to the occasion.'

If Campbell Logan was happy with the first transmission from the Intimate, the local reporter in the *Gazette* (6th Dec. 1946) was ecstatic:

Enthusiastic Looker-In Writes

With a cup of coffee near to hand, a soft carpet beneath my feet and a fire glowing rosily, testing the shadows' depths with its lazy flickering, I saw and heard *George And Margaret* in comfort in the home of a friend on Monday evening.

In other words, I was at the receiving end of the Intimate Theatre's televised comedy – and a grand experience it was. One revelled in the success so clearly attending the efforts of the players; indeed, recalling the hazardous nature of the Intimate's brave re-opening during the war years and being deeply appreciative of the quality productions, which distinguish our own little theatre, one's enjoyment was not unmixed with emotion.

Successes Of Friends

I risk a charge of sentimentality. No matter, if you agree with me that there is happiness to be won from consciousness of the successes of friends.

That the Intimate has achieved fame from Monday's unique occasion there is no room to doubt. No better choice of play could have been made than *George And Margaret*, Gerald Savory's titillating story of a delightful family whose idiosyncrasies – and the manner of their interpretation – were so exactly pictured by colleague V.V.D. in her criticism last week.

There were five of us looking-in, and all were impressed by the brilliance of the Intimate players' bubbling enthusiasm, skill and polish. So well did they perform that they might have been in the middle of a long run, instead of at the beginning of a second week! The action rippled like a laughing stream, evenly and joyously.

All Were First-Rate

Ernest Haines and Marjorie Wilde were outstanding and were supported with such verve and spirit as to arouse one's unstinted admiration. Reception was admirable: the sound perfect. The laughter of the fortunate audience heartily coincided with our own less dignified outbursts as the gems of dialogue flowered.

We missed, perhaps, those close-ups, which would have admitted us even more intimately to the family circle, but only those acquainted with television would have noted it.

Enthusing over *George And Margaret,* I remembered that behind the scenes were quality producer and actor of note, Ronald Kerr, the stage captains and artists and the ever-eager Frederick Marlow.

The Future

In warmly commending everyone concerned with Monday's eminently satisfying achievement, I would add this. The combined work of our own theatre and the BBC has surely established something, which as the years roll on, will immeasurably benefit both the Theatre and the television service.

They have so much in common, that the development of this week's experience will bring increased pleasure to the growing number of lookers-in and, who knows, impart new life and vigour to the stage.

Television viewers did not have to wait long for a second visit to the Intimate as cameras were installed in the circle again at the end of the month when the BBC broadcast *Junior Miss* by Jerome Chodorov and Joseph Fields on 30th December. Campbell Logan was a little more critical this time of the finished product. In his programme report he pointed out that he had only three days in which to see the show before actual production, which he felt was not long enough. The sound, he thought, was not as good as for *George And Margaret* and the cameras missed some of the action. Even so, the BBC was very keen to continue with outside broadcasts from the Intimate, even increasing the facilities fee from £59 to £84 plus stage labour costs, and plans were made for the cameras to visit the theatre on a regular basis. A potential fly in the ointment was the Middlesex County Council who raised doubts about the adequacy of protection to the public against any possible risks arising out of the lighting installation but that problem was eventually solved to everyone's satisfaction.

The third play to be televised was St. John Irving's *Anthony And Anna* on Friday 18th April 1947. The BBC had hoped to show *French Without Tears* but a revival in the West End scuppered that plan and the Irving play was selected. David Garth, Peggy Thorpe Bates and Ann Castle headed the cast for this drama which was directed, not by Ronald Kerr who was away working briefly at the Lyric Theatre, Hammersmith, but by one of the Intimate's favourite actresses, Sheila Raynor. The BBC's production report was very critical of this play, claiming it was 'badly cast and poorly acted.' As for Sheila Raynor's direction, the report, while admitting she was a capable actress, declared that she 'has had no experience of production at all and this obviously reacted on the performance.'

The report went on: ' With regard to the view that it would have been better produced in the studio, I think if such a bad performance had been given in the studio, it would have been quite unbearable, whereas with a very live audience reaction, I felt it was entertainment value!'

It is also clear from BBC memos that the Intimate Theatre was facing opposition from some play agents owing to their association with television. These agents resented this new medium and quiet often refused to give permission for a play to be televised, thus limiting the theatre's choice. Fred Marlow confided to Campbell Logan that 'heavy guns had been produced 'about his allowing television from his theatre but that he did not propose to give way in this matter, as he believed that 'there must always be pioneers of new things if we are to have any progress.' Logan was concerned that the Intimate was being victimised and made to suffer because of its association with the Corporation and asked for the situation to be thoroughly investigated.

With this mostly negative feedback it may come as a surprise to discover the BBC persevering with these broadcasts but continue they did. On Friday 27th June 1947 the BBC screened *The Family Upstairs* by Harry Delf. Ronald Kerr was back as stage producer and Campbell Logan once again directed for television. In a letter to Fred Marlow after the broadcast, Logan claimed everyone was delighted with the play but added a word of caution 'I think next time it would be well to choose a British play and avoid American accents!' After a summer break the broadcasts resumed on Friday 5th September when Terence Rattigan's *French Without Tears* was finally able to be shown. Ronald Kerr was once again in the stage producer's chair and Harold Cox directed the television version with Intimate regulars David Garth and Ann Castle leading the cast. There was obviously a slight problem with actors paraphrasing and possibly using words not acceptable to the Corporation at that time, as a BBC memo to the television staff working on these plays makes clear. The memo stressed that the BBC should adopt the same practice for theatre outside broadcasts as studio plays: 'These plays must be scrutinised for offensive or dangerous words, phrases, expressions, sentences, etc and if necessary, a blue pencil used....As you know, it very often happens that actors slip in words, expletives and expressions, which are not in the original script. This is very noticeable in rep companies where the casts seldom manage to be word perfect. I think this happened a lot in *French Without Tears!*'

No further outside broadcasts were made from the Intimate that year but Tuesday 6th January 1948 found the cameras once more in the circle for Madeline Bingham's play *The Man From The Ministry*. Campbell Logan returned as TV director whilst Jimmy Grant Anderson was now the resident director at the theatre. In the cast were Diana Fairfax and Jack Howarth, who was to achieve fame in old age playing *Albert Tatlock* in *Coronation Street*. The television slot was from 7 pm until 9.15 pm with the play commencing at 7.15 pm. To the dismay of the BBC the play under ran and finished at 8.58 pm leaving the BBC with seventeen minutes to fill! The BBC was convinced that the play had been 'cut mercilessly by the theatre' but on the credit side, they regarded the picture quality as the best yet.

The Winslow Boy - January 1948

A week later the cameras were back for *The Winslow Boy* on Tuesday 13th January. In the cast were Intimate regulars David Raven and Ernest Haines. Campbell Logan thought the acting in this production was above average for the Intimate and reserved special praise for the actress Monica Stutfield who played *Catherine Winslow.*

The Engineer-In-Charge of television outside broadcasting, however, was concerned about the state of the grid over the stage, which he felt was in a dangerous condition and should be replaced before any further outside broadcasts were contemplated. The theatre management immediately placed a contract for the existing wooden beams to be replaced by steel girders, thus satisfying the fears of the BBC.

The Corporation was obviously impressed with these screenings from Palmers Green and Logan was asked by his superiors to conclude an agreement with Fred Marlow whereby the BBC would contract a regular series of broadcasts at roughly monthly intervals. The BBC was also willing to pay an appreciably higher fee on condition that the Intimate engaged 'higher grade artists' for the televised plays. As far as choice of plays was concerned, the Corporation felt the accent should be on comedy where there was a noticeable audience reaction. The BBC was keen to set up a television set on the premises so that West End managers, such as 'Binkie' Beaumont, doyen of impresarios and manager of the powerful H.M. Tennent organisation, could see what the viewers were seeing and hopefully encourage other theatres to allow cameras in.

Logan also suggested to Fred Marlow that the theatre employ guest stars for these televised dramas but Fred felt that this would damage their regular policy. Marlow pointed out that the theatre audience was purely local and if he presented well-known names one week there would be a falling-off in attendance on the other weeks.

On Friday 20th February 1948 *The Ghost Train* by Arnold Ridley was televised with Ridley also appearing in the cast. Arnold Ridley would later achieve fame as the loveable but dithery *Private Godfrey* in *Dad's Army*. The transmission was felt to be 'not as good as usual' as a problem with the sound on the night meant that the Act 2 climax with the sound of the 'ghost' train and the breaking of the glass in the station waiting-room window was unheard by the viewers!

The Shop At Sly Corner - March 1948

The Shop At Sly Corner by Edward Percy was the next play to be selected for screening on Thursday 8th April with Myrtle Reed and David Raven heading the cast but Campbell Logan felt the performance was 'indifferent' with 'some very bad miscasting'. This did not deter the BBC and cameras could be found in the circle on Thursday 13th May 1948 for Esther McCracken's *Quiet Wedding*, Thursday 8th July for James Parish's *Distinguished Gathering* and Thursday 16th September for *Acacia Avenue* by Mabel and Denis Constanduros.

Quiet Wedding - May 1948

Distinguished Gathering involved a much larger cast than usual and, as it was only staged at the Intimate because it was being televised, the BBC agreed to pay an extra £25 to cover the costs of five extra actors. The BBC's internal report on the transmission pointed out that 'owing to the large number of dinner jackets being worn, some of the pictures were not up to the usual standard'. The cast for that play was headed by Leonard White, who, prior to joining the Intimate company for seven productions, had played Malcolm to Michael Redgrave's *Macbeth* at the Aldwych Theatre, and Roger Delgado, known to *Dr. Who* fans everywhere as *The Master*, while *Acacia Avenue's* cast included Noele Gordon and John Barron.

Acacia Avenue - September 1948

Children To Bless You by G. Sheila Donisthorpe, the television company's choice on Thursday 14th October, posed a few problems for the BBC of 1948 but Campbell Logan, in a letter to Fred Marlow, felt that 'if we do not stress the nymphomaniac aspect and cut out reference to the deity, it should prove another winner.'

Children To Bless You - October 1948

Whether it was a winner or not, the BBC did not televise another Intimate production until August of the following year when Kenneth Horne's comedy *Two Dozen Red Roses* was screened on Monday 15th August 1949. Fred Marlow had managed to negotiate an increase in the fee to £150, which included the hire of the theatre, stage labour and the artists. The television director on this occasion was Peter Dimmock, a famous name in sports broadcasting. His debut at the helm at Palmers Green was not without incident, as recorded in John Swift's book *Adventure In Vision,* published in 1950:

> He (Peter) saw the play six times before he had finally worked out his treatment. He spent the entire afternoon on transmission day rehearsing a close-up sequence of two people on a settee. One minute after the broadcast started there was a black-out on the camera set up for the close-up shots. While the fault was being traced the scenes were transferred to another camera. By the time the fault was found – it was in the circuit, not the camera – there were only twenty minutes of the play left! *Two Dozen Red Roses* was a thoroughly enjoyable broadcast, but the pictures were not quite those the producer intended. He made the best of two cameras, and few viewers were aware of the hitch or that, as they were watching, engineers were stumbling in the dark across cabbage patches and gardens trying to trace any faults between the theatre and the mobile unit.

The next play to be chosen by the BBC was *Mountain Air* by Ronald Wilkinson on Tuesday 22nd November 1949 and with it came a major problem. At the very last minute the theatre management discovered a clause in the playwright's contract forbidding the televising of his play from any theatre. To save the situation the production, cast and settings were transferred to a studio at Alexandra Palace in front of an invited audience and relayed from there whilst the Intimate Theatre stood in darkness. Not an auspicious end to the BBC's relationship with the Intimate. For whatever reason no further plays were screened from the venue but the Intimate had certainly been a pioneer in the live transmission of complete dramas to a television audience over two years and had paved the way for other theatres to allow television cameras in to their buildings.

Mountain Air - November 1949

ACTORS APPEARING AT THE INTIMATE 1946 – 1950
(Not Already Mentioned In The Text)

Regular members of the acting company during these years included well-established character actors Ernest Haines and Marjorie Wilde as well as Ann Castle, Jane Hilary, David Crosse, Margaret Pepler, Pauline Loring and John Wentworth. The aforementioned David Garth and David Raven were also familiar faces during this period.

Gerald Campion, later to score a great success as television's *Billy Bunter,* appeared in *The Hasty Heart* with Nicholas Parsons (Jan 1947). This play proved so popular that it returned for a second week's run the following month. Gerald returned to the Intimate the following year in *The Girl Who Couldn't Quite* (Nov 1948).

John Barron made frequent visits to the Intimate during these years, featuring in such plays as *We Proudly Present* (May 1947), *And The Music Stopped* (Aug 1948), *Children To Bless You* (Oct 1948) and *Dr. Angelus* (Jan 1949). A frequent face on television he is fondly remembered for his portrayal of *C.J.,* Leonard Rossiter's boss in *The Fall And Rise Of Reginald Perrin,* where his catchphrase was 'I didn't get where I am today by…'

Noele Gordon visited the theatre in 1948 and could be seen in such plays as *The Last Of Mrs. Cheyney* (Aug 1948), *Acacia Avenue* (Sept 1948) and *To Kill A Cat* (Oct 1948). The following year Miss Gordon was starring in the West End in the original London production of the Lerner and Loewe musical *Brigadoon*, playing the female comic lead. Later, of course, she played *Meg Richardson* in the television soap *Crossroads*.

The noted actress Isabel Dean made several appearances in 1946 including *Lover's Leap* (Jul 1946), *After October* (Aug 1946) and *The Silver Cord* (Oct 1946). Isabel had been a member of John Gielgud's Repertory Company in 1944 and she later played in Osborne's *The Hotel In Amsterdam* and Rattigan's *The Deep Blue Sea* at the Royal Court Theatre.

Jack Howarth, later known to millions as grumpy pensioner *Albert Tatlock* in ITV's *Coronation Street,* was another frequent visitor in plays such as *Whiteoaks* (May 1947), *The Man From The Ministry* (Jan 1948) and *Queen Elizabeth Slept Here* (Aug 1950).

Bill Travers could be seen in several productions during 1950 including *The Light Of Heart* (May 1950), *Young Wives' Tale* (Jun 1950) and *Other Men's Wives* (Jun 1950). Bill later married the actress Virginia McKenna and appeared with her in such successful films as *The Smallest Show On Earth, Born Free* and *Ring Of Bright Water.*

Roger Delgado, later to achieve celebrity as *The Master* in the cult television series *Dr. Who,* was seen in less threatening roles at the theatre in 1948 when he was a member of the cast of several plays including *A Man About The House* (Jul 1948) and *The Distaff Side* (Aug 1948).

Clifford Williams appeared as an actor at Palmers Green in *The Corn Is Green* (Sept 1948) and *Peace Comes To Peckham* (Sept 1948). Mr. Williams later became a playwright and a celebrated director working with the Royal Shakespeare Company and the National Theatre.

One-Off Appearances

Brenda De Banzie, remembered fondly as the headstrong *Maggie* in the film *Hobson's Choice,* appeared in *The Girl Who Couldn't Quite* (Nov 1948).

Comic actor and raconteur par excellence Kenneth Williams briefly trod the Palmers Green stage in *Born Yesterday* (Jan 1949). Williams scored a great success in the radio series *Beyond Our Ken* and *Round The Horne.* Two of the unforgettable characters from the latter show were the camp duo *Julian and Sandy.* Partnering Williams in these skits was Hugh Paddick, who also paid a brief visit to the Intimate in 1950 in the play *Other Men's Wives* (Jun 1950).

Three other comic actors made one-off visits in 1950: Ray Cooney, later a very successful writer of farces, featured in the cast of *A Poor Weak Woman* (Sept 1950) and two months later Leo Franklyn, mainstay of many a Brian Rix Whitehall farce, appeared in *We Laugh And Live* (Nov 1950) while Kenneth Connor, star of many a *Carry On* film, appeared in *A Lady Mislaid* (Nov 1950).

Ewen Solon, later to be Rupert Davies sidekick *Lucas* in the television series *Maigret,* was in the cast of *Living Dangerously* (Apr 1946).

Distinguished actor Peter Barkworth had a featured role in *Young Woodley* (Jul 1947) whilst attractive Sheila Shand Gibbs fleetingly visited the area for *Moonlight Is Silver* (Aug 1949).

Noele Gordon

Gerald Campion

John Barron

THE FIFTIES

When Ronald Kerr left the Intimate in 1947 to work at Bromley, Jimmy Grant Anderson took his role as resident director. Anderson was a very experienced actor and director who had founded the Indian National Theatre in Bombay, for the playing of English and Indian classics in English with all-Indian casts. When Noel Coward met him in Singapore in 1930, Anderson was in charge of an English theatrical touring company called *The Quaints,* which had a very young John Mills as one of the troupe. Coward reported in his autobiography that Anderson was 'rich in quality; he was "of the dust the theatre bore, shaped, made aware," his blood was the best greasepaint.' Coward went on to say: 'I had the feeling that even after his (Anderson's) own death he would merely retire to some celestial dressing-room and take off his make-up.' Noel even described Jimmy as 'Ham – but prime York!'

Jimmy remained at the Intimate until Ronald Kerr's return in May 1950 and actually directed Kerr in several plays early in 1950 before Kerr resumed control of the productions. Pamela Gatward remembers working with Jimmy at the Intimate when, as Pamela Yeomans, she became ASM in the late 1940s. It was her first job after leaving RADA and she recalls telephoning Fred Marlow continuously until he offered her a job! At first she worked for nothing but later was paid the priceless sum of £1 per week. She remembers Jimmy had a soft spot for the young actor John Clark when he appeared in *All Rights Reserved* in June 1948. Clark, according to the programme, was 'known to millions of listeners as *William Brown* of *Just William* fame ' and much later married the actress Lynn Redgrave, from whom he was divorced very acrimoniously a few years ago.

Pam also remembers Jimmy shouting at a very young Roger Moore. Roger, later to find fame as *Ivanhoe* and *The Saint* on television and *James Bond* on film, was just out of the army and desperate for work: 'When I first emerged from the mob, resplendent in a demob suit and comprising a nothing-green sports coat and a nothing-brown pair of trousers, all I could get was repertory work at the Intimate Theatre, Palmers Green. The Intimate at least gave me a haven. I think the first play I did there was Noel Coward's *Easy Virtue.* The leading lady was Noele Gordon, now fondly remembered as *Meg Richardson* in the television soap opera *Crossroads.* Jimmy Grant Anderson was the director. He was God at the Intimate. But I was working and making about £10 a week.'

Roger Moore

Roger's memory was quite correct as his first play was indeed the Coward comedy in August 1948 followed by roles in *Acacia Avenue, Green Laughter, Children To Bless You* all in the autumn of 1948. Work was obviously still hard to come by elsewhere as he returned the following spring to appear in *Easy Money, Flat To Let, Trespass, While Parents Sleep, I Have Been Here Before* and *Rebecca*. His last appearance at the Intimate was in February 1950 when he played the role of *Jimmy* in Daphne Du Maurier's *September Tide*.

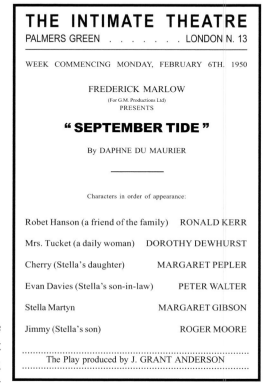

THE INTIMATE THEATRE

PALMERS GREEN . . . . . LONDON N. 13

WEEK COMMENCING MONDAY, 16th MAY

FREDERICK MARLOW

(For G.M. Productions Ltd)
PRESENTS

" REBECCA "

By DAPHNE DU MAURIER

Characters in order of appearance:

Frith .... FREDERICK MORANT
Mrs. Danvers .... UNA VENNING
Beatrice Lacy .... RUTH GORB
Giles Lacy .... ERNEST HAINES
Frank Crawley .... ROGER MOORE
Robert .... RICHARD PRESTON
Maxim de Winter .... STEPHEN WARD
Mrs. de Winter .... GENINE GRAHAM
Jack Favell .... JOHN WENTWORTH
Colonel Julyan .... FRED McNAUGHTON
William Tabb .... CLEMENT HAMELIN

The Play produced by J. GRANT ANDERSON

A 1949 production of *Rebecca*

THE INTIMATE THEATRE

PALMERS GREEN . . . . LONDON N. 13

WEEK COMMENCING MONDAY, FEBRUARY 6TH. 1950

FREDERICK MARLOW

(For G.M. Productions Ltd)
PRESENTS

" SEPTEMBER TIDE "

By DAPHNE DU MAURIER

Characters in order of appearance:

Robet Hanson (a friend of the family)   RONALD KERR

Mrs. Tucket (a daily woman)   DOROTHY DEWHURST

Cherry (Stella's daughter)   MARGARET PEPLER

Evan Davies (Stella's son-in-law)   PETER WALTER

Stella Martyn   MARGARET GIBSON

Jimmy (Stella's son)   ROGER MOORE

The Play produced by J. GRANT ANDERSON

Roger Moore in *September Tide*.
His last play at the Intimate Theatre

Another famous British film star could be found at the theatre in 1949 but he did not actually appear on stage. In early May John Mills spent some time at the Intimate assisting Jimmy Grant Anderson with the production of Mary Hayley Bell's drama *Dear Enemy*. There was good reason for this as John and Mary were, in real life, husband and wife! Just to keep it in the family the programme pointed out that 'the melody which runs throughout the play is especially composed by Annette Mills.' Annette, who brought *Muffin The Mule* to television screens in the 1950s, was John's sister!

The following week a curious ban led to a plaintive request from the management to the audience:

In common with other theatres we can no longer play any British made gramophone records. Foreign records are free from this ban, but, of course, are difficult to obtain. Should any of our patrons have a surplus of such records (non-vocal) and would like to dispose of them, the management will be pleased to hear from them.

One of the last plays directed by Anderson during his tenure at the Intimate was a brand new drama by J.B. Priestley called *Bright Shadow*. This was another coup for the theatre and warranted a review in *The Times* on Tuesday 11th April 1950. Sadly the critic found the play, a detective drama, had nothing like Priestley's usual zest and concluded: 'It is thus a piece that leaves rather more to the actors than is altogether fair but some of them get along very nicely with it. Mr. David Garth, for instance, conducts the investigation with as much aplomb as if the investigator had a moral right to be there, and Mr. John Barron made the most of one of Mr. Priestley's over-strung young men.'

1950 also saw the first appearances of an actress who was to become something of a legend at the Intimate, Margaret Gibson. Margaret soon became a mainstay of the repertory company, playing leading roles week after week and she remained with the company until 1967.

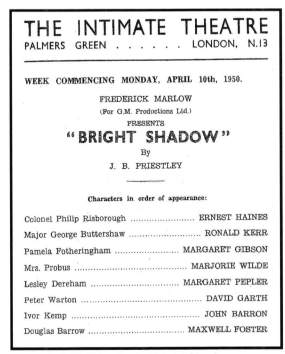

THE INTIMATE THEATRE
PALMERS GREEN . . . . . LONDON, N.13

WEEK COMMENCING MONDAY, APRIL 10th, 1950.

FREDERICK MARLOW
(For G.M. Productions Ltd.)
PRESENTS

"BRIGHT SHADOW"
By
J. B. PRIESTLEY

Characters in order of appearance:

Colonel Philip Risborough	ERNEST HAINES
Major George Buttershaw	RONALD KERR
Pamela Fotheringham	MARGARET GIBSON
Mrs. Probus	MARJORIE WILDE
Lesley Dereham	MARGARET PEPLER
Peter Warton	DAVID GARTH
Ivor Kemp	JOHN BARRON
Douglas Barrow	MAXWELL FOSTER

**J. B. Priestley's *Bright Shadow*
had its premiere at the Intimate in April 1950**

A regular member of the repertory company in the late 1940s was David Raven, who also directed a couple of productions. In April 1948 he appeared in the play *Spring Meeting* where he was joined on stage by the actress Mysie Monte. Little did they know then that they were destined to see quite a lot of each other professionally as both actors appeared for a considerably long period in Agatha Christie's long running thriller *The Mousetrap* as *Major Metcalf* and *Mrs. Boyle*. On 22nd July 1967 David celebrated ten years in this role. It was the longest single engagement by any actor in the world in one part and consequently his achievement entered *The Guinness Book Of Records* as 'Most Durable Actor for 4,575 performances as *Major Metcalf*.' He finally left the thriller, after being in it for more than eleven years, claiming: 'I'm too old for the part!'

Peter Coleman

81

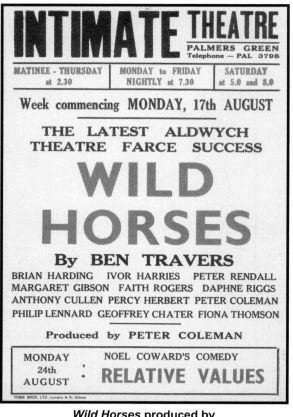

INTIMATE THEATRE
PALMERS GREEN
Telephone — PAL 3798

| MATINEE - THURSDAY at 2.30 | MONDAY to FRIDAY NIGHTLY at 7.30 | SATURDAY at 5.0 and 8.0 |

Week commencing MONDAY, 17th AUGUST

THE LATEST ALDWYCH
THEATRE FARCE SUCCESS

WILD
HORSES

By BEN TRAVERS

BRIAN HARDING   IVOR HARRIES   PETER RENDALL
MARGARET GIBSON FAITH ROGERS   DAPHNE RIGGS
ANTHONY CULLEN   PERCY HERBERT   PETER COLEMAN
PHILIP LENNARD   GEOFFREY CHATER FIONA THOMSON

Produced by PETER COLEMAN

| MONDAY 24th AUGUST | NOEL COWARD'S COMEDY RELATIVE VALUES |

TRIBE BROS. LTD., London & St. Albans

**Wild Horses produced by
Peter Coleman, August 1953**

Mysie actually beat David Raven's length of service staying with the play for a mind-boggling twelve and a half years but as she had a break of a year during that time she lost her claim to a Guinness record. She finally left the play stating: 'I think I have earned a rest!'

Jimmy Grant Anderson returned to the Intimate for a few weeks, on the death of Ronald Kerr, to keep the theatre's productions running smoothly, and then, in 1951, a new resident director arrived at the theatre – Peter Coleman. Peter, who directed virtually every play from June 1951 until June 1956, maintained the Intimate's reputation for hiring colourful, larger than life characters when he featured in a news report in the *Palmers Green and Southgate Gazette* on 28th December 1951. Mr. Coleman had apparently been bold enough to inform a Communist Party speaker in Hyde Park on the previous Saturday evening that the speaker's version of the Korean Campaign was 'a lot of absolute rot'. Two burly men then assaulted Peter; one grabbing him by his scarf while the other struck several blows on his face and head. Half-blinded by a rapidly closing eye, Coleman retaliated with a few punches. He later had his wounds stitched at St. Mary's Hospital and was told to rest for a couple of weeks. However, in the usual theatrical tradition, Peter was back at the Intimate on the Monday!

It is astonishing to discover looking through the list of productions that apart from one week at Christmas in 1948, the Intimate presented a different play every week from 1941, when it reopened, until 1952, when the management decided to introduce a summer closure, which lasted for four weeks. This closure became an annual event usually taking in the month of July and any renovation work that was needed was therefore timetabled for that period.

Sadly Peter Coleman died suddenly in the summer of 1956 whilst the theatre was closed for its annual break. When the Intimate reopened on 6th August with Alan Melville's *Mrs. Willie,* a new producer was at the helm – Frederick Tripp. Aubrey Woods, a leading actor and a great favourite at the Intimate in the mid-1950s remembers Tripp as 'a small dapper man dressed always in suit and tie but with an uncertain temper bubbling beneath the veneer. This erupted on an average of once per production and always with good cause.

Freddie did not suffer fools gladly and was also frustrated by the transient nature of the staff. On one occasion the scene painter walked out and the management had need to beg assistance from the first year students at the Hornsey School Of Art. The play was a farce set in a country vicarage but the students had taken the "vicarage" idea rather too literally: on the flats the woodwork was painted dark, dark brown, and the walls were stippled purple. When I dropped in on the Sunday afternoon to check my props, the set was glowering away on the stage.

"Freddie", I cried, "we can't play a light hearted farce in this. It looks like a Victorian mausoleum."

"Don't worry", said Freddie, "I quite agree. No time to repaint so I've been to Old Times and got a lot of very tall furniture."

By dress rehearsal time on the Monday hardly a square inch of the set was visible. Welsh dressers, tallboys, high-backed armchairs, grandfather clocks, towering bookcases and huge gold framed paintings jostled each other for position.

"There you are", said Freddie. "I've done my best, now it's down to you. Go on and be farcical!"

Aubrey pointed out that the actors 'generally rehearsed from French's Acting Editions of the plays, but we were once or twice faced with cue scripts, which printed each character's lines in full in separate flimsy scripts but with only the line preceding each speech as the actor's cue. And nothing at all if you weren't in any particular scene: so the first time many of us knew the plot when saddled with these scripts was on the first read through on the Monday.

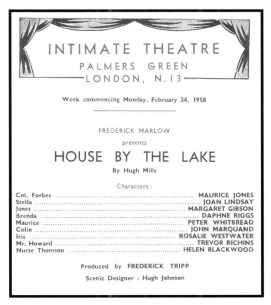

House By The Lake February 1958
Cloud Across The Moon April 1957
Two of the many productions
directed by Frederick Tripp

'Freddie stuck as far as possible to the printed stage instructions, copied by Messrs. French from the original productions, but varied them if the set or size of the stage at the Intimate so dictated, or he so wished. At one rehearsal he stopped me in mid move with the instruction: "No, no, don't go round the back of the sofa, you did that last week." '

David Forder recalls Freddie as 'a brisk, dapper little Londoner in his fifties, who regularly directed pantomimes at the Bradford Alhambra (a venue famous for its Christmas shows). He was completely efficient at getting the production on in the time available. Freddie gave us the minimum direction – usually just correcting moves, or encouraging pace. I remember Freddie suddenly, without warning, clapping his hands very loudly and shouting " Come on, come on. We've had an awful lot of slow plays lately." ' The actor John Hart Dyke remembers Tripp as being 'very serious. There were not many laughs with Freddie!'

Freddie Tripp remained at the Intimate until the end of June 1959 when ill health forced him to retire. His place was taken by John Maxwell. Maxwell commenced his career with the Oxford University Dramatic Society in 1935 alongside Michael Denison and Nora Pilbeam. Three years later he became a member of the Oxford Playhouse Company, working with Pamela Brown and Christopher Fry, and staying with the company until 1943. He then joined the Arts Theatre Company before achieving his ambition to become a producer. Before arriving at the Intimate he had produced plays all over the country. John's stay at Palmers Green as resident director was fairly brief, his last production being *Claudia* by Rose Franken in February 1960.

Margaret Gibson and friend a at social function in March 1974

Margaret Gibson was fast becoming one of the Intimate's most popular actresses, building up a sizeable devoted following. This band of supporters obviously numbered the local paper's theatre critic as the headline for the review of Felicity Douglas's play *It's Never Too Late* on 28th January 1955 read:

Margaret Gibson's Beautiful Performance At The Intimate

The following week the review for Rhys Davies' drama *No Escape* announced:

Another Brilliant Study By Margaret Gibson

And went on to say:

> The main role provides for yet another brilliant study by Margaret Gibson, who again on Monday at curtain call had to wait for prolonged applause to die down before she could speak. When one recalls that last week she was playing an equally demanding part while acquiring this one, that in both cases she could not be faulted on a line and that she got right under the skin of two quite dissimilar characters, one realises that no ovation can do justice to her powers. How she does it is nobody's business – it is just a miracle.

When one looks at the substantial roles Margaret Gibson played week in, week out, with the occasional free week, for an incredible seventeen years at the Intimate, one has to agree that it was indeed miraculous! Leslie Parnell pointed out that Margaret was ' a very quick study' which meant that she learned her lines easily. In the hard work of weekly rep, being a quick study must have been a blessing!

David Forder MBE, who from 1983 to 1990 was Director of the Colchester Rep and the Mercury Theatre, played the Intimate as an actor in two productions in 1959, *On Approval* (March 1959) and *Eden End* (April 1959). He recalls: 'I remember with affection and admiration the leading lady in each of these productions, Margaret Gibson. She was a favourite with the regular audience and rightly so. She was elegant, rock sure of her lines always, and completely assured, with a gracious personality off-stage as well as on. She was resourceful too. I remember in *Eden End,* James Irwin missed an entrance one night, and to cover we had to improvise about a page of dialogue. Ironically, the line I had to speak to him on his entrance was "Where have you been?" We fought to avoid corpsing!

'People speak dismissively now of standards in weekly rep and there's no doubt that they varied from week to week because of casting limitations and from theatre to theatre. But they would be astonished at the consistently high level of accomplishment that such actresses and actors maintained week after week, keeping their commitment without growing disillusioned or careless.'

On Approval - March 1959
featuring David Forder & Margaret Gibson

The deep affection that Margaret Gibson was held in by the local playgoers was clearly obvious in 1958 when, after a performance of Noel Coward's *Private Lives* in which Miss Gibson played the leading role of *Amanda,* she was presented with an illuminated address by a group of old age pensioners. *The Palmers Green and Southgate Gazette* reported the event on 20th June under the headline:

To Margaret – With Love
Surprise Presentation To Intimate Favourite

Margaret Gibson, who has moved so many audiences to tears and laughter, struggled with tears in her own voice when, after the show on Monday, she declared, "This is the most touching thing that ever happened to me in my life. I cannot thank you enough for all your kindness."

She had just received from the hands of Mr. William Budd, the manager, a surprise presentation – an illuminated address from the group of old age

INTIMATE THEATRE

PALMERS GREEN
Telephone — PAL 3798

MATINEE - THURSDAY at 2.30	MONDAY to FRIDAY NIGHTLY at 7.30	SATURDAY at 5.0 and 8.0

Commencing MONDAY, SEPTEMBER 7th

DIRECT FROM THE HAYMARKET THEATRE
THE OUTSTANDING SUCCESS

WATERS OF THE MOON

By N. C. HUNTER

Margaret GIBSON   Phyliss MONTIFOIRE

Pauline LORING   Peter COLEMAN   Margaret PEPLER

Philip LENNARD   Fiona THOMSON   Andrew LAURENCE

Gordon DAISLEY   Eileen BRADY

Produced by PETER COLEMAN

MONDAY 14th SEPTEMBER	From ST. MARTINS THEATRE — THE COMEDY
	## CLAUDIA
	By ROSE FRANKEN

TRIBE BROS. LTD., London & St. Albans

Waters Of The Moon - September 1953
One of the many productions featuring Intimate favourite Margaret Gibson

pensioners who regularly attend the Intimate and who are among her most ardent admirers.

The pensioners, to whom the management allows price concessions, had inscribed their address simply 'Margaret 1958'. The text, read by Mr. Budd from the stage, included the words "We greatly appreciate the atmosphere you are able to create in so many varied roles and recognize your great power in presenting emotional and intellectual characters of the first order. These gifts, together with your outstanding memory and clarity of utterance, have endeared you to our hearts."

It is safe to say that no actress ever received a more genuine or spontaneous tribute nor has it ever been more deservedly won than by Margaret Gibson, who never spares herself in giving unstintingly to her public.

It is fitting too that the presentation should be made in a week when she is taking a leading and exacting role, that of *Amanda* in a revival of Coward's wittily wicked comedy of a marital imbroglio.

Margaret remained at the Intimate until 1967, clocking up an amazing number of performances but then she was rather an amazing lady. The actress Muriel Barker pointed out that Margaret lived for many years in Teddington and used to catch the tube back to Richmond each day and then cycled from the station to her home. She probably used the underground journey to learn some lines! Her great friend, the actress Daphne Hanson pointed out that Margaret lived with her mother and her daughter, her husband having been killed during the war. 'I first met Margaret at the Theatre Royal, Stratford. She was not much older than me but I felt she was much wiser', said Daphne, 'and she was one of those women who were good at anything they tackled. She made her own clothes, cooked, painted and decorated. She was not in the least theatrical or 'actressy' and did not come from a theatrical family. When her mother died Margaret moved to Notting Hill and I remember that she used to give a Christmas Eve party every year. She was a very kind person with a lovely sense of humour. Sadly she died, far too young, of cancer.'

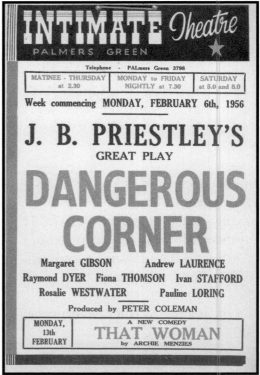

Dangerous Corner - February 1956
Margaret Gibson leading the cast once again

The actor Michael Knowles pointed out that Margaret Gibson was never under long term contract at the Intimate despite being there for so many years. 'It was a very casual business then with the manager popping into her dressing room and asking if she would be available for such and such a play in a couple of weeks time! When Maggie finally left Palmers Green she worked for a time as an understudy at the National Theatre.'

Another member of the Intimate team, much loved by the local audiences, was the manager William Budd. Bill Budd lived at Edenbridge Road in Bush Hill Park. His parents had been members of Charlie Chaplin's company *The Karno Mumming Birds* and Bill's first job was callboy at the Theatre Royal, Drury Lane. He was later promoted to stage manager there and stage director for a couple of the Ivor Novello musical spectaculars, which he later took on tour. He was a very keen magician and presented his illusionist act all over the world. He also worked for a time in America on Shirley Temple films before becoming general manager for orchestra leader Maurice Winnick. He became company manager of the Intimate in 1951 and soon developed a close personal contact with the Palmers Green playgoers. The first play produced under his management was *The Man With A Load Of Mischief.* By some quirk of fate when Budd was made a director of GM productions in the late 1960s the first show to be staged was a musical version of *The Man With A Load Of Mischief*! In the film *30 Is A Dangerous Age, Cynthia* one of the scenes shows the Intimate Theatre in the background with Bill Budd standing on the theatre steps behind the star of the film Dudley Moore.

The actor Aubrey Woods remembers Budd with affection: 'William Budd was the company manager and formed an excellent liaison cum buffer between the management and the rest of the world. The way he balanced the varying demands of Frederick Marlow, Frederick Tripp (the director), the Church Authorities, the ever-changing casts, the Old Times Furnishing Company, costumiers, wigmakers, printers and theatre staff, and could still don the bow tie and dinner jacket each evening and charm the patrons front of house was amazing!'

Bill Budd brought a welcome chatty style to his weekly letters in the printed programmes. He would keep the audiences up-to-date with the career developments of actors who had recently played the Intimate and would also mention any improvements to the theatre. This engendered in local playgoers a sense of belonging and a community-feel lacking in many other theatres, thus ensuring a loyal audience base. In many ways it recalled John Clements' similar efforts in the theatre's early days.

A popular move by Bill was announced in the theatre programme for *Who Goes There?* on 3rd March 1952:

> The management wishes to have it known that on and after March 10th they
> will be allowing OAPs and members of the Golden Link Clubs into the Monday

and Tuesday night performances at a nominal payment of 1/-. I feel that there are many who love the theatre but cannot attend as often as they would like.

In August 1956 Bill, in his programme notes, notified the local playgoers of the latest improvements to the theatre:

> The Middlesex County Council have made us carry out extensive alterations to comply with the latest regulations. In the first place we have a new safety curtain that now goes up through the roof, worked by electricity. To carry the extra weights new supports have been placed under the stage and a four-inch water main with hose attached for use in case of fire. Also over the safety curtain we have a large water pipe that sprays water over the stage, again in case of fire. Altogether we must be the most up-to-date equipped theatre in the country.

The Intimate Theatre, like a lot of other theatres at that time, served tea and coffee to patrons in their seats in the interval which explains this plea from Bill in a programme in 1958:

> It would help the staff if the patrons would kindly pass the cups and saucers to the end of the row, so that they may be collected without too much discomfort to the other patrons.

The feeling that the theatre was part of the local community was further demonstrated by Bill's notes in the programme for *Plan For A Hostess* in March 1959:

> Now that "Spring-cleaning" time is almost with us, may I make an appeal for any article that you may be throwing out and you think it may be useful as "props" for us, do let us know. We would always be glad of pictures and vases, and that sort of thing. Thank you.

The proximity of the Intimate to the West End certainly proved advantageous on several occasions in acquiring leading actors to recreate their West End roles for a further week in Palmers Green. In May 1950, when the company staged *The Perfect Woman,* the management was able to avail themselves of the services of Honor Shepherd, who recreated the role of *Joan Merrifield,* which she had played recently in town, and in September 1954 the actor Hugh Latimer appeared in *Birthday Honours,* in the same role he had played at the Criterion Theatre.

The convenient location of the playhouse to the West End also meant that well-known actors were willing to guest in the Intimate's productions. During the 1950s several then-famous names visited the Palmers Green theatre. Erstwhile minor film stars Bessie Love and Chili Bouchier led the way in 1952 with Bessie taking leading roles in *The Green Pack* in April and *Red Letter Day* in September followed by Chili in *White Cargo*. Claude Hulbert starred in *Nothing But The Truth* in November 1952 and Lupino Lane, the original star of the musical success *Me And My Girl*, did likewise the following March in *Twenty To One*. Derek Bond, who played the title role in the film *Nicholas Nickleby*, was the name above the title when the Intimate staged Dorothy L. Sayers' detective drama *Busman's Honeymoon* in May 1953 and in October of that year Charmian Innes featured in *To Christabel*.

Sonnie Hale who made a guest appearance in *Nest Of Robins* December 1955

1954 brought the radio and television personality Anona Winn in *The Orchard Walls* (February) and Valentine Dyall, of *The Man In Black* fame, in *Full Circle* (March), whilst 1955 found Sonia Dresdel in *This Was A Woman* (March) and Sonnie Hale in *Nest Of Robins* (December).

In September 1957 the Intimate's production of *The Day Nursery* proudly announced the appearance of Nancy Roberts, then at the height of her fame having played *Gran* in *The Grove Family* for the last three years on BBC Television. *Worm's Eye View*, the Christmas attraction in December 1957 boasted the presence of the actor Jack Hobbs, who had appeared in the original West End run of R. F. Delderfield's play. Not only did he recreate his role of *Pop* at Palmers Green but he also directed the production, earning fulsome praise from the local newspaper critic who declared that 'it showed how deeply he (Jack Hobbs) is steeped in both the part and the play as a whole'. Rounding off the decade was Jack Hulbert's guest appearance in *Not In The Book* in November 1959.

As had been the case in previous decades, many later to be well-known actors appeared in the rep company during the 1950s. The young Vivien Merchant made many appearances in 1954 and 1955, her first appearance being in James Leggatt's play *Chance Of Happiness* (March 1954). Vivien, whose real name was the less than glamorous sounding Ada Thomson, had been a member of Donald Wolfit's company before appearing at the Intimate and whilst at Palmers Green played leading roles in a variety of plays including *Job For The Boy* (May 1954), *Dial 'M' For Murder* (August 1954), *Dear Charles* (October 1954), Graham Greene's *The Living Room* (November 1954), *The Merchant Of Venice* (November 1954) and *I Capture The Castle* (February 1955).

Vivien Merchant later became one of the country's leading actresses before tragically committing suicide in 1982. From 1956 to 1980 she was married to the playwright Harold Pinter, who also made several appearances at the Intimate as an actor in the late 1950s under the name David Baron. His first appearance was in the 1957 Christmas production of *Worm's Eye View* by R.F.Delderfield and he later played roles in *Subway In The Sky* (January 1958), *The Vanity Case* (March 1958), *The Chalk Garden* (August 1958), *The Bride And The Bachelor* (September 1958) and *The Key Of The Door* (September 1958).

When one looks at the British theatre scene of the '50s and '60s two playwrights stand out from the crowd – John Osborne and Harold Pinter, so it is intriguing to find Mr. Pinter appearing at the Intimate as the second male lead in his contemporary's most famous play *Look Back In Anger.* As David Baron he played *Cliff Lewis* to Aubrey Woods' *Jimmy Porter,* the original 'Angry Young Man'. Aubrey recalls that at that time Harold was finishing off his script for *The Birthday Party,* which was to be produced at the Lyric, Hammersmith. *The Palmers Green and Southgate Gazette* for 24th March 1958 was greatly impressed with this production of Osborne's play, referring to 'the tremendous impact of Aubrey Woods' performance' and his 'lean and hungry charm' and claiming: 'This is one of the best, if not the best, of all the things he has done at the Intimate.' The reviewer also felt that David Baron gave ' a real gem of a performance.' At one point in the script the two men had to sing

The playwright Harold Pinter made many appearances at the theatre under the name David Baron

a music-hall ditty. Aubrey recalls: 'The score of the music-hall number which our two characters sing onstage was not included in the script and as getting this would not only have cost time but also composer's royalties, my wife, Harold and I dreamed up a tune and the necessary choreography – my wife had trained as a dancer – and included it in the play. Sadly no record of this tune remains.'

Aubrey, himself, was a leading player at the Intimate in the mid –1950s, joining the company after the summer break in 1956 and staying until August 1958. His first appearance was in *Murder When Necessary* (October 1956) and he followed this with roles in many productions including such repertory classics as Rattigan's *Separate Tables* (October 1956), *Pink String And Sealing Wax* (October 1956), *Sweet Aloes* (November 1956), written, incidentally, by the actress Joyce Carey under her nom de plume Jay Mallory, *The Late Christopher Bean* (March 1957), *Black Chiffon* (February 1958), *An Inspector Calls* (February 1958) and the inevitable Agatha Christie *Towards Zero* (April 1958).

Aubrey made his film debut as *Smike* in the 1947 version of Charles Dickens' *Nicholas Nickleby* and later had featured roles in such diverse films as *The Queen Of Spades, School For Soundrels, Wuthering Heights, Willy Wonka and The Chocolate Factory, Up Pompeii, Loot* and *The Abominable Dr. Phibes.* His stage and television roles have been equally varied with seasons at Stratford-Upon-Avon and the Open Air Theatre,

Regent's Park and even a period in the Tardis as *The Controller* in television's *Dr. Who.* Musicals have featured strongly in Aubrey's career. He replaced Ron Moody as *Fagin* in the original London production of *Oliver!* and also featured in *Valmouth, I And Albert, Mardi Gras, The Four Musketeers* and the 1991 revival cast of *Joseph and His Amazing Technicolor Dreamcoat.* Aubrey also collaborated with the composer Julian Slade on a musical retelling of Pinero's classic *Trelawny Of the Wells.* Called simply *Trelawny,* the musical had a successful run at Sadler's Wells and the Prince Of Wales Theatre after a pre-London run at the Bristol Old Vic, and is highly regarded by British musical theatre enthusiasts.

Aubrey Woods

Aubrey has many memories of his time at the Intimate: 'Due to the fact that the theatre was available to the company throughout the day, Frederick Marlow, who ran the Intimate, was not overjoyed when members of the company, most of whom lived far from Palmers Green, asked if rehearsals could take place in central London. A rehearsal room was found above the Albemarle public house in Soho, but the cast was informed that the rental would have to be paid by themselves as there was a perfectly good rehearsal space onstage at the theatre. This revelation had mixed response as we were all on Equity minimum salaries and every penny counted. Also two of us, Peter Whitbread and myself, lived in Winchmore Hill and in Palmers Green and were now saddled with fares to and from Soho every day instead of either cycling or walking to the theatre.'

Mishaps on stage always make entertaining reading and Aubrey recalled two that happened during his time at the Intimate.

'I remember on one memorable occasion, on a set with only one door, the door jammed. The actor onstage had to leave the actress to herself for her big soliloquy scene so, nothing daunted, he bade her farewell and exited through the fireplace!

'The theatre, as a former church hall, was still church property and was watched over diligently by the churchwarden. Coming in one afternoon and finding lights burning but no one present and wishing to be electrically economic, he operated a switch he thought to be the culprit. It was, however, connected to the sprinkler system, which burst into life. By the time the error had been righted the stage, the set, the furnishings and all the auditorium seats were dampened. Frantic efforts by the staff, the management, the actors and any of the audience who were unlucky enough to arrive early and be pressed into service, succeeded in mopping up the worst of the water and tea-towels, sheets of cardboard, plastic sacks and the curtains from the previous week's production were used to cover the audience's seats. Lack of time and further cover-up materials meant that the stage furniture remained waterlogged and tell-tale patches appeared on the gentlemen's trousers and ladies' frocks when they rose from the armchairs and sofas. The rest of the play was performed standing.'

Vivien Leigh, William Budd and Peter Whitbread pictured during one of the intervals in *Spring At Marino* (*Palmers Green Gazette* 15th November 1957).

Peter Whitbread, like Aubrey, lived in close proximity to the theatre and was a regular face in the productions of this period. When he gave a talk to the Playgoers Society on the actor's craft called *Mirror Up To Nature,* the local newspaper described him as 'the young actor who has been delighting Intimate audiences with a wide variety of character roles in recent weeks.' When Peter tackled the leading role in the play *Spring At Marino* in November 1957 his friend the actress and film star Vivien Leigh made a special visit to see him in the part. That evening Miss Leigh also renewed acquaintance with another old friend, manager William Budd. They had first met in the Western desert when Bill was in the forces and Vivien had gone out there to entertain the troops.

Another regular member of the company in the 1950s was Raymond Dyer. Raymond was also a playwright and whilst at the Intimate had six of his plays produced there. At first these plays were listed as written by Raymond Dyer or C. Raymond Dyer but later plays were listed under the name Charles Dyer. One of these later plays, which achieved great success, was *Rattle Of A Simple Man.* The original West End production starred Harry H. Corbett and Sheila Hancock and it was later filmed with Corbett recreating his stage role opposite actress Diane Cilento. The film also features a screen appearance by Mr. Dyer himself. The play was recently revived in the West End with Stephen Tompkinson and Michelle Collins in the starring roles.

Charles Dyer also scored a success with his play *Staircase,* which starred Paul Schofield and Patrick Magee in the West End in 1966, in a production directed by Sir Peter Hall, and Richard Burton and Rex Harrison in the subsequent film.

Stage setting by John Mellon for *Who On Earth!* by Charles Dyer - June 1952

**Charles Dyer and his future wife,
actress Fiona Thomson
beside the steps of the Intimate Theatre
11th May 1956**

**Miki Iveria and Raymond Dyer in
Dear Charles by Alan Melville
October 1954
Miki was the wife of theatre director
Peter Coleman**

THE INTIMATE THEATRE

Raymond Dyer is grand in 'Dry Rot'

"Dry Rot," by John Chapman. Produced by Frederick Tripp at the Intimate Theatre this week.

Raymond Dyer is back, after a year's absence from the Intimate stage, for one all-too-shot week. Without him, John Chapman's broad farce from Whitehall Theatre would have been in danger of crumbling. Where others in the cast fall into the trap of hamming unashamedly to draw the laughs, Raymond Dyer relies on his innate sense of fun and goonery, his so comic facial expressions and his ability to look quite at home in the most outrageous of costumes.

The scene where, as Flash Harry the dim spiv, he tries to drink a cup of tea, sugar it, and eat a cream horn, all at the same time, is the funniest thing I have seen on the stage for a long time.

GUEST HOUSE

"Dry Rot" is the story of a retired Colonel (Hedley Colson), his wife (Pauline Loring), and attractive daughter, (Valerie Kirkbright) who open a guest house near a race-course hampered rather than helped by housemaid Fiona Thomson, expecting their first guests to be ordinary clean-living patrons of the turf.

But they are assailed by crooked bookie Alfred Tubbs (John Ringrose), his henchman Fred (Peter Whitbread) and their newly-engaged Harrow-educated secretary, played by Aubrey Woods – not to mention Flash Harry, and the French jockey who is to ride the favourite the gang plan to switch (a masterly portrayal here by Geoffrey Sasse), and a policewoman (Sylvia Osborne).

For some reason, the play took time to warm up at Tuesday's performance, Peter Whitbred and John Ringrose not entering wholeheartedly into their roles until the third act; but once it was under way, the laughs, titters and sometimes guffaws, came fast and furious.

A LESSON

Peter Whitbread's dunderheaded stooge was a bold attempt by an actor more accustomed to straight acting; he certainly appeared to shake off any discomfort in his scene with Alfred, where he takes a lesson in horse-riding, using the sofa as his mount and a French phrase-book as his instructions.

There is the usual run of farce dialogue, ranging from jokes about drawers to humourisms like "If he made a doughnut out of his brains, there wouldn't be enough for the hole in the middle!" but that is as farce should be.

It is all good clean fun – just the thing to put you in the holiday mood. – **W. R. B.**

Raymond Dyer scored a great sucess in *Dry Rot* by John Chapman - August 1958. The review above appeared in the Palmers Green Gazette 8th August 1958.

Geoffrey Sasse as *Albert* and Raymond Dyer as *Flash Harry* in a scene from the play.

Wanted One Body! by Charles Raymond Dyer
Raymond Dyer as Mr Mickleby - 3rd September 1956

>>>>>>>>>><<<<<<<<<<

Stage setting by Edward Furby for *Wanted One Body!* by Charles Dyer
Intimate Theatre 23rd April 1956

Dyer's first play at the Intimate was *Who On Earth!* in June 1952. Charles was also in the cast and recalls a troublesome 'prop' on the first night: ' Wax bottles were a required prop for my first Intimate play. During the action I smashed a bottle over the head of a Martian giant, played by Andrew Lawrence. Regrettably on the night, the wax prop had been over-cooked (at Covent Garden workshops) and wouldn't smash. So, as a serious actor dedicated to truth, I kept hammering at Lawrence's head until the bottle did shatter – slightly before Lawrence's head! Poor Andy carried the bumps for several weeks. It earned him a dramatic paragraph in the *Palmers Green Gazette* though!'

Although Charles was kept extremely busy as a regular member of the rep company he still found time to write more plays. *Turtle In the Soup* was staged at the Intimate in December 1953 and the following December saw *The Jovial Parasite.* In April 1956 his farce *Wanted- One Body!* was premiered at the Intimate. This play later achieved great success when it was staged at the Whitehall Theatre as one of Brian Rix's celebrated farces. The BBC subsequently televised it with Brian Rix and Dora Bryan leading the cast.

**Raymond Dyer's comedy *Turtle In The Soup*
had its premiere at the Intimate Theatre in December 1953**

Charles has very fond memories of the Intimate: not surprisingly since he met his future wife there, the actress Fiona Thomson, another regular member of the rep company at that time. As Charles recalled: 'We became engaged during the fifth of six plays I wrote there (*Prelude To Fury*) in November 1959 and married in 1960. Forty six years and still going strong!'

Dyer's sixth play to be produced at Palmers Green was his great success *Rattle Of A Simple Man,* which opened on 30th December 1963 with Charles Dyer himself playing the leading role opposite a comely television quiz show hostess called Nancy Roberts.

**Charles Dyer's hit play
Rattle Of A Simple Man
played for a week in December 1963
with the author in the leading role**

Another local playwright featured at the Intimate around this time was Sutherland Scott. This was the nom de plume for Dr. Clunie Harvey who was Southgate's Medical Officer Of Health at that time. He had five of his plays staged at the theatre: *Suspended Sentence* (April 1955), *Unseen Among Us* (May 1956 and again in May 1961), *Checkmate* (May 1957), *As It Happened* (May 1958) and *Fog* (September 1959).

David Forder only made two appearances at the Intimate but remembers his brief time there vividly:

'Having left RADA in 1957 at the late age of 30 and gone straight into two seasons as actor and then director at the Byre Theatre, St. Andrews, I was inexperienced in the ways of agents and managements. The agent John Penrose, whose office was just off Cambridge Circus, said he couldn't take me on as a client, but suggested I went round the corner to the office of a management who were casting a production in Palmers Green of *On Approval*. Actors recently out of drama school in those days could only expect to be taken on as juveniles, so looking younger than my age, I had told him I was 24. "Tell 'em you're 30", he said.

'The office round the corner was a run-down one, up a dimly lit flight of concrete stairs smelling of cats. Behind a large desk sat two unnervingly inscrutable middle-aged men in well-worn business suits. Only one of them spoke, finally offering me the part of Richard. I think the salary was to be £12 per week. I accepted.

'I was told that to save travelling each day during the rehearsal week rehearsals would be held in a room over a pub in the Euston Road. I presented myself there on the Tuesday before the Monday of the opening date. I discovered that there would be only four days' rehearsals, as there was no rehearsal on matinee day, which was a Thursday. I think we began at 10 am, and finished about 3.30 or 4 pm, with a brief lunch break. Then came the discovery that we were expected to club together to pay for the cost of the rehearsal room hire – it was alleged that after all, we didn't have to pay fares each day out to Palmers Green. More dismaying was the discovery at the end of the week that as we were in London, there was no rehearsal pay. According to Equity agreement, in London we were paid only for playing. To cap everything, when I finally received my pay packet a week later via Bill Budd, ten per cent had been deducted. I was told that it had been taken by the man who hadn't spoken during my interview, who was an agent!

'*On Approval* has two sets. They were made up of stock flats cleated together, which had been painted horizontally in a space under the stage. The first act was set inside the second act set. It was a very small stage and I remember closing the door after making an exit in the first act, and having to walk sideways between the two sets, squeezing my tummy in, to reach the wings, and then brushing scene paint off my suit (which was my own – in rep we had to provide our own costumes except in period plays)

'I thought I did rather well on the first night, not drying, and getting several exit rounds. But all Freddie Tripp (the director) said was "Oh well, it seems to have woken you up a bit". However I was invited back to play in the next but one production, Priestley's *Eden End.*'

'The dressing room tables were covered with newspaper. There was no running hot water, and there was a notice pasted up saying "Hot water may not be fetched from the kitchen". I did just that saying loftily that I should refer anyone taking me to task to 8, Harley Street (Equity's head office), but nobody did.

'A regular actress at the Intimate at that time was Adele Strong who appeared with me in *Eden End.* She was a good-natured soul, a thoroughly competent character woman of middle years, plain of face, hair straight and in an untidy bun. She might have passed for a cook-housekeeper, and no doubt specialised in that line of parts, which we called "character bags". She arrived for rehearsal one morning rather flustered, but looking radiant, and ten years younger. "A man tried to interfere with me on the train," she said.

'I owe a lot to Pearl Catlin, another regular at the theatre, because I told her I really wanted to direct and she chivvied me ceaselessly until I reluctantly wrote to Derek Salberg of the Birmingham Alexandra Theatre, as she knew he was looking for a Company Manager who would also act and occasionally direct for his Wolverhampton company, which she was to rejoin in a few weeks time. I discovered what I didn't know when Pearl chivvied me, that his was a highly reputable management, so his taking me on gave me just the step up the ladder I needed'.

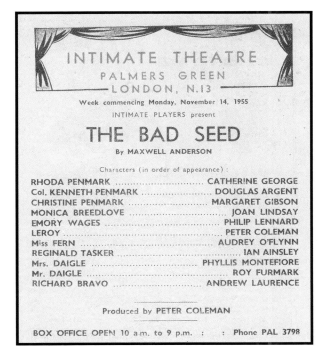

INTIMATE THEATRE
PALMERS GREEN
—— LONDON, N.13 ——

Week commencing Monday, November 14, 1955

INTIMATE PLAYERS present

THE BAD SEED

By MAXWELL ANDERSON

Characters (in order of appearance) :

RHODA PENMARK	CATHERINE GEORGE
Col. KENNETH PENMARK	DOUGLAS ARGENT
CHRISTINE PENMARK	MARGARET GIBSON
MONICA BREEDLOVE	JOAN LINDSAY
EMORY WAGES	PHILIP LENNARD
LEROY	PETER COLEMAN
Miss FERN	AUDREY O'FLYNN
REGINALD TASKER	IAN AINSLEY
Mrs. DAIGLE	PHYLLIS MONTEFIORE
Mr. DAIGLE	ROY FURMARK
RICHARD BRAVO	ANDREW LAURENCE

Produced by PETER COLEMAN

BOX OFFICE OPEN 10 a.m. to 9 p.m. : : Phone PAL 3798

**Cast list for
The Bad Seed
November 1955**

Local actress Catherine George joined the company as Assistant Stage Manager at the end of this decade. Cathy had started young as a child actress understudying the important role of *Rhoda* in the West End production of Maxwell Anderson's *The Bad Seed*. When the Intimate decided to stage this play in November 1955 Cathy, then only twelve years of age, was delighted to be asked to play the role.

The critics were ecstatic as this extract from the *Gazette* of 18th November 1955 proves:

Child Actress In Amazing Study

Forget all you ever heard about child actresses. Almost unbelievable for a child of twelve, utterly fascinating, and terrifyingly convincing is the performance given by Catherine George at the Intimate this week… what other child player, no matter how well versed, could convey its subtleties, or leave one with a sense of cold horror transcending anything put over by adults in the more usual, more obvious, thriller!

'I had a fabulous week', recalls Cathy, ' and had my photograph on the theatre gate as well as in the foyer. I was even presented with flowers on the Saturday night and Maggie Gibson gave me a beautiful make-up tray, which I used for many, many years. I returned to the theatre on a few occasions as a 'child actress', appearing as *Eve* in *Pink String And Sealing Wax* (Oct 1956) and the daughter in Patrick Hamilton's *The Governess* (Apr 1959), and then worked as an ASM from the age of 17 for two and a half years, also playing a few more parts as and when I was required.'

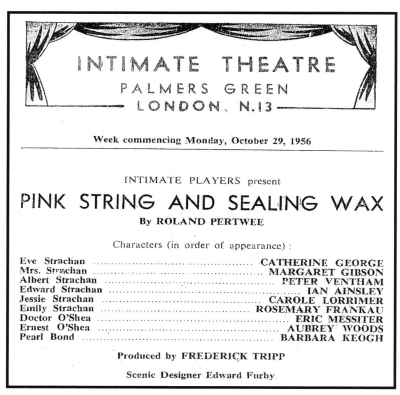

INTIMATE THEATRE
PALMERS GREEN
— LONDON, N.13 —

Week commencing Monday, October 29, 1956

INTIMATE PLAYERS present

PINK STRING AND SEALING WAX

By ROLAND PERTWEE

Characters (in order of appearance) :

Eve Strachan	CATHERINE GEORGE
Mrs. Strachan	MARGARET GIBSON
Albert Strachan	PETER VENTHAM
Edward Strachan	IAN AINSLEY
Jessie Strachan	CAROLE LORRIMER
Emily Strachan	ROSEMARY FRANKAU
Doctor O'Shea	ERIC MESSITER
Ernest O'Shea	AUBREY WOODS
Pearl Bond	BARBARA KEOGH

Produced by FREDERICK TRIPP

Scenic Designer Edward Furby

Cast list for *Pink String And Sealing Wax* October 1956

Cathy's performance in *The Governess* once again stole the review headlines:

Child Dominates The Stage

....This role supplies another opportunity for a visit to the Intimate of young Catherine George, who was last in Palmers Green to play the murderous child in *The Bad Seed*. Once again she dominated the stage getting right inside a difficult and involved personality. Given only the modicum of luck that even the outstanding player needs, she must surely have a brilliant stage career before her.... (*Gazette* 17th April 1959)

Cathy remembers her period as ASM at the Intimate as 'two and a half years of fun and laughter mixed with extremely hard work.' The weekly schedule of weekly repertory had barely changed since the war years. 'Rehearsals during my time', said Cathy, ' took place in a room above a public house near Warren Street station. We rehearsed on Tuesdays, Wednesdays and Fridays plus Saturday mornings.' The weekly rehearsal routine was as follows:

Tuesday
Read through of play and we also marked the moves of all three acts.

Wednesday
Rehearse Act 1 without scripts (usually twice through)

Thursday
Matinee Day

Friday
Rehearse Act 2

Saturday Morning
Rehearse Act 3 followed by run through of play.

Cathy remembers that 'all the stage management team were present at these rehearsals and we took it in turns to prompt the play. On a Saturday night after the performances we struck the set and set up the flats for Monday's play. We quite often worked until 2 a.m. or 3 a.m. which was rather tiring!

'On Monday I would get to the theatre around 10 a.m. to start collecting props for the current play. I would go out into Palmers Green and borrow china, glasses, pictures, etc. from Lawleys and Courts. All the stores were very helpful regarding this. The dress rehearsal usually began about 2 p.m. followed by the first performance at 7.30 p.m. These dress rehearsals were often chaotic with scenery still being painted at 7 p.m.! I remember that I used to prompt Act 1 and Act 3. Some plays were a nightmare for props such as Agatha Christie's *Murder At the Vicarage,* which we staged one Christmas. Act 1 saw a complete dinner at the table – meat, vegetables, etc. I improvised very well but there was so much china which all had to be cleared and washed in the interval ready to be re-used in Act 3. I really hated Agatha Christie!

'Of course with this hectic weekly schedule problems often occurred. I remember one play where a scene in Act 1 was very similar to a scene in Act 3. Needless to say at one performance two actors in the first act went straight into the words for the third act with me making frantic gestures from the prompt corner to alert them! The actors involved spent the entire interval trying to re-write the third act so that the audience would not notice!

'On one occasion we staged a wonderful play called *The Long And The Short And The Tall*, which had a jungle type setting. The stage manager and myself collected a car full of long, dry grass and somehow we made the most super woven roof for the set. I am pleased to say that the set received a round of applause when the curtains opened. What the audience didn't know was that we nearly had to dismantle the set, as we had not given a thought to any fireproofing! Luckily our fire officer was friendly and we managed to spray the grass with some sort of anti-flame liquid and the show went on!

'The actors were a great bunch and a lot of them stayed for a couple of years before moving on to television or radio. They worked hard particularly our leading lady Margaret Gibson. Because Maggie lived so far away she really looked forward to playing the occasional role that did not appear in Act 3 so that she could leave the theatre and get home just a little bit earlier! Everyone loved Thursday matinee days and Saturday evenings as these always seemed to supply the best audiences, especially for comedies. Thursdays found most of the elderly community at the matinee and they always 'oohed and aahed' in the right places. A great audience!'

An innovation in the '50s was the introduction of the *Festival Of Drama* for various amateur dramatic societies. The first festival was held in June 1956 when three different societies staged plays for two nights each and it was proudly advertised as the first of its kind in North London. The festival idea was obviously a success and was repeated under the title *Southgate Theatre Week* in 1957 and 1958. Most years afterwards saw an amateur drama group occupying the theatre immediately before the summer break.

If the actors at the Intimate were still finding fulfilment playing to audiences not yet completely entranced by the rival delights of television, they experienced a fruitless trip to Central London in May 1955 when Rita Weeks, an actress in the company, was due to marry her agent Vincent Shaw at Caxton Hall. The actors arrived to find Rita had gone home to Bournemouth. In an interview with the newspapers Rita confessed: 'We had a slight difference but the wedding is only postponed, we're still engaged!'

 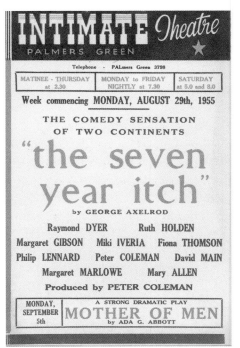

Two posters from 1955

ACTORS APPEARING AT THE INTIMATE 1951-1960
(Not Already Mentioned In The Text)

In addition to the afore mentioned Raymond Dyer, Fiona Thomson, Aubrey Woods, David Baron, Peter Whitbread and the indefatigable Margaret Gibson regular names cropping up in the weekly programmes included Margaret Pepler, Faith Rogers, James Irwin, Joan Lindsay, John Hayter, Pearl Catlin, Adele Strong and Diana Van Proosdy.

Nicholas Courtney, another actor, like Roger Delgado, to find lasting fame with the television series *Dr. Who* when he played *The Brigadier,* made many appearances with the company in the late 1950s. He featured in such diverse productions as *Doctor In The House* (Dec 1956), *The Whole Truth* (Apr 1957), *Private Lives* (Jun 1958) and *The Glass Cage* (Jan 1959). Nicholas received a glowing notice from the local press for his role in Leslie Sands' thriller *Something To Hide* (Sept 1958). As the personable villain of this whodunit the critic found that 'Nicholas Courtney has mastered the trick of chilling with a mere glance that he makes oddly disturbing to the nerves…'

Arthur Lowe, unforgettable as *Capt. Mainwaring* in the much-loved comedy classic *Dad's Army,* could be found at the Intimate around this period appearing in such plays as *To Christabel* (Oct 1953), *The Mannion Mystery* (Nov 1953) and *Witness For The Prosecution* (Aug 1955).

Two actors, who later found television fame in soap operas, joined the company in the early years of the decade. Edward Evans, who later portrayed *Mr. Grove* in British television's first soap opera *The Grove Family,* could be seen in *Lace On Her Petticoat* (Aug 1951) and *Who Is Sylvia?* (Sept 1951) whilst Doreen Keogh, destined to play barmaid *Concepta Hewitt* in the early days of *Coronation Street,* had roles in *A Priest In The Family* (Mar 1952) and *Women Of Twilight* (Dec 1953).

Barry Foster, remembered fondly as the television detective *Van Der Valk,* featured in *Dear Charles* (Oct 1954) and *Serious Charge* (Oct 1955) and Cockney character actor Percy Herbert joined the acting company for such plays as *Of Mice And Men* (Nov 1952) and *The Merchant Of Venice* (Nov 1954).

Glamour in the shape of Vanda Godsell and Melissa Stribling was also on display at the Intimate. Vanda appeared in *Fair And Warmer* (Oct 1951) and *Full Circle* (Mar 1954) and Melissa appeared in *Down Came A Blackbird* (Mar 1954) and *Murder Out Of Tune* (Apr 1954).

Mark Eden, now indelibly associated with the villainous character *Alan Bradley* in *Coronation Street,* had featured roles in *Variations On A Theme* (Nov 1958) and *Late Love* (Dec 1958).

Terence Alexander joined the company for *What Anne Brought Home* (Oct 1951) and returned for *Sleeping Out* (Mar 1953) whilst Anthony Bate could be found in such repertory classics as Emlyn Williams' drama *Night Must Fall* (Jun 1957) and Terence Rattigan's *While The Sun Shines* (May 1958).

The noted actor Geoffrey Chater appeared in *Busman's Honeymoon* (May 1953) and *The Deep Blue Sea* (Aug 1953) and the following year Peter Vaughan could be seen in *Trouble At No. 13* (Jan 1954) and *Shadow Of A Man* (Apr 1954).

The actor Arthur Barrett, later better known as Tim Barrett, made the first of many appearances at the Intimate in 1959 appearing in such plays as *To Dorothy, A Son* (Oct 1959) and *Pot Luck* (Dec 1960). His last appearance at the theatre was in 1969, shortly before the theatre closed as a full-time professional venue, when he starred in the farce *See How They Run*.

Janet Butlin joined the company in 1960 appearing in *This Thing Called Love* (Oct 1960) and *The Tender Trap* (Oct 1960). Over the next few years Jan became a regular face at the Intimate before branching out into directing and scriptwriting.

One-Off Appearances

Roy Dotrice briefly visited the theatre to appear in Noel Coward's *South Sea Bubble* (Mar 1957). Dotrice later joined the Royal Shakespeare Company and achieved great success in the West End and on Broadway playing *John Aubrey* in his one-man tour de force *Brief Lives*.

Barry Foster

Geoffrey Chater

Terence Alexander

THE SIXTIES

As the Intimate entered a new decade it was clearly obvious that the glory days of weekly rep were firmly past. Audiences were now being enticed by the wonders of television, both BBC and ITV, and were not so willing to venture out every week to the local playhouse. The management, ever mindful of other claims on the audience's leisure time, did its best to maintain standards at the Intimate. The annual holiday break at the theatre in the summer of 1960 was put to good use as Billy Budd reported in the programme of Agatha Christie's *The Unexpected Guest,* the first play of the autumn season:

> The theatre has been completely redecorated at considerable cost. We are quite sure that as soon as you enter the theatre you will realise what has been done to bring the Intimate up to the highest pitch of elegance. New, carefully chosen colour schemes, the most modern lighting, a completely renovated bar – the changes will give you some idea of the vast amount of work which has gone into this year's exceptional redecoration.

A more controversial innovation was the Bingo and Social Club, introduced by the theatre in August 1961.

The Wood Green Weekly Herald for Friday 25th August 1961 decided to make this their main news story on page one:

BINGO BROUGHT TO INTIMATE

Don't really want it, says director, but it's coming

Although London's last surviving repertory theatre – the Intimate Theatre at Palmers Green, is introducing Bingo three afternoons a week it is definitely not a last-ditch attempt to keep the Theatre solvent. The Managing Director of the company, which runs the Intimate, Mr. Frederick W. Marlow, said: "We are determined that this theatre is to continue whether bingo is a success or not."

Mr. Marlow told the Weekly Herald, "We don't really want to do this but, like so many other theatres and cinemas, we have decided we must. Television has hit the live theatre as well as the cinema. I think Bingo is a form of escapism – people are sick and tired of sitting and watching television every evening."

He added, "We are the only repertory theatre left in London. We have been here for twenty years and we hope to be here another twenty years." Both he and Mr. William Budd, the Theatre Manager, emphasised that Bingo had been introduced not to save the Theatre but only to add to its funds....

...Mr. Budd pointed out another advantage of the bingo sessions: "One of the things we hope to do is to draw in people who would come to the Bingo but not to the Theatre. Perhaps they would then come along to the evening performance. After all there must be thousands and thousands of people in the area who have never been to the Theatre."

On the cost of running the Theatre Mr. Marlow said that although the cost of living had gone up over 300 per cent since the war the seat prices at the Theatre had only risen by around two shillings – from 3/6d to 5/6d. In addition to this, the cost of light, heat, gas and advertising had all risen and the Theatre was completely redecorated last year.

On the question of Bingo he commented, "It is a reluctant decision but if this is a success it will help. We have always given the public good clean entertainment and we are definitely not altering our policy."...

B I N G O

TUESDAY, WEDNESDAY & FRIDAY
at 2.30

H

£87 SNOWBALL NOW!

Application Forms at the Box Office. Members and Guests must be over 18 years of age.

FREE MEMBERSHIP

ALL STAKE MONEY RETURNED AS BIG CASH PRIZES

Bingo sessions took place every Tuesday, Wednesday and Friday afternoon at the theatre (the theatre had matinee performances on Thursdays and Saturdays). Membership of the bingo club was free but members could not use the club premises until twenty-four hours after the application. Each member was allowed two guests, over eighteen years of age, and admission was 2/6d. Letters soon appeared in the local press, some bemoaning the introduction of bingo whilst others were more philosophical, accepting the idea if it meant keeping the theatre's doors open.

In *The Palmers Green and Southgate Gazette* for 8th September there was a letter from Eric Batson of Steeplestone Close, N18, complaining about the choice of plays at the Intimate. He had moved to the Enfield area eleven years ago and had looked forward to attending the theatre 'made famous by John Clements and Ronald Kerr'. However, he pointed out that

I have not been there above a dozen times since I came. Week after week goes by with the same sort of rehash of West End hits and near hits, not to mention the near misses and worse. I cannot recall a single announcement at any time of a play by one of the more significant dramatists of our own day: Anouilh, Beckett, Sartre, O'Casey, Osborne, Mortimer, Pinter, etc...

He concluded his letter with a suggestion that the theatre should establish a repertory company with two or three week runs of more adventurous plays.

More letters followed, praising the actors and Billy Budd, although a couple pointed out that some of the plays seen at the Intimate were not worthy of producing. Eve Shirley of The Trent Players, came to the theatre's defence when she explained in her letter how hard it was to find an audience for 'intelligent plays.' The Editor of *The Palmers Green and Southgate Gazette* joined in the debate devoting his Opinion column on 15th September to the subject of bingo and subsidies for the theatre, stating that there was only a limited audience for good drama.

The following week Mr. Batson was back on the letters page of the *Gazette* reiterating that he blamed playgoers for concurring the theatre's current policy. He also blamed a 'negligent borough'. He pointed out that although people say 'good drama doesn't pay, it is obvious the current policy doesn't pay either or else why introduce bingo!' This set off another flurry of correspondence, both attacking and defending the Intimate's play policy. The theatre's management obviously took notice of the criticism and the following year experimented with Harold Pinter by staging *The Caretaker*. This prompted a letter of praise from one member of the audience in the local paper on 15th June 1962, although the letter writer did point out that some of the audience walked out after Act 1.

It wasn't just the television and other attractions keeping audiences away from the Intimate. The appalling winter of 1962/1963 had such an adverse effect on audience numbers that the management decided to close the theatre for three weeks. Interestingly the bingo sessions continued uninterrupted! *The Palmers Green and Southgate Gazette* for 1st February 1963 reported the closure and concluded their article with:

> ...The management regrets that necessity has enforced the temporary closing but feels confident that patrons, by then rid of their own troubles, caused by the freeze-up, will respond to the special attraction arranged for them when the theatre opens again.

This special attraction was the thriller *Distinguished Gathering* by James Parish and featured a guest appearance by the famous stage, radio and television personality and comedian, Vic Oliver. Vic was born in Vienna in 1898 and achieved fame in the wartime radio series *Hi Gang* with Ben Lyon and Bebe Daniels.

Vic Oliver

His stage act was in the same mould as comics Ted Ray and Jimmy Wheeler in that he cracked jokes in-between bursts of violin playing. In the 1950s he was one of the regular comperes of the Home Service's immensely popular Saturday evening show *Variety Playhouse* and achieved another claim to fame when he chose Winston Churchill's daughter Sarah as his second wife. His role that week at the Intimate was probably one of his last stage appearances, as he died the following year in 1964.

Two regular faces in the acting company during this period were Linda James and Michael Knowles. Linda first met Michael when they played opposite each other at the Intimate in *Little Women* when Linda played *Meg* and Michael played *John Brooke.* 'We were both shy', said Linda, 'but the play required us to have a chaste kiss. At one performance, as we moved towards each other, Michael stood on my foot (I was only wearing ballet pumps so it was rather painful) and when I came offstage I declared to anyone in earshot " He really is the clumsiest actor I have ever met. I hope he doesn't come here again!" I was to eat those words as like our characters in *Little Women,* we eventually married. Incidentally in the sequel *Good Wives Meg* and *John Brooke* have twins and, by a strange coincidence we also were blessed with twins.'

Two scenes from the February 1967 production of *Jane Eyre*
featuring Linda James as *Jane Eyre* and Barry Sinclair as *Mr. Rochester*
Michael Knowles is second from the left in the right hand photograph.

Michael was asked to work at Palmers Green by the director Douglas Emery, who first worked with him at Bognor Regis. Michael remembers that he was paid the princely sum of £9 per week. Rehearsals were still held in the West End and the actors still had to pay towards the costs of the rehearsal room. The actor Roy Hepworth, another regular face at Palmers Green, once admitted to Michael that he had to pawn his watch in order to get to rehearsal!

Towards the end of his time at the Intimate Michael was getting some television work on educational programmes. 'I often had to ask Douglas Emery for a day off to record the programme,' recalled Michael, 'I probably would not be allowed to do that today but Douglas was kind and let me go. Luckily, like Maggie Gibson, I was blessed with a photographic memory.'

The actor and film star Bob Hoskins worked for a short while as a student assistant stage manager during the 1960s. He asked Billy Budd for a job and Billy offered him the post of ASM – unpaid! Linda asked Bob why he was working for nothing and Bob replied that he was learning so much from just being there. 'I thought he was a very nice man', said Linda, 'but as most plays in those days required what was called Received Pronunciation, I thought Bob, with his rough voice, would not go far in the profession. How wrong I was!'

Michael and Linda look back on their days at the Intimate as one of the happiest times of their lives. 'Everyone worked together', said Linda, ' with the actors all helping each other. Working with the same faces every week meant that you soon learnt when someone was going to 'dry' and you did all you could to assist them. The audiences were very loyal, often sitting in the same seats week after week. We often had long chats with some of the regulars at the stage door or in the bar.'

Some members of the audience would also write to the actors but not necessarily in complimentary terms. One week a theatre patron wrote to Linda saying that he did not think she had been as good as she could have been in that week's role. 'I was incensed when I read that', recalls Michael, ' and instead of ignoring it as I should have done, I wrote back to the man saying, "How dare you criticise my wife!" '

Like most actors, Michael and Linda love to recall the mishaps that occurred from time to time. Michael recalled a couple of problems encountered by Margaret Gibson:

'In one play Maggie was required to play, or rather mime playing, the piano while the ASM played a sound effects disc. Unfortunately at one performance the ASM was not on the ball and did not stop the disc when he should have. Poor Maggie was forced to stay at the piano for the remainder of the scene, whilst delivering her lines over her right shoulder!

'Doors in stage sets could often pose a problem. On one occasion as Maggie entered, the door came away altogether. Maggie, completely unfazed, gave her opening lines whilst propping the door against the set! On another occasion Maggie was waiting behind the set door sometime before her entrance cue when the door suddenly opened revealing her to the audience. Maggie just walked onto the stage saying "I couldn't help overhearing!" much to the bemusement of the rest of the cast on stage.'

Billy Budd would often be called upon to play small roles on stage but as Michael pointed out 'He was a lovely man but not much of an actor. I remember in *Barefoot In The Park* Billy played a janitor and was so concerned about his lines that when he finally appeared on stage he said all his lines at once not waiting for anyone else to speak.'

Michael and Linda also worked for Jimmy and Gilda Perry at Watford. 'The money was much better than the Intimate', recalls Michael, 'and Jimmy was very good at remembering actors he had worked with when casting his television comedy series.' That was certainly the case with Michael as he went on to play *Captain Ashwood* in BBC's very successful *It Ain't Half Hot Mum.*

Kay Patrick

Kay Patrick was another regular member of the company in the 1960s. She remembers that the director Douglas Emery had a habit of putting cocoa powder on his hair, which would come off in clouds whenever he inadvertently patted his head! Kay also recalls an occasion when Emery was called upon to appear on stage:

'Duggie was playing a detective inspector in an Agatha Christie type play. Unfortunately Duggie was quite deaf and the actor he was on stage with, even more unfortunately, had forgotten his lines. We had this bizarre and rather hilarious situation where Duggie was asking the suspect various questions and responding to the answers that the other actor should have given but hadn't!'

Kay now works as a freelance television director and her name can often be seen on the credits for *Coronation Street.* It was Kay who directed the episode in 2006 when long time Street character Mike Baldwin died in Ken Barlow's arms on the famous cobbled road.

The playwright and comedy writer David McGillivray worked for six months as an ASM at the Intimate in the mid-1960s. David was brought up in Palmers Green and on leaving school worked for a time at Gateway Films, an industrial film company, based in Green Lanes. 'I had only been to the Intimate on about six or seven occasions but I actually made my film debut at the theatre when Gateway produced a film called *Grooming For A Career,* sponsored by Horne Brothers. One sequence was shot in the Intimate Theatre with Gateway staff as the audience!'

William Budd's son also worked for Gateway and when David met William one day he told him that he would like to work at the Intimate. He was immediately offered a job and started work as an ASM the following Monday. David remembers, 'It was the most exciting period of my life. I could hardly believe it was happening. It was so easy to get a job there that it lulled me into a false sense of security and I thought all jobs were that easy to find! I was really a "gofer", cadging props from local shops in exchange for a credit in the programme; acting as prompt for rehearsals and performances and also activating the sound effects, such as once when they had a working sink on stage I was kept busy pouring water down a funnel! I remember clearly that the prompt corner was on stage right not the usual prompt side. I also occasionally made brief appearances on stage when someone was needed as a policeman or similar.' For this David was paid £5 a week, half of what he had received at Gateway.

'I remember noticing immediately the smell of size. This smell was omnipresent during the weekly rep days. The set was painted usually in the room under the stage and quite often completed in one day. At the time I thought the sets looked perfectly acceptable. Sets shook but then they did on television at that time! Later, when the theatre ceased to be a fulltime professional venue, I had connections with an amateur drama company called The Trent Players who staged plays at the Intimate on a regular basis. As soon as I entered the theatre I sensed something was missing and then I realised the smell of size had gone.'

Having encountered derision when, later in his career, he mentioned that he had worked at the Intimate, David came to the conclusion that the Palmers Green playhouse's reputation was not considered that high as far as the theatrical profession was concerned. However, at the time, David was oblivious to the quality of work being produced. 'I was new to it all and therefore had no standards to judge it by and I was having the most wonderful time. Despite the hectic schedule with actors carrying lines for up to three plays in their heads and the production team planning even further ahead with sets, nothing seemed to go drastically wrong and there were no arguments or temper tantrums. In fact everything ran remarkably smoothly. The director, Douglas Emery, gave practically no direction to the actors, relying instead on the moves given in Samuel French's Acting editions of the plays. He obviously knew what his regulars were capable of!'

David remembers particularly the old lighting gantry above the stage where both hands were needed to operate the huge wheels, which tightened the lights. 'I was amazed when I worked at another theatre and found a modern lighting deck as I thought all theatre lighting was like the Intimate's!'

After six months David moved on to Golders Green Hippodrome as ASM and then enrolled at drama school. Later he ran his own theatre company and wrote a series of very popular plays about the Farndale Avenue Housing Estate Townswomen's Guild Dramatic Society. In addition to his playwriting, David works for various national newspapers as an obituaries writer as well as contributing comedy material for performers such as Julian Clary. He regrets not going to more productions at the Intimate when he was growing up. 'I tended to take it for granted as it was on my doorstep. Looking back now the Intimate played a very important part in my life. I felt that Palmers Green was too suburban for my tastes. The Intimate offered the only excitement in the area and working there gave me the impetus to get out and explore. It was a wonderful period of my life.'

Guest artists were being employed more and more often to boost the flagging fortunes of the playhouse. Jack Hulbert, Sonia Dresdel, Henry Kendall and Bill Owen all made appearances in 1960. Sonia Dresdel featured in the Dorothy and Campbell Christie play *Come Live With Me* in January and the following month Bill Owen guested in his own drama *Breakout.* April saw Henry Kendall in William Douglas Home's play *Aunt Edwina* and in August Jack Hulbert starred in Ian Hay's *The Housemaster* alongside a then unknown actor called John Inman. Twelve years later, of course, Inman would be known to all and sundry through his camp antics and constant cry of 'I'm Free!' in the comedy series *Are You Being Served?*

Jack Hulbert

Henry Kendall

Guest stars at the Intimate
in the early 1960's

Jessie Matthews

Bill Owen

Derek Bond returned to the theatre in January 1962 to star in *The Marriage Go Round* by Leslie Stevens and the following month saw Frank Williams, later to achieve television fame as the vicar in *Dad's Army,* head the cast in his own thriller *The TV Murders.* Two weeks later the legendary musical comedy star Jessie Matthews graced the theatre's boards in Guy Bolton's play *Larger Than Life,* based on the W. Somerset Maugham novel. A fortnight later saw Ruth Dunning, alias *Mrs Grove* of BBC's *The Grove Family* (British television's very first soap opera), appear in Ted Willis's drama *Hot Summer Night.*

1963 saw television personality and quizmaster Jeremy Hawk appear in Rex Howard Arundel's *The Final Twist* in May and the year ended with the afore-mentioned *Rattle Of A Simple Man* written by and starring Charles Dyer. Playing opposite him was Nancy Roberts. This was not the Nancy Roberts who had appeared earlier at the Intimate and who achieved fame as *Gran* in *The Grove Family,* but a younger more attractive lady who was known to audiences at that time as a hostess on the popular television quiz show *Double Your Money.*

David McGillivray remembers these guest artists very clearly. 'Every few weeks a guest star would appear with the company. These guests behaved differently to the regular company members and acted as if they were very important. I must admit I was in awe of these visitors and as I was passionately interested in the stage and television I knew all their names as opposed to the rest of the backstage crew who quite often had not heard of these 'stars'. I remember one week when the actress Miki Iveria appeared at the Intimate. She was a lady noted for playing characters like exotic gypsies. She may only have been a character actress among many on television and stage but at the Intimate that week she was a star and how she revelled in her newfound role.'

September 1964 saw the end of an era at the Intimate with the death of Frederick Marlow, whose company GM Productions had run the venue since 1941. *The Palmers Green And Southgate Gazette* reported his death in their issue dated 2nd October:

Death Of Mr. Frederick Marlow

Frederick Marlow

Frederick Walter Marlow of 48, Bramley Road, Southgate, died in Highlands Hospital on Friday 23rd September 1964 aged 61. A true man of the theatre from an early age and a resident of the borough most of his life.

He is best known locally, of course, as the inspiration, which has kept the Intimate going at a time when other rep theatres all over the country have been closing their doors.

Born in Edmonton, he went to work at the old Empire there when he was 14 and was only 19 when appointed manager. In 1932 he set up in business as a variety agent in London.

After the Intimate closed, in common with most other theatres, on the outbreak of war, Mr. Marlow, as managing director of G.M. Productions Ltd showed tremendous courage and faith in opening it up again a year or so later to provide much-needed relaxation for the war-weary people of the district.

Although dogged by ill-health and suffering far more pain than most men are called upon to endure, Mr. Marlow spent a lot of time at the theatre until recently.

About three weeks ago he became ill and while being nursed at home for pneumonia, had a heart attack and was taken to Highlands Hospital.

Mr. Marlow leaves a widow and two sons, Peter, who is married and lives at Ponders End, and Christopher, who is still at home. There are two grandchildren.

The funeral took place at All Saints Church, Edmonton on Wednesday 30th September.

Fred's sons, Peter and Christopher, vowed to continue running the Intimate, although they faced an uphill struggle as by December of that year, the Intimate was listed as the only existing professional repertory theatre in the whole of the London area.

Three variations to the week-in, week-out diet of three-act plays were introduced by the new regime in 1965. The first was the introduction of a week of old time music hall entertainment in February. Presented by Horace Mashford, who for many years staged this style of entertainment at the Alexandra Palace, and featuring well-established variety artists such as Larry Parker and Billy Wells, this proved to be highly successful with the paying public. So much so that the management decided to stage *The Intimate Revue* in March featuring members of the resident company, including Billy Budd, in a programme of songs and sketches. In May a second week of music hall appeared at the theatre. The company in this production, headed by Ken Barnes and Brenda Armstrong, was previewing the show that would play a summer season on the Isle Of Wight before returning to the Intimate for a two-week season in September where they staged two completely different programmes.

Olde Tyme Music Hall programme February 1965

Another innovation, introduced to broaden the theatre's audience base, was on view in November when the Intimate staged a musical – Leslie Bricusse and Anthony Newley's *Stop The World, I Want To Get Off* with Jimmy and Gilda Perry in the leading roles. Jimmy, of course, is now famed for devising and writing some of the most famous comedy series of recent years, such as *Dad's Army, Hi-De-Hi, It Ain't Half Hot Mum* and *You Rang, M'Lord.* He and Gilda would become familiar faces at the Intimate in the mid-1960s, appearing in various productions. On one memorable occasion in January 1967 Jimmy actually tackled the role of *Hercule Poirot,* Agatha Christie's famous Belgian detective in *Black Coffee* in January 1967.

Although *Stop The World* was the theatre's first full-scale musical, the company had staged *Me And My Girl* in 1961. On closer inspection though, this turned out to be the play version with songs inserted just for the leading couple and was not the full blown musical version first seen at the Victoria Palace in 1937 and later revamped so successfully by Robert Lindsay and Emma Thompson at the Adelphi Theatre in 1985.

Gilda and Jimmy Perry in a scene from *Stop The World, I Want To Get Off* November 1965

The final innovation of 1965 was the presentation of the Intimate's first-ever pantomime in December, when the resident director Douglas Emery staged *Cinderella*. It featured the ever-versatile rep company with Intimate favourite Margaret Gibson donning fishnet tights to play *Dandini*. The initial fortnight's run proved so popular that a third week was swiftly added.

The first Intimate pantomime - December 1965

No one can accuse the management of not trying to whip up enthusiasm for the Intimate .In a bid to attract a new kind of audience to the theatre, a club was formed for young people called *Theatre 32*. It ran a programme of Sunday afternoon performances of classic and modern plays, poetry, jazz and folk music. The members even helped with cleaning the theatre when it was closed for its summer break. The Playgoers Society was also still going strong with monthly meetings and fund-raising efforts for the theatre. However, with no grants or sponsorship the theatre was still struggling.

1966 began on a more optimistic note when *The Palmers Green and Southgate Gazette* for 28th January reported that Billy Budd was having discussions with Enfield Council on the possibility of council support for the theatre. This proposal was to be considered by the Education Committee, who pointed out that, in return for financial support, they would like to see the Intimate stage classical plays and plays with appeal for schoolchildren. In the event, Enfield Council agreed to subsidise eight productions in an attempt to save the Intimate. During the course of 1966 and the first few months of 1967, the theatre presented such plays as Christopher Fry's *The Lady's Not For Burning,* Shaw's *Arms And The Man, The Snow Queen, Jane Eyre,* Wilde's *The Importance Of Being Earnest* and Robert Bolt's *A Man For All Seasons.*

As for the rest of the year's offerings, a couple of guest artistes livened up the weekly play cycle when Betty Alberge, billed as '*Florrie Lindley* from *Coronation Street*', starred in *So Many*

Arthur English

Children and comedian Arthur English took top billing in John Waterhouse's play *Just The Ticket*. Betty Alberge as *Florrie Lindley* was featured in the very first scene in the very first episode of *Coronation Street* in 1960. *Florrie* was owner of the famous corner shop and in that opening scene encountered the infamous *Ena Sharples* played by Violet Carson. Arthur English was a well-known comedian, who dressed as a 'spiv' in his variety act, complete with kipper tie and padded shoulders. His catchphrase was 'Open The Cage!' and he was billed as *The Prince Of The Wide Boys*. In later years Arthur became a regular member of the comedy programmes *Are You Being Served?* and *In Sickness And In Health*.

Variety and music hall returned for odd weeks with Lesley Welsh, the memory man, making an appearance in October. Jimmy and Gilda Perry joined forces with resident director Douglas Emery to stage a two-week season of Sandy Wilson's musical pastiche *The Boy Friend* in November and then the couple returned to the theatre in December to present the pantomime *Dick Whittington*.

Jimmy and Gilda Perry as *Captain & Mate* in *Dick Whittington*, December 1966

Sizeable audiences, however, were still elusive. When *Pinch And Run,* written by and starring Clive Elliott, opened on the 6th June the *Gazette's* critic commented that the theatre was half-empty on opening night. By January 1967 things had worsened when the newspaper review of the play *Ask Me Tomorrow* pointed out that there was a near empty house on the first night.

It was clear that something drastic had to be done to revive the fortunes of the ailing theatre. Christopher Marlow announced in April 1967 that productions would now run for two or three weeks, thus giving more rehearsal time to each play and hopefully a higher standard of performance. He also brought in a new Director Of Productions and Publicity in the person of Ernest Dudley, a well-known radio broadcaster and dramatist who was known to the general public as BBC's *Armchair Detective*. Dudley's policy was not to have a resident company of actors but to recruit each cast separately with, hopefully, a star name in each show. Overnight the theatre lost its director, Douglas Emery, who had replaced John Maxwell back in 1960 and had directed virtually every play since then, its scenic designer, David Vickers and its company of well-loved faces, much to the dismay of the regular playgoers.

The first production under this new regime was Julian Slade and Dorothy Reynolds' musical *Salad Days* followed by a three-week presentation of the farce *Boeing-Boeing* with comedian Charlie Chester heading the cast. The third production to open before the summer break was Sutton Vane's *Outward Bound* with radio and television personality Jimmy Hanley leading a cast that included a return of Intimate favourite Margaret Gibson.

Salad Days
April 1967

At first there was an air of optimism about the scheme, exemplified by the *Gazette* reviewer in the issue for 21st April 1967:

> At last the Intimate comes to life and takes its rightful place in the Greater London theatre scene ….A different spirit seems to pervade the whole theatre both in front of, and behind, the footlights, and for the first time, in my admittedly short recollection, the actors and actresses actually seem to be enjoying what they do… The only department to which this euphoristic state of affairs had not yet permeated, apparently, was the bar and where I was told, quite sharply, to wait, when I had the temerity to request a pre-show drink before the attendant, Hebe, had finished taking orders for the interval!

That edition of the *Gazette* also posed the question:

Will Intimate Be Borough's First Civic Theatre?

When asked by a reporter whether the Council was likely to have any further financial interest in the Intimate, Cllr. Eric Smythe, leader of the Labour majority on the council, said: ' The council's policy is to have a civic theatre locally and at the moment we have helped the Intimate with certain of its productions to the tune of £3,000 in the last year, though not all of it was used.' Cllr. Smythe pointed out that the council had had discussions with Ernest Dudley and had agreed to spend some more money on the theatre. 'It is early days to say that the council is likely to take over', said Smythe, 'we are still very interested in helping the local theatre in the borough.'

The following week's *Gazette* reported that Enfield Council hoped to sponsor twenty two-weekly productions during the coming year and that negotiations were still in progress with Christopher Marlow, Ernest Dudley and the Arts Council of Great Britain regarding the financial aspects of the proposed arrangements.

In the *Gazette* for the 12th May further details of the council's sponsorship were given. Enfield Council's proposed outlay on the twenty productions was given as £24,000. As the paper explained:

The council would receive 80% of the box office revenue and with contributions from the Arts Council, the actual cost to Enfield would be £4,000. If the box office income did not cover the original outlay the loss, up to a maximum of £10,000, would be shared equally by the Arts Council and the local council. But it was thought that the council's receipts would amount to £16,000 leaving an £8,000 deficit, of which the Arts Council would pay £4,000.

The usual summer closure stretched to an unprecedented nine weeks that year. New seating, curtains and lighting were supposed to be installed during the closure but when the theatre re-opened on 26th August the *Gazette* critic's searching eye noted only ' a few licks of paint, some reinforced (not replaced) seats and a face-lift generally.' Ernest Dudley apologised for the delay in re-opening claiming that his aim was to try and build a permanent rep company 'but this takes time.' He also said: 'It is a question of giving the public what it wants and so we are moving away from the previous type of production and presenting a new and much broader field of stage entertainment. In other words, we are moving with the times.'

If Mr. Dudley was moving with the times he certainly wasn't taking the audience with him as the *Gazette* critic noted when reviewing the opening production of *A Midsummer Night's Dream,* with Charlie Chester returning to the Intimate as *Bottom*: '…Increasingly familiar wide empty spaces out front and many of the people who were there appeared to be friends of the rather large cast.'

Sadly Mr. Dudley's decision to dismantle the old resident company had alienated a large number of local people who still supported the Intimate and he had not attracted a new audience to replace them - a fact seized upon in the editorial column of the local paper on 29th September. That edition of the *Gazette* also announced that Enfield Council had approved an advance of £2000 for first aid improvements and would be financing future productions at a rate of £1000 per production. It seemed that the Arts Council was no longer providing any assistance. GM Productions were also required to submit a list of future productions for the council's approval. One councillor spoke out against this, horrified at the idea of the council vetting or determining what plays should be staged. He told the paper that he could not think of a worse body to do such a thing than seventy councillors and added 'I tremble at our knowledge of the theatre!'

Dudley's autumn season of plays continued with Shaw's *Candida,* Wilde's *Lord Arthur Savile's Crime, Wuthering Heights* plus thrillers such as *Dial 'M' For Murder, Gaslight* and *The Ghost Train* but sadly there was no sign of the well-known guest artists promised for each production.

Jimmy and Gilda Perry returned for a short, successful pantomime season of *Mother Goose* and then Dudley staged a two-week presentation of the hit revue *Beyond The Fringe.* Unfortunately the weather was against him and on the opening night, because of the arctic conditions and the snow, no one turned up to attend the performance and only twenty hardy souls made the journey on the second evening. Not an auspicious start to 1968.

By March Ernest Dudley had left the Intimate and the local council had decided to end its financial aid. Things looked bleak indeed but Peter Marlow was still trying to be upbeat. He told the *Gazette:* 'We are going to reshape and revert to the weekly rep system.' He had requested financial assistance from the council for the new financial year but had been refused. 'We are not going to say "No, that is the end". We are going to do our very best as we have done in the past.' The Federation of Ratepayers and Civic Associates asked the council to reconsider their decision of withdrawing support from the Intimate but the council was busy choosing a site for a civic theatre, an activity thought inopportune by the Federation as it felt the Intimate already served the needs of the borough and was, most definitely, in a prime site.

Douglas Emery and David Vickers were persuaded to return to help put the theatre on its feet again and several well-loved names from the old resident company made welcome reappearances but no amount of goodwill could revive the fortunes of the ailing theatre. The venue's recent trail of bad luck with the elements also continued when a fire broke out in the theatre's boiler room on Monday 17th June. The play was stopped during the first act and the audience told to vacate the building. Actors and actresses in full make-up and costume formed a chain to pass buckets of water into the boiler room. Bill Budd, after evacuating the theatre, went back to the boiler room and found himself trapped when the door closed behind him. He panicked when he could not find his way out through the smoke but was luckily rescued by a fire-fighter.

One artist who appeared at the Intimate during this troubled period was none other than David Bowie, who appeared with Lindsay Kemp's company in *Pierrot In Turquoise* in March. One can only imagine how different the audience figures would have been if Mr. Bowie had achieved his worldwide fame by March 1968!

David Bowie

Week commencing Tuesday 26th March, 1968

G.M. Productions Ltd. by arrangement with Richard Jackson

present

PIERROT IN TURQUOISE

by

LINDSAY KEMP

Cloud .... **DAVID BOWIE**
Harlequin .... **JACK BIRKETT**
Pierrot .... **LINDSAY KEMP**

They play with him.
He comes from the moon
They play with Masks, flowers, gestures; through them he sees Columbine.
He performs with knives, birds, apples, gargoyle angels .....
They play with him.
They move in and out of costumes, in and out around Pierrot.
Mesmerised.
Harlequin the bright shadow.
Cloud the changing ..... flowerseller, policeman, spectator, chorus,
Pierrot's voice,
They do not leave the theatre.
Columbine is a husk and bits of black string.
They play with him.

There will be an interval of twenty minutes.

Lindsay Kemp

By July the theatre was no longer controlled by the Marlow family, who had been at the helm since 1941 and who had done so much to keep the Intimate Theatre alive and flourishing. To add to the sadness, Billy Budd, the popular manager, was also leaving. The *Gazette* (28th June 1968) critic, reviewing the final production of the Marlow reign, *The Seventh Veil,* paid tribute to the old regime:

…When the takeover is completed however, it seems that the Intimate will be the Intimate Theatre in name only and little else will remain. To the Intimate's friends this must be a regrettable thing… Week after week manager Bill Budd and the people at the Intimate struggled to present the best they could with severely limited resources. Director, designer and casts seemed to work minor miracles.

The new group in control of the Intimate was called Intimate Theatre (PG) Ltd with Donald Nash (Chairman), Frances O'Hanlon (General Manager), Glyn Johnson (Assistant Manager), Rolf Kruger (Casting Advisor) and Howard Kent (Administrator). Kent was a former local journalist and a one-time editor of the *Wood Green Observer*, who had been full-time in the entertainment business since 1961. He announced that he was going to spend £5,000 on redecorations during the theatre's annual summer break and promised local theatregoers 'a West End style of entertainment' with fortnightly productions and star names. He also declared that the theatre would be opening its doors to welcome local companies for an amateur season. In the programme for his opening production he stated that ' the new policy for the Intimate is to blend together those who are already established stars in their profession with the most promising new talent. Similarly the play policy is to provide proven successes and classic revivals mixed with new plays which may well include among them the outstanding successes of the future.'

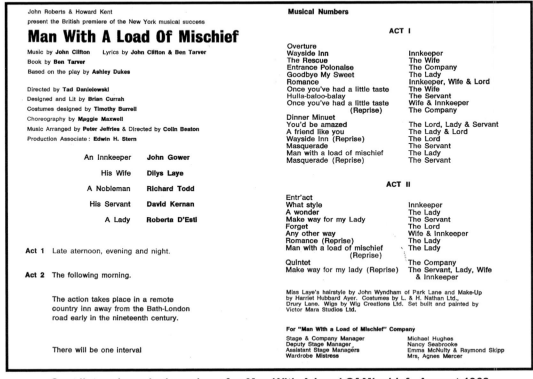

Cast list and musical numbers for *Man With A Load Of Mischief* - August 1968

Kent's opening attraction was a musical version of *Man With A Load Of Mischief,* starring Richard Todd, David Kernan, Dilys Laye, Roberta D'Esti and John Gower. By some strange coincidence the play version of *Man With A Load Of Mischief* was the very first production that Billy Budd oversaw as house manager back in 1951 and now the musical version was the first production to be staged at the Intimate since Budd's departure.

Man With A Load Of Mischief - August 1968

This American mini-musical was a British premiere and it eventually transferred to the Comedy Theatre in the West End albeit with a different cast. The Intimate's production ran for three and a half weeks and the theatre's publicity machine certainly worked overtime for this opening show, giving away free bottles of 'Mischief' perfume and selling a 'Mischief' cocktail in the theatre bar. There was even a recipe for the cocktail in the programme so that playgoers could go home and make their own!

Have A 'Mischief' Cocktail

A special 'Mischief' cocktail has been created especially for this production and is on sale in the bar of this theatre. Try one tonight – and then serve it at home for all special occasions.

The ingredients are:-
      1 measure Booth's Gin (or 'High and Dry' Gin)
      1 measure fresh lemon juice (or PLJ)
      ¾ measure Martini sweet vermouth
      ½ measure Blackcurrant cordial (or Ribena)

Stir with ice and strain into glass – on the rocks.

The theatre had been redecorated by a young designer, Mark Dalton, and performances were now at 7.45 pm from Monday to Friday and 5 pm and 8 pm on Saturdays. The Thursday matinee was at 2.30 pm. Ticket prices were 12/6, 9/6 and 7/6 except for Saturday when they were 15/-, 9/6 and 7/6. Cheaper prices were available for the Thursday matinee at 7/6 and 5/-.

The *Gazette's* (16th Aug. 1968) critic was extremely enthusiastic about the new regime at the Intimate:

> It is a splendid sight to see on a wet, out of season, Wednesday night. People, that is, by the hundred, crowding in the rain, filling up the stalls and the balcony, jamming shoulder to shoulder in the bar. The Intimate theatre bar, which a few wet Wednesday nights ago, would cater for only about as many people as the launderette across the road…. Crowds applauding, bouquets, star cast and celebrity studded audience: this is the new image of the old Intimate Theatre.

Alan Ayckbourn's popular comedy *Relatively Speaking* was the new company's second production followed by the distinguished actress Yvonne Mitchell in C.K. Simon's play *Out Of Order*. Joining Miss Mitchell in the cast was Carole Ann Ford, well known to television viewers and science fiction fans as the Doctor's granddaughter in the very first series of *Dr. Who* when William Hartnell portrayed the Tardis time traveller.

Two tried and tested thrillers occupied the Intimate during October when *Wait Until Dark* and *Ten Little Niggers* were staged and then a new play by Roger Milner called *The Upper Crust* brought actresses Gwen Watford and Penelope Keith to Palmers Green in a production directed by Donald Sinden.

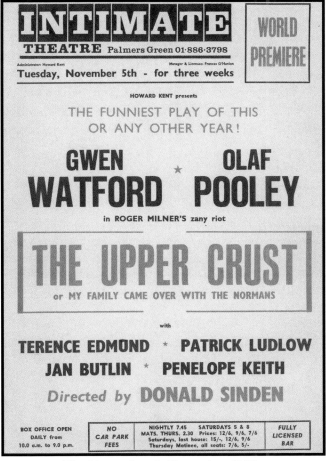

THE INTIMATE

THEATRE Palmers Green 01·886·3798

Administrator: Howard Kent   Manager & Licensee: Frances O'Hanlon

Tuesday, November 5th - for three weeks

HOWARD KENT presents

THE FUNNIEST PLAY OF THIS
OR ANY OTHER YEAR!

GWEN ★ **OLAF**
WATFORD POOLEY

in ROGER MILNER'S zany riot

THE UPPER CRUST

or MY FAMILY CAME OVER WITH THE NORMANS

with

TERENCE EDMOND ★ **PATRICK LUDLOW**
JAN BUTLIN ★ **PENELOPE KEITH**

Directed by **DONALD SINDEN**

| BOX OFFICE OPEN DAILY from 10.0 a.m. to 9.0 p.m. | NO CAR PARK FEES | NIGHTLY 7.45   SATURDAYS 5 & 8 MATS. THURS. 2.30   Prices: 12/6, 9/6, 7/6 Saturdays, last house: 15/-, 12/6, 9/6 Thursday Matinee, all seats: 7/6, 5/- | FULLY LICENSED BAR |

WORLD PREMIERE

The Upper Crust - December 1968

June Ritchie, perhaps best known for her leading role opposite Alan Bates in the film version of Stan Barstow's *A Kind Of Loving,* joined the cast of Bill Naughton's *Alfie* and then on 10th December the Intimate presented the premiere of the play *Angie And Ernie.* The comedian Peter Jones, known to millions at that time as *Mr. Fenner* in the television situation comedy *The Rag Trade,* and later a regular member of the radio panel game *Just A Minute,* co-wrote the play with Kevin B. Laffan. Peter also starred in the production alongside Elspeth March, Leslie Dwyer and Johnny Briggs, now best known as *Mike Baldwin* in *Coronation Street.* Posters for the play also advertised pre-show music from 7.30 pm nightly from Reg Varney and his Trio. Reg, a well-known comedy actor whose biggest success was ITV's *On The Buses* and, at that time, an Enfield resident, was a great friend of Peter Jones and appeared with him in *The Rag Trade.*

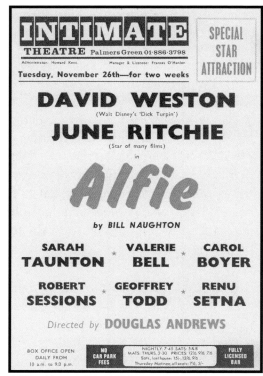

Alfie - November 1968

Angie And Ernie - December 1968

The programme for *Angie And Ernie* also advertised another innovation by the new management – Intimate Theatre Gift Vouchers.

AN UNUSUAL GIFT

Why not give relatives and friends a really unusual and welcome gift this Christmas – Intimate Gift Vouchers. Vouchers can be bought at the box office for any multiple of seat prices from 15/- upwards (i.e. two seats at 7/6d). The voucher itself costs 1/-. The recipient merely exchanges the voucher at the box office for tickets to the value shown – or pays the balance if more seats, or more expensive ones, are required.

For Christmas, birthdays, anniversaries, etc. these Gift Vouchers provide an ideal simple gift for all who enjoy the theatre.

The year ended with a five week run at Christmas of *Where The Rainbow Ends* starring

1968's Christmas attraction

television's *William Tell,* Conrad Phillips.

The new management had now been at the helm for five months and a mood of cautious optimism prevailed. Howard Kent told the *Gazette* in January 1969 that he 'had been able to prove that the district needed a decent theatre. Business had improved tremendously but it had to increase even more…there are thousands and thousands who do not know that we are here and what we are doing.' He emphasised that 'big name artists are happy to play at Palmers Green.'

The first three productions of 1969 were billed together as *The Intimate Festival Of Laughter.* This season consisted of Michael Pertwee's *Together We Did It* starring Lynda Baron and Jimmy Thompson; Francis Matthews and Dilys Laye, making a welcome return after her

appearance in *Man With A Load Of Mischief,* in Frank Barbera's *Faithful In My Fashion,* directed by another Intimate favourite Bill Owen, and Trevor Peacock's *Collapse Of Stout Party.* This final play was originally to have starred Terry Scott, but Mr. Scott had to withdraw because of ill health. Nevertheless the cast was a strong one with Bill Fraser, of *The Army Game* and *Bootsie And Snudge,* revue star Joan Heal and Peter Jones. Also in the cast was the playwright, who had been a pupil of Enfield Grammar School and who, at that time, lived, with his wife and two children, in Hadley Road, New Barnet. Trevor, of course, has had a distinguished career on stage and television, scoring a great success as *Jim Trott* in *The Vicar Of Dibley.* Trevor's local connections probably account for the fact that the area gets a mention in the play. In Act 3 the character of *Lieutenant Barrow,* the fire prevention officer (played by Bill Fraser) enters:

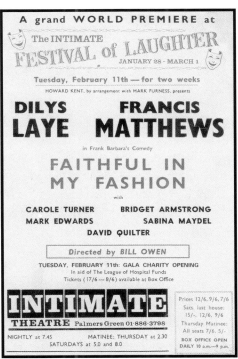

A 1969 World Premiere for the Intimate

RIMBOLD: Hallo Lieutenant – you're back then.

BARROW: Yes. I was suddenly called away to Palmers Green.

Working backstage at the theatre at that time was Simon Barry. Simon had been a member of Enfield Youth Theatre in 1968 when the theatre was in need of an assistant stage manager for the production of *The Upper Crust.* Simon expressed interest and was rewarded with the job, receiving £5 a week, even though he was still at school at the time. Luckily games afternoon fell on Thursdays so Simon was able to attend the matinee performances. He worked at the theatre for two years before carving a career as an actor and impresario. Simon had a particular love of pantomime and quite often appeared as dame including appearances in the Intimate pantomimes. Simon's production company is now responsible for staging several pantomimes each year throughout the British Isles. Simon remembers with some embarrassment the production of *Collapse Of Stout Party* and, in particular, the actor Bill Fraser:

'Bill had a habit of lying on the floor of the dressing room to relax between shows. On one occasion I dashed into the darkened room not seeing Bill, knocked his hand and managed to push his finger up his nose causing a nosebleed. I don't think I was too popular that evening!'

By April, goodwill and optimism were in short supply. Letters of complaint had been printed in the local press concerning the music hall show starring Maxine Audley, which had followed the three-play season, and the ticket prices for the children's entertainment *Brer Rabbit and Uncle Remus.* Howard Kent replied to the criticism admitting 'we have so far run at a loss and the only way we can continue and develop is by attracting bigger audiences.' He explained that *Brer Rabbit* 'has quite a substantial cast and a small orchestra. This plus all the overheads, which go on week after week, means that we must take something in the region of £1500 per week if we are to pay our way. We are trying to produce shows of West End standards with top quality performers at the very lowest possible price. We charge approximately one third of current West End prices, though with only 442 seats at our disposal we can never take a large amount in any one week.'

After a week of two one-act plays by Walter Winward, *Absente Rea* and *A Game Of Chess,* which saw the return of June Ritchie to the Intimate, there was a two-week run of Frank Barbera's play *Forever April* starring comedian Dickie Henderson and noted comic actor, Henry McGee. Dickie, of course, was a famous name in light entertainment, probably remembered today for his classic routine as a would-be Sinatra style crooner singing *One For My Baby* whilst battling with temperamental bar stools and packets of cigarettes. McGee was a familiar television face from his many appearances on *The Benny Hill Show.* The combination of Henderson and McGee promised much but sadly the play received a very negative review in the *Gazette* (2nd May 1969), whose critic stated

> By far the most entertaining part of this new farce by Frank Barbera was actor and comedian Dickie Henderson's impromptu speech to the audience after the final curtain.

This poor press notice stung Howard Kent into writing to the paper complaining about the unfair criticism and pointing out that the box office was hit badly in the second week by the paper's review. He warned that the Intimate was the only public theatre in North London and one of very few theatres in the whole country mounting productions in this way: 'If audiences are kept away from the Intimate there will be no theatre at all for the people of the area. I believe the Intimate is a very tangible amenity for the district. I want it to play an important part in the life of the area. I want not only to provide first-class entertainment but

also to help amateur companies and to play our part in the local community. Unless we can make both ends meet we shall be quite unable to fulfil these ambitions.' Kent then suggested that local critics had a responsibility to help local theatre.

Not surprisingly the paper's theatre reviewer replied in the following week's *Gazette* (23rd May 1969) pointing out to Mr. Kent that critics had responsibilities to their readers and therefore had to give an honest opinion!

After a two-week run, from the 13th to 24th May, of Henry Cecil's play *Hugo* with Ellen McIntosh, there was a three week season of guaranteed old-fashioned 'crowd pleasers', *Arsenic And Old Lace,* the farce *See How They Run* and Agatha Christie's *Spider's Web.*

Regular playgoers were no doubt delighted to see the return of Douglas Emery to direct *See How They Run* whilst another popular member of the erstwhile rep company, Janet Butlin directed the Christie comedy-thriller.

Music Hall entertainment returned in June when *Palace Of Varieties* played for two weeks with two completely different bills. The first week's show was topped by the veteran jazz singer Adelaide Hall whilst the second week saw Leon Cortez heading the cast. The *Gazette* (27th June 1969) critic, attending the second week's show, was in vitriolic mood:

> One gets the idea that the show has been thrown together and the fact that two different comedians told the same joke tends to confirm this impression.

He went on to describe the general presentation of the show as 'shabby' and added:

> The presenters of this show might well take heart from the fact that although audiences now may not join in the banter and choruses with such inhibition as of old, they are not so quick to throw things either!

Summer variety 1969

The season ended with three three-night productions from local drama groups. Southgate Jewish Literary Society presented *The Anniversary* by Bill McIlwraith, Trent Players offered Leslie Sands' thriller *Intent To Murder* and St. Monica's Players followed with Shaw's *Pygmalion*.

The Intimate then closed for its summer break, a normal feature of the theatre's year. However, this year was rather different for although the local playgoers did not know it at the time, they had just witnessed the end of the Intimate as a full-time professional repertory theatre. The first hint of closure appeared in *The Stage* newspaper for 14th August when the main headline on the front page of the paper was

The Intimate:
No Re-Opening For Some Time

The following day the local *Gazette* (15th August 1969) declared:

Theatre Trust Only Hope For
Re-Opening Intimate

Howard Kent announced that the Intimate would not re-open as a full-time theatre in the immediate future but he planned to hold a public meeting at the theatre in September when the idea of setting up a trust would be discussed. He went on to say:

> For the past three months I have been working on a proposition for saving the Intimate. We have arranged with our landlords for the premises to be let for a short while to an organisation with strong theatrical interests.

This organisation called WPC Associates consisted of scene builders and costumiers who would use the Intimate as a showcase. Kent hoped that a trust would take over the lease, operating the theatre professionally for the main part of the year and making the venue available for amateur companies during the remaining months. He declared:

> We have none of us taken one penny out of the company by way of fees and remuneration and our principal aim is now to see the theatre's future secured.

He said that he had attempted to put the Intimate 'on the map' but had found it difficult to build up sufficiently large, regular audiences. He felt that without the 'cushion' in the way of grant aid and public support, the theatre was not a viable proposition.

Mr. Kent told *The Stage*:

> Our opening production ran for four weeks in August and early September and we grossed about £1,300 per week during that time, compared with approximately £340 per week grossed by the previous management for a regular weekly change of programme. What has emerged from our experience is the difficulty of building up either a sufficiently large, regular audience or an audience big enough overall so that even if many do not come regularly there is still a strong enough potential for each production. To this, other factors have been added, the most important of which has been the growing economic uncertainty of the country this year.

Theatre business has declined in many areas and we, at the Intimate, suffered a particularly heavy decline from April on. The productions staged were, by and large, of a high standard but business generally fell off disastrously.

The following week's local paper included a letter from Douglas Emery who felt that the theatre should have continued with a resident rep company ' where familiar faces were seen every week', as well as an article claiming the borough council would do everything it could to help the Intimate survive, short of actually giving a grant. The Council would try and make the theatre pay its way by encouraging amateur societies, affiliated to the borough's arts council, to hire the Intimate. There was also a hint that the Entertainments Department might use the venue for one-day events.

David McGillivray sent a letter to the *Gazette* the following week claiming there was only one reason the theatre closed - Howard Kent had failed to keep his promise to bring West End entertainment to Palmers Green.

After that flurry of interest it all went ominously quiet and the theatre's doors remained closed. At the end of October the *Gazette* (31st Oct. 1969) proclaimed

Rep To Come Back At The Intimate

and claimed that Bill Costello and Ray Millichip, directors of WPC, planned to form a rep company by February 1970. Local amateur companies would be allowed to use the theatre between professional productions.

Sadly, that plan did not come to fruition and the Intimate remained dark all through the autumn. Like so many other playhouses throughout the country had already discovered, the days of weekly or even fortnightly rep were a thing of the past. The Intimate had managed to cling on for longer than most venues but rival forms of entertainment and audiences' changing tastes had finally secured its demise as a full-time professional theatre.

To young actors starting out in the profession today, the world of weekly rep is an alien land but if you speak to any of the actors who worked at the Intimate or similar theatres the sense of loss is immediately apparent. Aubrey Woods spoke on behalf of many of those actors when he said:

' The loss of the Intimate as a repertory venue was felt not only by its patrons but by the acting profession as well. Weekly rep has now almost vanished from the theatre and as a consequence actors have one less training ground and have to spend their first years in the profession picking up walk-on parts in television plays where possible and appearing for little or no money in fringe theatre, instead of doing the rounds of the London and provincial reps and gaining their experience on a regular basis.

'Sudden fame did not spring from these companies, but the grounding found there gave a solid basis for many a career which has then gone from juvenile to character performances and is in many cases still continuing. Future generations of actors will, of course, train and many will prosper, but without the hothouse of weekly rep which was hard work, frustrating, rewarding, successful, disastrous, tearful, hysterical but never boring and which never left any of the cast on Saturday night after the final performance feeling that the week had been wasted.'

THE PLAYS YOU HAVE ASKED FOR!

Monday, May 26th - one week only

The finest comedy thriller of them all

ARSENIC AND OLD LACE

BANK HOLIDAY MONDAY at 6.0 & 8.45 p.m.

Monday, June 2nd - one week only

There isn't a funnier farce than . . .

SEE HOW THEY RUN

Monday, June 9th - one week only

AGATHA CHRISTIE'S

THE SPIDER'S WEB

INTIMATE

THEATRE Palmers Green 01·886·3798

| Prices: |
| 12/6 9/6 7/6 |
| Sats. last house: |
| 15/- 12/6 9/6 |
| Thursday Matinee: |
| All seats 7/6, 5/- |
| BOX OFFICE OPEN |
| Daily 10 a.m.—9 p.m. |

NIGHTLY at 8.0   MATINEE: THURSDAY at 2.30

SATURDAYS at 6.0 and 8.45

BOOK FOR ALL THREE AND SAVE MONEY — Full details at the Box Office

ACTORS APPEARING AT THE INTIMATE 1961-1969
(Not Already Mentioned In The Text)

In addition to regulars Margaret Gibson, Janet Butlin, Joan Lindsay and James Irwin, Anthony Dutton, Anthony Shirvell, Ralph Broome and Phyllis Totten all became familiar faces during this period.

Colin Bean, who became a regular member of television's *Dad's Army* platoon playing *Private Sponge*, made several appearances at the Intimate in this decade including *Dear Delinquent* (Apr 1963), *The Man With Red Hair* (Jan 1966) and *A Man For All Seasons* (Nov 1966).

Edward Petherbridge visited the area for roles in *Simple Spymen* (Dec 1961) and *Watch It Sailor* (Jan 1962), whilst Kenneth Waller, perhaps best known as *Grandad* in the television comedy series *Bread,* could be found in *Dr. Brent's Household* (Aug 1962) and *Don't Listen Ladies* (Dec 1962).

Simon Williams, son of playwrights Hugh and Margaret Williams and one of the stars of the hit television series *Upstairs, Downstairs,* appeared in *Candida* (Sept 1967) and *Lord Arthur Savile's Crime* (Sept 1967) whilst Clive Russell, who played *Phil* the reflexologist in *Coronation Street*, could be seen in several productions including *Time To Kill* (Aug 1961) and *The Family Upstairs* (Nov 1962).

One Off Appearances

The film and stage star Anthony Hopkins could be seen briefly at the Intimate in 1962 when, as a twenty-four year old unknown actor, he appeared in the comedy *The Amorous Prawn* (Aug 1962). Hopkins has enjoyed a distinguished stage career appearing at the Royal Court and the National and an equally successful film career with starring roles in *The Remains Of The Day, Shadowlands* and *Silence Of the Lambs.* He was made a CBE in 1987 and knighted in 1993.

Keith Pyott, who was in John Clements' company at the Intimate back in 1936, made a welcome return to the theatre in 1962 when he took a role in Agatha Christie's courtroom thriller *Witness For The Prosecution* (Jan 1962).

Steven Berkoff made a fleeting appearance at the theatre in 1962 when he played the role of *Laurie* in a dramatisation of Louisa M. Alcott's book *Little Women* (Feb 1962).

Anthony Hopkins

Colin Bean

Simon Williams

THE LATTER YEARS

On 24th December 1969 the Intimate opened its doors for the first time since productions ceased in the summer. In association with WPC, Alexander Bridge's pantomime *Cinderella* took to the stage for three and a half weeks. It boasted no star names and had a rather mixed reception with complaints in the local press over the 'blue' nature of some of the jokes.

The sad decline of the theatre continued until the church terminated WPC's lease in March 1970 when the venue reverted to a parish hall once again. The *Palmers Green and Southgate Gazette* reporting this fact on 13th March 1970 managed to sound an optimistic note in its *Opinion* column. Under the headline 'Curtain Up On A New Era', it went on to say: 'The regret at the passing of what was the last remaining rep theatre in London will be tempered somewhat by the renewed hope of local amateur societies that the parish hall might become available for bookings.'

The paper was quite correct in its prediction and for the next eighteen years the theatre found a new lease of life, albeit not so glamorous as those heady days of the '30s and '40s. At first, though, there was only a slow trickle of amateur drama groups using the venue and in September the *Gazette* reported that the future of the Intimate Theatre was still in the balance. It appeared that for several months a four-man parish hall committee had been closely investigating the future use of the hall following a decision that the parish should try to run the centre itself. This committee had concluded that in its present condition the theatre could not be used as anything other than a theatre and any suggestion that it be converted for social activities would have to be supported by strong evidence of demand before its function as an amateur theatre was destroyed. A couple of weeks later on 2nd October the *Gazette* quoted an unnamed parishioner who claimed the Intimate was a 'white elephant' that should be redeveloped or sold and at a parish meeting quite a few people thought the theatre should be turned into a social centre.

Despite these threats theatre business slowly improved as more and more amateur companies began to use the Intimate as their regular venue. Most of these companies staged at least two productions a year and brought with them their loyal audience base so the theatre was soon open for business on most weeks of the year and companies were playing to full or almost full houses. This upturn in the theatre's fortunes is due in no small measure to Ellen Trigger, the new manager. Ellen had no background in theatre; in fact, she had been a chauffeuse for fifteen years and had only worked in the box office for Billy Budd. When Ellen was asked by the church to take over the management of the venue she agreed with some trepidation. She remembers that she was given £100 for stationery to write to all the amateur groups inviting them to stage productions at the Intimate. In an interview with the *Wood Green Weekly Herald* on 7th June 1979 Ellen recalled: 'They

(The church authorities) gave me two years and a couple of hundred pounds to play with. If it paid for itself we would keep it open.' She admitted to the reporter that running a theatre was a frightening prospect: 'I only know about the box office'. Ellen, however, was successful and the church loan was soon paid back and enough profit was made to make improvements to the building. Ellen later arranged a loan of £3,500 from Enfield Council to renew the lighting, which had not been updated since the '30s. So successful was the venue at that time that the loan was repaid within a year!

Amateur drama groups using the Intimate on a regular basis during the 1970s included Group 12, Entens, Southgate Jewish Literary Society, St. Monica's Players and Trent Players The first musical society to perform at the theatre during this period was Risley Operatic Group when it staged Franz Lehar's *The Count Of Luxembourg* in October 1970. Other societies soon followed including Enfield Grand Opera Society, Chandos Operatic Society, Choreodrama, Enfield Light Operatic and Dramatic Society and Green Room Operatic Society.

Risley Operatic Group in Lehar's operetta
***The Count Of Luxembourg*, October 1970**

In the book *Once Upon A Time In Palmers Green,* Alan Dumayne recalled that the Intimate 'became the home of many of our local societies whose productions were invariably of the highest standard. My wife and I remember especially some superb musical shows, abounding in talent.'

Whilst amateur shows were predominant at the Intimate, professional entertainment had not disappeared entirely as the theatre was home to several 'one-nighter' type concerts each year as well as providing the area's only professional pantomime.

A roll call of the stars appearing at the venue in concert during these years would include Cleo Laine and John Dankworth, Frankie Howerd, The King's Singers, The Worzels, Kenny Ball, Jake Thackeray, Acker Bilk, Marian Montgomery, The National Youth Jazz Band, George Melly, George Chisholm, The Temperance Seven, Peter Sarsted, Margaret Savage, of TV's *Black And White Minstrels* fame, Frank Carson, The Searchers, Matt Monro, Jack Warner, Gerry And The Pacemakers, Joe Brown, Clodagh Rodgers, The Bachelors, Derek Batey with a stage version of the TV show *Mr. And Mrs.,* Charlie Smithers, Jack Parnell, jazz trumpeter Kenny Baker, classical pianists Joseph Cooper and Walter Landauer, ventriloquist Terry Hall with Lenny The Lion, Bernie Winters, Moira Anderson (replacing another Scottish singer Kenneth McKellar who had suffered a heart attack), clown Charlie Cairoli, Rosemary Squires, The Yetties, The Cambridge Buskers, jazz musicians Betty Smith and Don Lusher, Clown Cavalcade, Stu Francis and veteran comic Tommy Trinder.

In April 1982 the Cambridge Footlights revue *Beyond The Footlights* played one performance at the theatre where the audience could catch early career appearances of Emma Thompson, Robert Bathurst, Hugh Laurie and Stephen Fry. In contrast, in 1971, theatregoers were able to see two grand old music-hall stars in the twilight of their careers. Wee Georgie Wood was seventy four when he appeared in June and the great male impersonator Hetty King was an amazing eighty-nine years of age when she took to the Intimate stage in an old time show in September with impresario John Farrow as chairman and Billy Whittaker and Mimi Law heading the support bill.

Billy Whittaker, Hetty King and John Farrow backstage at the Intimate in 1971

141

Jimmy Wheeler

The music hall and variety comedian Jimmy Wheeler, whose catch phrase was 'Aye, Aye, that's your lot!' topped the bill in an Old Time Music Hall that ran for three nights in September 1973 with the legendary "Mrs. Shufflewick" in support. Colin Fenn, who was a reporter working for the local *Gazette* at that time, recalls arranging an interview with Jimmy at the theatre prior to his performance:

'I was nervous as I approached the dressing room door. This was, after all, a major comic who had appeared in variety shows all over the world, including many top-of-the-bill performances at the prestigious London Palladium.

'A member of the theatre's staff announced: "Mr. Wheeler – it's Mr. Fenn, from the newspaper, to see you.

'I expected to see a towering figure cracking jokes and acting very quick-witted. But I was in for a big shock. Sat by the dressing room mirror was a tired-looking, frail old man. He looked weary and he spoke quietly.

'I began the interview asking about his long and varied career in show business. His replies were brief and lacking in any kind of humour. I asked him about the great comics with whom he had worked and the venues he had played.

'His replies were polite but he lacked any enthusiasm. He could have been talking about working in an amateur panto. Between questions he sipped from his glass of whisky and he spoke in a croaky voice.

'As the interview was coming to an end I was finding it hard to believe that in five minutes this sad, weak, frail old man would walk on stage to entertain a packed theatre. As we shook hands Jimmy said: "Could you pass me my hat, son." Together with his tiny moustache, his hat made him instantly recognizable to audiences.

'I got back in my seat just as the lights went down. "Ladies and Gentlemen", said the compere, "the legendary Jimmy Wheeler." My jaw dropped as onto the stage came an upright-looking man with a twinkle in his eye, cracking extremely funny jokes at a breakneck pace during a brilliant thirty-minute routine. It was as if the lights went on and the entertainer went into auto-pilot, rattling off his highly rehearsed performance.

'Three days later I was driving my car in Enfield. A newsreader announced: "The comic Jimmy Wheeler died today." I had just done the last interview with a real trouper.'

**Hinge & Bracket relaxing between shows
with Theatre Manageress Ellen Trigger**

The drag act Hinge and Bracket proved to be great favourites at the Intimate and in 1976 they were resident for the Christmas season appearing in their *Evening Of Memories* after the evening performances of the Tony Blackburn pantomime *Jack And The Beanstalk*. Dame Hilda Bracket and Dr. Evadne Hinge were, in real life, Patrick Fyffe and George Logan and had started out working in gay venues. Their popularity was such that they soon had their own radio and television series, made several recordings and even appeared at the Royal Opera House, Covent Garden as guest performers in *Die Fledermaus* and at Dame Eva Turner's 90th birthday celebrations. Sadly Patrick died in 2002, aged just sixty. Incidentally, his sister, the soprano Jane Fyffe appeared at the Intimate in the 1970s on a variety bill headed by Jack Warner, *Dixon Of Dock Green,* himself.

The set for Hinge and Bracket's show was supposed to represent their drawing room and at the end of the evening Dr. Evadne Hinge placed an old record on their wind up gramophone and the two ladies would listen to it as the lights slowly lowered. The record in question was Bertha Lewis, a contralto from the D'Oyly Carte Opera Company as *Katisha* from *The Mikado*. At one performance the record player had not been wound up so the record played very slowly. Dame Hilda immediately ad-libbed 'It sounds more like Leo Sheffield, dear!' (Sheffield was a bass-baritone from D'Oyly Carte).

Another great Intimate favourite was the Australian soprano June Bronhill, who appeared at the venue on no less than four occasions in the mid-1970s, selling

INTIMATE THEATRE
Green Lanes, Palmers Green, N.13
01-886 3798

JOHN FARROW PRESENTS
FOR ONE NIGHT ONLY
Saturday, September 25th at 7.30 p.m.

T.V's 'Dixon of Dock Green'

JACK WARNER

IN

OLDE TYME
MUSIC HALL

WITH

JANE FYFFE, West End Star of 'ROBERT & ELIZABETH'

| Mr. DAVID HAMILTON | Mr. JOHN FARROW |
| Broadcasting and Recording Organist | YOUR WORTHY CHAIRMAN |

The Lovely Jenny Set Dancers

Miss MIMI LAW
Revue's Star Comedienne

| POPULAR PRICES | £1.20 | 90p | 60p |

REDUCTIONS OAP's AND PARTIES

BOOK EARLY

Printed by Beacon Press Ltd. (T.U.), 129 Stoke Newington Church Street, N.16. 254 7000.

Saturday 25th September 1976

143

out the theatre on each visit. Her first appearance was in March 1973 with a programme devoted to Ivor Novello's melodies. Joining her that evening was the contralto Olive Gilbert, who had been a great personal friend of Ivor's and had appeared in several of his spectacular musicals such as *The Dancing Years, Perchance To Dream* and *King's Rhapsody.*

1976 June Bronhill's last appearance at the Intimate

June Bronhill

The *Gazette* reviewer (*Gazette* 9th March 1973) was full of praise for the evening stating:

> June gave a splendid performance of Novello songs. She was witty, charming and in magnificent voice…At the end of her performance the audience gave June a standing ovation and she came back for four or five encores.

The key to June's success at the Intimate was not hard to discover. Anyone lucky enough to have witnessed June Bronhill in concert will know that she was the complete opposite of the usual image of an operatic prima donna. No standing on ceremony for her. Her charm, warmth and great good humour combined with that wondrous voice won an audience over in minutes. The Intimate theatregoers were no exception with cheers and laughter being the order of the day. In March 1976, her fourth visit, she presented *Another Night In Vienna.* The curtain went up a few minutes after the appointed time and June came on to apologise for the delay. She explained that she had only arrived back in this country at lunchtime, having been on a working cruise that had docked at Southampton. She had then had to rush to a television studio to rehearse an appearance on *The David Nixon Show*, which was being screened on ITV the following evening. This meant that she had not had any time to see her hairdresser so she had done her hair backstage with an egg whisk! With a hope that she looked presentable, she launched into a medley from her big success *The Merry Widow* and the audience was with her every step of the way from then on. True star quality!

The Imperial Opera Company under the leadership of Vere Laurie occasionally visited the theatre. Cyril Foley, a backstage worker, remembers Laurie as 'a gentleman of the old school who would order tea from outside whenever he had visitors at the theatre'. Cyril remembers vividly that the company's production of *La Boheme* actually used Melba's third act costume as Cyril's wife was entrusted to iron it! On the last night of one of the company's visits Cyril encountered a man at the stage door asking to see Mr. Laurie and claiming to be his cousin. Cyril duly knocked on Vere Laurie's dressing room door and told him. Mr. Laurie, in the process of packing away all his costumes, boomed 'Cousin! I have no cousins on get-out nights!'

THE INTIMATE THEATRE

GREEN LANES, PALMERS GREEN — Telephone: 01-886 3798

THE IMPERIAL OPERA COMPANY

(Under the Direction of Vere Laurie)

present

FOR TWO NIGHTS ONLY, THURSDAY, JUNE 12th and FRIDAY, JUNE 13th at 7.30 p.m.

GRAND OPERA GALA

FAUST
by CHARLES GOUNOD   (The Garden Scene)

LA BOHEME
by G. PUCCINI   Act III

RIGOLETTO
by G. VERDI   Act IV

FULL COMPANY CHORUS and CHAMBER ORCHESTRA
with

GUEST ARTISTS FROM ROYAL OPERA HOUSE COVENT GARDEN

Operas produced by VERE LAURIE

Conductor: ROY BUDDEN
(Leader: REGINALD MORLEY)

PRICES: £1.00, 80p, 60p (Senior Citizens Half Price at BOX OFFICE, THURS.)

— — — — — — Please tear off here — — — — — —

Name ....

Address ....

No. of seats required .... Price ....

Children/Old Age Pensioners .... Price ....

Date of Performance .... Time ....

This form and cheque or P.O. made payable to Intimate Theatre, Green Lanes, London N.13 enclosing s.a.e. for reply.

A 1975 visit by Vere Laurie's Imperial Opera Company

Two veteran artists encountered by Cyril at the Intimate on variety bills were singer Lester Ferguson and comic Sandy Powell. Cyril recalls that Lester was very reluctant to leave the stage at the end of his act and would always find an excuse for singing one more song! Sandy Powell gave his usual polished performance but Cyril was intrigued to see how calm and collected he was prior to his performance. Curiosity eventually got the better of Cyril and he asked Powell how he kept so cool to which Sandy replied: 'That's fright, lad!'

Patrick Newley, who now writes for *The Stage* newspaper as well as various national dailies, appeared at the theatre in 1978 with the company Clown Cavalcade. 'At that time I was still an actor', recalls Patrick, 'and I was booked to appear at the Intimate in a touring pantomime called

Clownerella, written and produced by Carol Crowther. I played one of the Ugly Sisters and I remember thinking it was a bit of a comedown as the previous year I had been Dame opposite the comedian Ken Platt in *Babes In the Wood* in Barrow-In-Furness! (All these No. 1 dates!)

Mrs. Shufflewick (Rex Jameson)

'The one thing I remember about the Intimate was that in my dressing room there was a big framed poster screwed to the wall of the drag comedian "Mrs. Shufflewick" (Rex Jameson) on a bill, I think, with Alec Pleon. It was a variety bill that had been on there in the 1960's or 1970's. At that time I knew "Shuff" well and he came round to have a look at it. He actually wanted to pinch it, but, as I said, it was screwed to the wall!'

Professional pantomimes were staged at the Intimate every year from 1969 until 1988. The impresario Alexander Bridge staged the afore-mentioned *Cinderella* in 1969 and *Mother Goose* in 1970 before Jimmy and Gilda Perry took over the reins in 1971 with *Babes In The Wood.* Jimmy Perry was, of course, no stranger to the Intimate and provided a strong cast for this Christmas entertainment including Bill Pertwee, otherwise known as *Warden Hodges* in Perry's sit-com *Dad's Army.* Two other members of the cast, Ruth Madoc and Michael Knowles, would later find success in comedy series written by Jimmy. Ruth would find fame as *Gladys Pugh* in *Hi-De-Hi* in the 1980s and Michael essayed the role of *Captain Ashwood* in *It Ain't Half Hot Mum* in the mid 1970s.

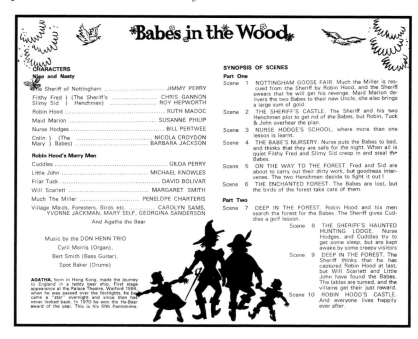

Programme One Shilling

BABES in the WOOD

INTIMATE THEATRE   PALMERS GREEN

Babes In The Wood 1971
Below: two back stage photos of Bill Pertwee as *Nurse Hodges*

Susanne Philip (*Maid Marion*), Jimmy
Perry and Ruth Madoc

Jimmy Perry as the *Sheriff Of Nottingham*

Backstage shots of the cast of
***Babes In The Wood* 1971**

Ruth Madoc as *Robin Hood*

Chris Gannon as *Filthy Fred* and
Michael Knowles as *Little John*

The following year's presentation of *Aladdin* with Benny Lee and Alec Pleon was reported to be the most successful Christmas show at the Intimate since *When the Rainbow Ends* in 1968.

The finale of the 1972 production of *Aladdin*

Local singer Anna Lethieullier played principal girl in 1973's *Dick Whittington* with noted drag artist Marc Fleming as dame whilst the following year's *Cinderella* saw the appearance of two more well-known drag performers when Chris Sheen and Vic Ford portrayed the *Ugly Sisters*. Bryan Johnson, the singer who had a big hit with the Eurovision Song Contest entry *Looking High, High, High,* tackled *The Prince's* role in 1975's *Snow White And The Seven Dwarfs*. Comedy was in the capable hands of veteran comic, George Williams, whose thin frame and pale face, enhanced by white makeup led naturally to his catch phrase 'I'm not well'.

The disc jockey Tony Blackburn proved a great success in *Jack And The Beanstalk* in 1976, so much so that he returned the following year as *Buttons* in yet another *Cinderella*. 1978 found the theatre playing host to 'Cheerful' Charlie Chester in *Humpty Dumpty*. A fellow cast member was Ann George, who achieved fame, or possibly notoriety, as *Amy Turtle* in

Anna Lethieullier

television soap opera *Crossroads.* Noted for the fragile hold she had on her lines, she unfortunately brought that same trait to her Intimate debut!

Far more secure performances were achieved by the stars of the following year's *Robinson Crusoe* when Clive Dunn, *Private Jones* in television's *Dad's Army,* and Lynda Baron, *Nurse Gladys Emmanuel* in *Open All Hours,* led the cast.

Bill Owen directed, wrote and starred in 1980's *Mother Goose* and fellow cast member, Marianne Price, recalls:

'It was virtually a sell-out from what I can recall because of Bill Owen's popularity as *Compo* in *Last Of the Summer Wine.* We even did some extra performances at 10 am some mornings to cope with the demand from local schools. It was a very good and enjoyable pantomime to be in and a very happy cast. Bill Owen was super, and such a nice man plus he made an excellent dame.

'I myself played the part of *Lady Mortice,* the wicked witch of the piece with strong overtones of *Cruella D'Evil* from the cartoon film *101 Dalmations.* As the wicked witch I was on the receiving end of lots of shouts and remarks from the audience including one very boisterous performance when cans and sweets were thrown! I immediately moved to the front of the stage and ad-libbed telling them to be quiet or "I'd poison their ice creams in the interval!" When the hissing, booing and noise at my entrances was too loud, I used another ad-lib, which became a permanent line, "Oh, it's so lovely to be hated!"

'As you probably know, to get from one side of the stage to the other during performances, you had to literally go outside the theatre. There was a door each side of the stage at the back wall, which opened to the outside. Along this was a small plastic lean-to roof (approximately 2 feet wide) held against the wall outside but apart from that you were

exposed to the elements. In the event of bad weather, umbrellas were placed by the doors either side for use, so that costumes and performers didn't get drenched. Both Bill and I had the most voluptuous costumes and I can remember lifting my skirt and many underskirts and ducking up close against the wall before I rushed to the other side to avoid getting wet! Once the show was up and running I soon understood why one canny individual in the pantomime had insisted on all his entrances and exits being on the same side near to his dressing room. He had claimed it was for convenience but it soon became clear that avoidance of the outside 'rat run' had been the main factor!'

1981 saw another production of *Dick Whittington,* directed by Tony Boden, who ran the local Boden Studios Stage School. Cross dressing was the order of the day in this pantomime with diminutive comic actress Sheila Bernette playing *Idle Jack,* Frank Williams (best known as *The Vicar* in *Dad's Army*) as *Sarah The Cook* and West End and cabaret star Joyce Blair, sister of Lionel, donning tights as *Dick.*

Stephen Lewis, of *On The Buses* fame, starred in the 1982 production of *Jack And The Beanstalk* with Anna Lethieullier and June Lewis in support. Helping the comedy along was Johnny Mans, who later switched to the other side of the footlights when he became Sir Norman Wisdom's agent. Mans returned the following year as *Buttons* in *Cinderella* which boasted a male and female principal boy with David Middleton as *The Prince* and Aimi MacDonald as *Dandini.* This pantomime also had one male ugly sister and one female in the form of Brian De Salvo and Sheila Bernette. Local girl Tracy Dee was the young choreographer of the production and during the run she took on the role of ugly sister *Tutti* for a week when Bernette lost her voice. As Tracy told the local Gazette: ' I have appeared as a dancer on stage and television but this was my professional acting debut and I really enjoyed it!' Although the pantomime attracted good audiences for the matinee performances the local paper reported that evening attendances were very disappointing.

Aladdin was the theatre's Christmas attraction in 1984 with Michael Robbins, from television's *On The Buses,* top billed as the wicked *Abanazar* while the following year's pantomime, *Snow White And The Seven Dwarfs* was noted for the appearance of actress Shirley Anne Field in the role of *The Wicked Queen.* John Noakes, well-known presenter of BBC's flagship children's programme *Blue Peter* was the star attraction of the 1986 pantomime which turned out to be yet another version of *Cinderella.* No doubt the auditorium echoed with the shout of "Down Shep!"

Tony Blackburn celebrating his pantomime success with colleagues including Ellen Trigger (Manageress), Director John Farrow (extreme right) and Simon Barry (extreme left)

The final professional pantomime to be seen at the Intimate was the 1987 production of *Jack And The Beanstalk* starring Bob Grant, yet another refugee from the comedy series *On The Buses,* and Joanne Good, an actress from the television soap *Crossroads*

Professional drama had not been completely forgotten and in the 1980s a few attempts were made to revive the drama tradition at the Intimate. This move coincided with a change of manager at the theatre. Mrs. Trigger retired as manager and the position went to Bob Dixon, who was at that time married to Mrs. Trigger's daughter Linda. Bob tried with varying degrees of success to bring more professional entertainment to the Intimate. Bill Owen's name appeared on the posters as playwright for a fortnight's run of his drama *In The Palm Of Her Hand* in June 1981. The cast was headed by Margaret Robertson and character actor Victor Maddern, a well-known face to television viewers and filmgoers.

Appearing at the Intimate Theatre for a two-week run in "Public Relations" are Julia Carey (left) Lisette Lecat, Richard Coleman, Jill Melford, George Flood and Kate Coleman.

Public Relations - March 1982

Gaslight - February 1983

Ready to take the stage at the Intimate in "Gaslight" are (front, left to right) Sue Shepherd, Mary Holland and June Lewis with Anthony Ingram, David Garth and Tony Adams.

Victor Maddern

Peter Simpkin's play *Double Exposure* took over the theatre for the following two weeks with Barbara Kellermann and Brian Croucher in the cast but neither play set the theatre alight and audiences were modest in number.

In September 1981 June Abbott brought Shakespeare's *The Taming Of The Shrew* for a two-week run and June returned the following year with Noel Coward's classic comedy *Private Lives* when she was partnered by Peter Gale.

The television actors Gerald Flood and Richard Coleman appeared for two weeks in the spring of 1982 in Trevor Cowper's play *Public Relations* and a two-week thriller mini-season in late June brought the actress Mary Holland to star as the blind heroine in Frederick Knott's gripping

Thriller

FREDERICK Knott's thriller "Wait Until Dark" is being presented this week at the Intimate Theatre, Palmers Green.

Mary Holland — known to millions as Katie in the Oxo ads — stars with Susan Shephard and David Redgrave in the professional production by Intimate Productions and Tumblehurst Ltd. It finishes on Saturday.

Mary Holland and David Redgrave in "Wait Until Dark."

Wait Until Dark whilst the second week featured Lewis Jones in *Echo Of Murder.* Mary Holland had achieved national fame by appearing as *Katie* in a series of television adverts for Oxo cubes and she returned to the Intimate in 1983 to play the role of *Mrs. Manningham* in Patrick Hamilton's chiller *Gaslight* opposite Tony Adams (*Adam Chance* in ITV's *Crossroads*). Also in the cast was David Garth who had last appeared at the Intimate in 1950 and who had taken part in the first play, *George And Margaret,* to be televised from the Intimate in 1946. Mr. Garth told the *Gazette* (11th Feb. 1983) 'I have got an enormous affection for this place. But it has changed. It is so tatty now!'

The comedy *Don't Start Without Me* starring Jennifer Wilson ran for a week in 1983 but the days of filling the theatre with a professional production were long gone as the *Gazette* reviewer noted in his critique. He found the actual play dated but admitted it 'delighted the mainly old audience who filled less than half the theatre on Monday's opening night.' The following year the Intimate staged three week-long productions during July as part of the Capital Radio Fringe

Festival. A thriller called *Murder Is Child's Play* saw the Palmers Green debut of Jack Wild. Wild, of course, had scored a great success as *Artful Dodger* in the film version of *Oliver!* Earl Okin took over the theatre the second week with his show *Hoagy Carmichael And The Songwriters*, whilst the final week saw a production about the music hall artiste George Leybourne called *The Life And Music Of Champagne Charlie* starring Chris Beeching. Sadly, none of these shows proved successful at the box office. Although professional entertainment was proving an extremely chancy proposition for the theatre's management the amateur companies were still doing well with good houses reported for most productions. This satisfactory state of affairs took a knock back at the beginning of 1987

GASLIGHT

By PATRICK HAMILTON

THE CAST

Mrs Manningham	**MARY HOLLAND**
Mr Manningham	**TONY ADAMS**
Rough	**DAVID GARTH**
Elizabeth	**JUNE LEWIS**
Nancy	**SUSAN SHEPHARD**
Policeman	**ANTONY INGRAM**

Standby for Mr Adams and Mr Garth **ANTONY INGRAM**
Standby for Miss Holland **SUSAN SHEPHARD**
Standby for Miss Shephard **JOAN BEVERIDGE**

Gaslight **February 1983**

when the *Enfield Independent* newspaper reported that the cost of the theatre's entertainment licence had quadrupled. The Greater London Council had established a fee of £300 but the GLC had now been abolished and responsibility for licensing had moved to the local borough councils. The new fee would be £1096. This triggered off a war of words in the local press between theatre manager Bob Dixon and Enfield Council with Dixon accusing the council of driving amateur groups away from the Intimate by imposing a massive increase in fees which would have to be recouped in theatre hire charges. The council retaliated by stating that Dixon's claims were 'a travesty of the truth' (*Enfield Independent* 21st January 1987). The council then explained to the reporter from the *Enfield Independent* that up until 1981 entertainments licences were held by the priests of St. Monica's Church and the theatre qualified for a nominal fee fixed by the GLC on the basis that any profits went to the church. When Bob Dixon became involved with the Intimate in 1981 a licence at a reduced rate was granted to him that year. Thereafter, because the theatre was operating independently of the church, the only basis for reducing the fee was on production of audited accounts showing financial difficulties. It appears that Bob Dixon was reluctant to show the council these accounts as, in his view, the council was in direct competition with him through the planned council theatre in Edmonton and revelation of the Intimate's full accounts would prejudice his business.

Worse news was to follow at the end of 1987 when the *Gazette* announced in December that the Intimate was to close as a theatre, much to the horror of the local playgoers and the many amateur groups that used it. Various reasons for the closure were bandied around. Bob Dixon, who had held the ten-year theatre lease for seven years, blamed the closure on the actual costs of running the theatre. He told the local press that 'rent and licence fees have become exorbitant' (*Enfield Independent* 30th December 1987). The church authorities claimed that Dixon owed them rent and had been slow in carrying out work on

Risley Operatic Group - *Fiddler On The Roof*

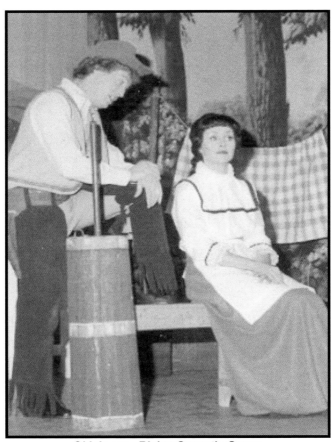

***Oklahoma* - Risley Operatic Group**

Enfield Light Operatic & Drama Society - *Sweet Charity*

The Boy Friend - Enfield Light Operatic & Drama Society

Entens Drama Group - *Crown Matrimonial*
With the play's author, Royce Ryton standing at the back

Chandos Operatic Society - *The Pirates Of Penzance*

Green Room Operatic Society - *South Pacific*

South Pacific **- Green Room Operatic Society**

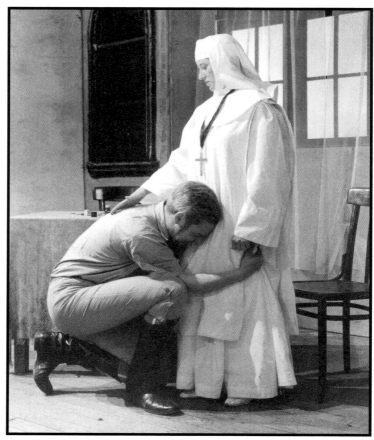

The Trent Players - *A Letter From The General*

Pink String And Sealing Wax **- The Trent Players**

***Bye Bye Birdie* - Choreodrama**

Choreodrama - *Irene*

161

Enfield Grand Opera - I Lombardi

St. Monica's Players - *The Winslow Boy*

162

the building. They were also keen to convert the building back to its original status as a parish hall as Father Robin Whitney of St. Monica's Church told the *Enfield Independent* (30th December 1987)

> The theatre, which is adjacent to the church, was originally built as a church hall but it was not used very much at first and was hired out as a theatre. Now we need it very urgently because our congregation has nowhere near the church to use as a meeting place. We did try to take it back some time ago but there was a great outcry because there was no alternative theatre in the borough. But now the situation is different. We have the Gladys Child Theatre at Southgate Technical College and the borough is building its own theatre at Millfield House in Edmonton.

> Another reason for acquiring the building is that our association with the present tenant Mr. Bob Dixon has been very unsatisfactory. We feel that the theatre has not been properly maintained.

Whatever the actual reason for the closure it looked like the end of the line for the Intimate. Alan Dumayne spoke for many when he wrote in his book *Once Upon A Time In Palmers Green*: 'There are many residents who feel a sense of great loss with the passing of this superb little theatre, here on our own doorstep.'

News of the Intimate closing also incensed the theatre fraternity. *The Stage* newspaper for February 4th 1988 carried the headline

Intimate Fight 'a nationwide issue'

and declared

> The Catholic diocese of Westminster has come under fire from theatre groups after its decision to close one of London's most popular small-scale venues.

> Its plan to effectively shut down the privately run Intimate Theatre in the borough of Enfield after fifty years has caused widespread concern among professional and amateur performers and is now threatening to become a nationwide issue involving even government ministers.

> Ranged against the church, which is the theatre's landlord, are the Theatres Advisory Council, the British Theatre Association and the Central Council For Amateur Theatre.

> TAC vice-chairman Charles Vance… warned that the theatre industry would fight all the way to save the Intimate.

Both the environment secretary Nicholas Ridley and the arts minister Richard Luce have been contacted by the growing lobby opposed to the Intimate's threatened shutdown.

In a compromise move the church has promised to include a small venue on the old site, most of which will be converted into a community hall.

Despite all this fighting talk, the theatre closed its doors at the end of January 1988 and the amateur groups made homeless by this action found temporary stages around the borough until the new council owned venue, the Millfield Theatre, based in Edmonton, opened its doors at the end of the year. Soon the larger musical societies were able to stage their productions at this new venue; the smaller drama groups sadly were not so lucky. A few of the groups did attempt to stage productions at the Millfield in the first few years but rising hire costs and smaller audiences made it well nigh impossible for drama societies to continue and other venues had to be found.

Russ Abbot and Roy Hudd in a scene from _The Last Detective_ filmed on the stage of the Intimate Theatre 2006
(Copyright ITV)

The conversion of the Intimate to a church parish hall meant the removal of the permanent stalls tip-up seating and local theatregoers were saddened by the sight of these seats stacked up outside the front of the theatre ready for disposal. It certainly looked as if the theatre had gone for good. However, that is not the end of the story for after a few years passers-by noticed that the odd week of theatrical activity was once again advertised outside the theatre. Probably the church authorities recognized that the parish hall was not bringing in as much revenue as they initially imagined. Whatever the reason, several amateur groups gradually returned to the Intimate stage and although the seating on the ground floor level was now rather basic, the old original tip-up seating in the circle was still intact.

A brief flash of its old glory days returned in 2006 when an episode of the television series *The Last Detective* used the theatre's stage for a scene involving two old time variety artists played by Roy Hudd and Russ Abbot. Seventy years after John Clements realised his vision of running a weekly repertory theatre, the Intimate is still struggling on. Long may it continue!

The Last Detective 2006 with Russ Abbot and Roy Hudd (Copyright ITV)

The Intimate Theatre December 1987
advertising *Jack And The Beanstalk*, the venue's last professional pantomime,

The Intimate Theatre June 2006

APPENDIX

A complete list of productions from 26th December 1935, when the theatre opened, to 19th July 1969 when the theatre ceased to function as a full time professional playhouse.

Plus a select list of professional attractions (those playing more than one performance at the venue) from 24th December 1969 to 16th January 1988 when the theatre reverted to its church hall status.

Please note that the date column lists the opening night of each production and it can then be assumed that the production played at the Intimate for the rest of that week. The only exception to this is the occasional 'Southgate Theatre Week' or 'Festival of Drama' when two or three local amateur companies took over the Intimate just before the summer closure, sharing the week between them.

Most of the productions listed, as one would expect with weekly rep, opened on the Monday but there are instances, especially in later years when fortnightly runs were introduced, when the opening night was later in the week.

There are a couple of occasions when two productions are listed for the same week. In January 1975 the pantomime *Cinderella* only played matinees for the last week of its run and the evenings were taken over by a music hall revue called *Palace Of Varieties* utilising the same cast, and in 1976, while the pantomime *Jack And The Beanstalk* played matinees and early evening performances, a late evening show starring Hinge and Bracket ran from 21st December to 1st January 1977.

YEAR	DATE	PLAY TITLE	YEAR	DATE	PLAY TITLE
1935	26-Dec	The Dover Road	1936	16-Nov	By Candlelight
1935	30-Dec	The Dover Road	1936	23-Nov	Hay Fever
			1936	30-Nov	The Letter
1936	6-Jan	THEATRE CLOSED	1936	7-Dec	Village Wooing
1936	13-Jan	Hay Fever	1936	7-Dec	The Man With A Load Of Mischief
1936	20-Jan	The Green Pack	1936	14-Dec	Sweet Aloes
1936	27-Jan	Sixteen	1936	21-Dec	Sweet Aloes
1936	3-Feb	Eight Bells	1936	26-Dec	The Middle Watch
1936	10-Feb	The Breadwinner	1936	28-Dec	The Middle Watch
1936	17-Feb	Dangerous Corner			
1936	24-Feb	Private Lives	1937	4-Jan	Heroes Don't Care
1936	2-Mar	The Cat's Cradle	1937	11-Jan	Dear Brutus
1936	9-Mar	A Murder Has Been Arranged	1937	18-Jan	The Marquise
1936	16-Mar	Mary Rose	1937	25-Jan	Dusty Ermine
1936	23-Mar	On Approval	1937	1-Feb	Autumn Crocus
1936	30-Mar	Eden End	1937	8-Feb	Payment Deferred
1936	6-Apr	The Passing Of The Third Floor Back	1937	15-Feb	The Dominant Sex
			1937	22-Feb	The Barretts Of Wimpole Street
1936	13-Apr	Meet The Wife	1937	1-Mar	London Wall
1936	20-Apr	The Circle	1937	8-Mar	The Sacred Flame
1936	27-Apr	Candida	1937	15-Mar	Rookery Nook
1936	4-May	Bird In Hand	1937	22-Mar	A Man's House
1936	11-May	On The Spot	1937	29-Mar	The Farmer's Wife
1936	18-May	A Minuet	1937	5-Apr	Libel!
1936	18-May	Canaries Sometimes Sing	1937	12-Apr	After October
1936	25-May	Musical Chairs	1937	19-Apr	The Silver Cord
1936	1-Jun	The Wind And The Rain	1937	26-Apr	The Ghost Train
1936	8-Jun	The First Mrs. Fraser	1937	3-May	Private Lives
1936	15-Jun	Ten Minute Alibi	1937	10-May	Richard Of Bordeaux
1936	22-Jun	The Late Christopher Bean	1937	17-May	Good Morning, Bill
1936	29-Jun	The Queen Was In The Parlour	1937	24-May	Young Society
1936	6-Jul	Tons Of Money	1937	31-May	Distinguished Company
1936	13-Jul	The Green Bay Tree	1937	7-Jun	To See Ourselves
1936	20-Jul	Mr. Pim Passes By	1937	14-Jun	Anthony And Anna
1936	27-Jul	The Outsider	1937	21-Jun	A Bill Of Divorcement
1936	3-Aug	Full House	1937	28-Jun	Aren't We All?
1936	10-Aug	The Two Mrs. Carrolls	1937	5-Jul	Mrs. Moonlight
1936	17-Aug	THEATRE CLOSED (Hols. & Renovat.)	1937	12-Jul	Young Woodley
			1937	19-Jul	Youth At The Helm
1936	24-Aug	THEATRE CLOSED (Hols. & Renovat.)	1937	26-Jul	Bees On The Boat Deck
			1937	2-Aug	Bird In Hand
1936	31-Aug	THEATRE CLOSED (Hols. & Renovat.)	1937	9-Aug	Yes And No
			1937	16-Aug	Wise To-Morrow
1936	5-Sep	Marry At Leisure	1937	23-Aug	The Young Idea
1936	14-Sep	The Shining Hour	1937	30-Aug	The High Road
1936	21-Sep	There's Always Juliet	1937	6-Sep	Petticoat Influence
1936	28-Sep	Yellow Sands	1937	13-Sep	Black Coffee
1936	5-Oct	Love From A Stranger	1937	20-Sep	Lady Precious Stream
1936	12-Oct	Marigold	1937	27-Sep	Dangerous Corner
1936	19-Oct	Outward Bound	1937	4-Oct	This Woman Business
1936	26-Oct	It Pays To Advertise	1937	11-Oct	A Hundred Years Old
1936	2-Nov	Laburnum Grove	1937	18-Oct	Nothing But the Truth
1936	9-Nov	Journey's End	1937	25-Oct	The Case Of The Frightened Lady

YEAR	DATE	PLAY TITLE	YEAR	DATE	PLAY TITLE
1937	1-Nov	Mademoiselle	1938	17-Oct	Time And The Conways
1937	8-Nov	The Rose Without A Thorn	1938	24-Oct	The Torch-Bearers
1937	15-Nov	See Naples And Die	1938	31-Oct	Love On The Dole
1937	22-Nov	Sixteen	1938	7-Nov	All Rights Reserved
1937	29-Nov	Hamlet	1938	14-Nov	Man And Superman
1937	6-Dec	Hamlet	1938	21-Nov	I Have Been Here Before
1937	13-Dec	Night Must Fall	1938	28-Nov	Comedienne
1937	20-Dec	Night Must Fall	1938	5-Dec	The Trial Of Mary Dugan
1937	27-Dec	Just Married	1938	12-Dec	Milestones
			1938	19-Dec	Milestones
1938	3-Jan	A Cuckoo In The Nest	1938	26-Dec	Ambrose Applejohn's Adventure
1938	10-Jan	Someone At The Door			
1938	17-Jan	Sarah Simple			
1938	24-Jan	Promise	1939	2-Jan	Ambrose Applejohn's Adventure
1938	31-Jan	Fresh Fields			
1938	7-Feb	Berkeley Square	1939	9-Jan	Alibi
1938	14-Feb	Only Yesterday	1939	16-Jan	Family Affairs
1938	21-Feb	The Outsider	1939	23-Jan	Mary Rose
1938	28-Feb	Death Takes A Holiday	1939	30-Jan	Devonshire Cream
1938	7-Mar	The Admirable Crichton	1939	6-Feb	Anna Christie
1938	14-Mar	Flat To Let	1939	13-Feb	And So To Bed
1938	21-Mar	The Queen's Husband	1939	20-Feb	The Fourth Wall
1938	28-Mar	Murder On The Second Floor	1939	27-Feb	Pygmalion
1938	4-Apr	Nine Till Six	1939	6-Mar	George And Margaret
1938	11-Apr	The Passing Of The Third Floor Back	1939	13-Mar	The Trespassers
			1939	20-Mar	The Skin Game
1938	18-Apr	The Importance Of Being Earnest	1939	27-Mar	Lovers Leap
1938	25-Apr	Quiet Is Best	1939	3-Apr	Traitor's Gate
1938	2-May	Living Dangerously	1939	10-Apr	Housemaster
1938	9-May	Little Women	1939	17-Apr	The Roundabout
1938	16-May	On Approval	1939	24-Apr	Romeo And Juliet
1938	23-May	Jane Eyre	1939	1-May	Romeo And Juliet
1938	30-May	I'll Leave It To You	1939	8-May	Winter Sunshine
1938	6-Jun	Busman's Holiday	1939	15-May	Fanny's First Play
1938	13-Jun	Third Time Lucky	1939	22-May	Glorious Morning
1938	20-Jun	Black Limelight	1939	29-May	The Sport Of Kings
1938	27-Jun	Thark	1939	5-Jun	Spring Tide
1938	4-Jul	Eight Bells	1939	12-Jun	Double Door
1938	11-Jul	Suspect	1939	19-Jun	The Rotters
1938	18-Jul	Home And Beauty	1939	26-Jun	The Cathedral
1938	25-Jul	Autumn	1939	3-Jul	Home Chat
1938	1-Aug	French Leave	1939	10-Jul	The Romantic Age
1938	8-Aug	Quality Street	1939	17-Jul	The Rivals
1938	15-Aug	Whistling In The Dark	1939	24-Jul	Nina
1938	22-Aug	Touch Wood	1939	31-Jul	Misalliance
1938	29-Aug	Passing Brompton Road	1939	7-Aug	The Astonished Ostrich
1938	5-Sep	Whiteoaks	1939	14-Aug	The Last Of Mrs. Cheyney
1938	12-Sep	The Brontes Of Haworth Parsonage	1939	21-Aug	Night Of January 16th
			1939	28-Aug	The Distaff Side
1938	19-Sep	Behold We Live	1939	4-Sep	PLAY POSTPONED - WAR DECLARED
1938	26-Sep	The School For Husbands			
1938	3-Oct	Sweet Aloes			
1938	10-Oct	I Killed The Count			

YEAR	DATE	PLAY TITLE	YEAR	DATE	PLAY TITLE
1939	11-Sep	French Without Tears	1940	19-Aug	The Lilies Of The Field
1939	18-Sep	Yes, My Darling Daughter	1940	26-Aug	People At Sea
1939	25-Sep	The Middle Watch	1940	2-Sep	Lot's Wife
1939	2-Oct	The Flashing Stream	1940	9-Sep	Full House
1939	9-Oct	Tonight At 7.15	1940	16-Sep	THEATRE CLOSED
1939	9-Oct	We Were Dancing	1940	23-Sep	THEATRE CLOSED
1939	9-Oct	Still Life	1940	30-Sep	THEATRE CLOSED
1939	9-Oct	Fumed Oak	1940	7-Oct	THEATRE CLOSED
1939	16-Oct	Seven Keys To Baldpate	1940	14-Oct	THEATRE CLOSED
1939	23-Oct	Parnell	1940	21-Oct	THEATRE CLOSED
1939	30-Oct	The Crime At Blossoms	1940	28-Oct	THEATRE CLOSED
1939	6-Nov	Goodness, How Sad!	1940	4-Nov	THEATRE CLOSED
1939	13-Nov	She Stoops To Conquer	1940	11-Nov	THEATRE CLOSED
1939	20-Nov	By Candlelight	1940	18-Nov	THEATRE CLOSED
1939	27-Nov	When We Are Married	1940	25-Nov	THEATRE CLOSED
1939	4-Dec	It Pays To Advertise	1940	2-Dec	THEATRE CLOSED
1939	11-Dec	Spring Meeting	1940	9-Dec	THEATRE CLOSED
1939	18-Dec	Springtime For Henry	1940	16-Dec	THEATRE CLOSED
1939	26-Dec	Plunder	1940	23-Dec	THEATRE CLOSED
			1940	30-Dec	THEATRE CLOSED
1940	1-Jan	Plunder			
1940	8-Jan	Little Women	1941	6-Jan	THEATRE CLOSED
1940	15-Jan	Gaslight	1941	13-Jan	THEATRE CLOSED
1940	22-Jan	Signature Tune	1941	20-Jan	THEATRE CLOSED
1940	29-Jan	Robert's Wife	1941	27-Jan	THEATRE CLOSED
1940	5-Feb	Saint Joan	1941	3-Feb	THEATRE CLOSED
1940	12-Feb	Grouse In June	1941	10-Feb	THEATRE CLOSED
1940	19-Feb	Autumn Crocus	1941	17-Feb	THEATRE CLOSED
1940	26-Feb	You Can't Take It With You	1941	24-Feb	THEATRE CLOSED
1940	4-Mar	The Venetian	1941	3-Mar	THEATRE CLOSED
1940	11-Mar	The Breadwinner	1941	10-Mar	THEATRE CLOSED
1940	18-Mar	Tobias And The Angel	1941	17-Mar	THEATRE CLOSED
1940	25-Mar	White Cargo	1941	24-Mar	THEATRE CLOSED
1940	1-Apr	Arms And The Man	1941	31-Mar	THEATRE CLOSED
1940	8-Apr	They Walk Alone	1941	7-Apr	THEATRE CLOSED
1940	15-Apr	Tovarich	1941	14-Apr	THEATRE CLOSED
1940	22-Apr	Strange Orchestra	1941	21-Apr	THEATRE CLOSED
1940	29-Apr	Interference	1941	28-Apr	THEATRE CLOSED
1940	6-May	Queer Cargo	1941	5-May	THEATRE CLOSED
1940	13-May	You Never Can Tell	1941	12-May	THEATRE CLOSED
1940	20-May	The Wind And The Rain	1941	19-May	THEATRE CLOSED
1940	27-May	Twelfth Night	1941	26-May	THEATRE CLOSED
1940	3-Jun	Twelfth Night	1941	2-Jun	THEATRE CLOSED
1940	10-Jun	Wasn't It Odd?	1941	9-Jun	THEATRE CLOSED
1940	17-Jun	Quiet Wedding	1941	16-Jun	THEATRE CLOSED
1940	24-Jun	Peg O' My Heart	1941	23-Jun	THEATRE CLOSED
1940	1-Jul	Yellow Sands	1941	30-Jun	THEATRE CLOSED
1940	8-Jul	The Dover Road	1941	7-Jul	THEATRE CLOSED
1940	15-Jul	The Man In Possession	1941	14-Jul	THEATRE CLOSED
1940	22-Jul	Saloon Bar	1941	21-Jul	THEATRE CLOSED
1940	29-Jul	The Two Mrs. Carrolls	1941	28-Jul	THEATRE CLOSED
1940	5-Aug	Richard Of Bordeaux	1941	4-Aug	THEATRE CLOSED
1940	12-Aug	Bats In The Belfry	1941	11-Aug	THEATRE CLOSED

YEAR	DATE	PLAY TITLE	YEAR	DATE	PLAY TITLE
1941	18-Aug	French For Love	1942	3-Aug	French Without Tears
1941	25-Aug	Thunder Rock	1942	10-Aug	Robert's Wife
1941	1-Sep	The Barretts Of Wimpole Street	1942	17-Aug	Payment Deferred
1941	8-Sep	Three Cornered Moon	1942	24-Aug	Sweet Aloes
1941	15-Sep	Pygmalion	1942	31-Aug	Dusty Ermine
1941	22-Sep	Call It A Day	1942	7-Sep	Love In A Mist
1941	29-Sep	Ah Wilderness	1942	14-Sep	The Admirable Crichton
1941	6-Oct	Suspect	1942	21-Sep	Yes And No
1941	13-Oct	Major Barbara	1942	28-Sep	Nine Till Six
1941	20-Oct	The Late Christopher Bean	1942	5-Oct	The Housemaster
1941	27-Oct	Jane Eyre	1942	12-Oct	They Fly By Twilight
1941	3-Nov	Accent On Youth	1942	19-Oct	The Amazing Dr. Clitterhouse
1941	10-Nov	Dear Brutus	1942	26-Oct	Whiteoaks
1941	17-Nov	The Light Of Heart	1942	2-Nov	The Last Of Mrs. Cheyney
1941	24-Nov	George And Margaret	1942	9-Nov	Bird In Hand
1941	1-Dec	Ladies In Retirement	1942	16-Nov	Rebecca
1941	8-Dec	Laburnum Grove	1942	23-Nov	Lady Windermere's Fan
1941	15-Dec	The Dominant Sex	1942	30-Nov	Anna Christie
1941	26-Dec	Goodbye Mr. Chips	1942	7-Dec	Almost A Honeymoon
1941	29-Dec	Goodbye Mr. Chips	1942	14-Dec	The Man With A Load Of Mischief
1942	5-Jan	Cottage To Let	1942	26-Dec	Dear Octopus
1942	12-Jan	Gaslight	1942	28-Dec	Dear Octopus
1942	19-Jan	Time And The Conways			
1942	26-Jan	Abraham Lincoln	1943	4-Jan	Rebecca
1942	2-Feb	No Time For Comedy	1943	11-Jan	Saloon Bar
1942	9-Feb	Fresh Fields	1943	18-Jan	Good Men Sleep At Home
1942	16-Feb	A Murder Has Been Arranged	1943	25-Jan	Outward Bound
1942	23-Feb	Hay Fever	1943	1-Feb	The Patsy
1942	2-Mar	The Shining Hour	1943	8-Feb	Green Waters
1942	9-Mar	She Stoops To Conquer	1943	15-Feb	Mr. Wu
1942	16-Mar	Full House	1943	22-Feb	Children To Bless You
1942	23-Mar	Love From A Stranger	1943	1-Mar	The Barton Mystery
1942	30-Mar	Devonshire Cream	1943	8-Mar	Grief Goes Over
1942	6-Apr	Quality Street	1943	15-Mar	Eden End
1942	13-Apr	Dangerous Corner	1943	22-Mar	To See Ourselves
1942	20-Apr	The Brontes Of Haworth Parsonage	1943	29-Mar	Murder On The Second Floor
			1943	5-Apr	The Corn Is Green
1942	27-Apr	After October	1943	12-Apr	Mary Rose
1942	4-May	The First Mrs. Fraser	1943	19-Apr	Other People's Houses
1942	11-May	The Wind And The Rain	1943	26-Apr	Yellow Sands
1942	18-May	The Devil's Disciple	1943	3-May	The Little Foxes
1942	25-May	Quiet Wedding	1943	10-May	Jupiter Laughs
1942	1-Jun	The Two Mrs. Carrolls	1943	17-May	The Corn Is Green
1942	8-Jun	On Approval	1943	24-May	On The Spot
1942	15-Jun	Double Door	1943	31-May	Actresses Will Happen
1942	22-Jun	Sixteen	1943	7-Jun	They Walk Alone
1942	29-Jun	The Bear	1943	14-Jun	Aren't Men Beasts
1942	29-Jun	Arms And The Man	1943	21-Jun	Wuthering Heights
1942	6-Jul	Spring Meeting	1943	28-Jun	The Doctor's Dilemma
1942	13-Jul	The Silver Cord	1943	5-Jul	Old Acquaintance
1942	20-Jul	If Four Walls Told	1943	12-Jul	Skylark
1942	27-Jul	Young Woodley	1943	19-Jul	To Have And To Hold

YEAR	DATE	PLAY TITLE	YEAR	DATE	PLAY TITLE
1943	2-Aug	Rookery Nook	1944	24-Jul	Family Affairs
1943	9-Aug	Granite	1944	31-Jul	Candida
1943	16-Aug	Ten Minute Alibi	1944	7-Aug	When Ladies Meet
1943	23-Aug	Lovers Leap	1944	14-Aug	Yes My Darling Daughter
1943	30-Aug	Muder Without Crime	1944	21-Aug	Gaslight
1943	6-Sep	Anthony And Anna	1944	28-Aug	Tell Me The Truth
1943	13-Sep	Night Must Fall	1944	4-Sep	The Importance Of Being Earnest
1943	20-Sep	Milestones	1944	11-Sep	Thou Shalt Not (Therese Raquin)
1943	27-Sep	Goodness How Sad	1944	18-Sep	Flat To Let
1943	4-Oct	I Have Been Here Before	1944	25-Sep	Lottie Dundass
1943	11-Oct	Men In Shadow	1944	2-Oct	Meet The Wife
1943	18-Oct	Michael And Mary	1944	9-Oct	Distinguished Gathering
1943	25-Oct	The Family Upstairs	1944	16-Oct	Grouse In June
1943	1-Nov	The Sacred Flame	1944	23-Oct	I'll Leave It To You
1943	8-Nov	The Dover Road	1944	30-Oct	Third Party Risk
1943	15-Nov	Why Not Tonight?	1944	6-Nov	A Bill Of Divorcement
1943	22-Nov	Play With Fire	1944	13-Nov	The Rotters
1943	29-Nov	The Astonished Ostrich	1944	20-Nov	The Second Mrs. Tanqueray
1943	6-Dec	The Living Room	1944	27-Nov	Love Isn't Everything
1943	13-Dec	The Merchant Of Venice	1944	4-Dec	The Wanglers
1943	20-Dec	The Merchant Of Venice	1944	11-Dec	Passing Brompton Road
1943	27-Dec	Charley's Aunt	1944	18-Dec	Canaries Sometimes Sing
			1944	26-Dec	Tons Of Money
1944	3-Jan	By Candlelight			
1944	10-Jan	Ghosts	1945	1-Jan	A Soldier For Christmas
1944	17-Jan	The Maitlands	1945	8-Jan	Poison Pen
1944	24-Jan	Private Lives	1945	15-Jan	This Happy Breed
1944	31-Jan	Dr. Brent's Household	1945	22-Jan	The Bread Winner
1944	7-Feb	Tony Draws A Horse	1945	29-Jan	Claudia
1944	14-Feb	The Good Young Man	1945	5-Feb	This Happy Breed
1944	21-Feb	Mademoiselle	1945	12-Feb	Acacia Avenue
1944	28-Feb	After All	1945	19-Feb	Suspect
1944	6-Mar	Short Story	1945	26-Feb	The Morning Star
1944	13-Mar	Rope	1945	5-Mar	The Outsider
1944	20-Mar	Mr. Pim Passes By	1945	12-Mar	The School For Husbands
1944	27-Mar	Someone At The Door	1945	19-Mar	Blithe Spirit
1944	3-Apr	The Queen Was In The Parlour	1945	26-Mar	Blithe Spirit
1944	10-Apr	The Ghost Train	1945	2-Apr	Pride And Prejudice
1944	17-Apr	Jane Eyre	1945	9-Apr	The Man From Toronto
1944	24-Apr	Without The Prince	1945	16-Apr	I Killed The Count
1944	1-May	They Came To A City	1945	23-Apr	Jane Steps Out
1944	8-May	Mrs. Moonlight	1945	30-Apr	This Is My Life
1944	15-May	Watch On The Rhine	1945	7-May	The Rising Generation
1944	22-May	Watch On The Rhine	1945	14-May	Britannia Of Billingsgate
1944	29-May	Busman's Holiday	1945	21-May	Hobson's Choice
1944	5-Jun	Craig's Wife	1945	28-May	The Barretts Of Wimpole Street
1944	12-Jun	Ambrose Applejohn's Adventure	1945	4-Jun	The Barretts Of Wimpole Street
			1945	11-Jun	This Was A Woman
1944	19-Jun	The Truth About Blayds	1945	18-Jun	Wasn't It Odd?
1944	26-Jun	Eliza Comes To Stay	1945	25-Jun	The Cat's Cradle
1944	3-Jul	Heaven And Charing Cross	1945	2-Jul	The Light Of Heart
1944	10-Jul	Lavender Ladies	1945	9-Jul	How Are They At Home?
1944	17-Jul	At Mrs. Beam's	1945	16-Jul	A Hundred Years Old

YEAR	DATE	PLAY TITLE	YEAR	DATE	PLAY TITLE
1945	23-Jul	Glass Houses	1946	22-Jul	The Crime Of Margaret Foley
1945	30-Jul	The Tolerant Husband	1946	29-Jul	The Shining Hour
1945	6-Aug	Kind Lady	1946	5-Aug	Sweet Aloes
1945	13-Aug	Getting Married	1946	12-Aug	If Four Walls Told
1945	20-Aug	Musical Chairs	1946	19-Aug	The Case Of Lady Camber
1945	27-Aug	Pink String And Sealing Wax	1946	26-Aug	After October
1945	3-Sep	Pink String And Sealing Wax	1946	2-Sep	Dangerous Corner
1945	10-Sep	Skylight	1946	9-Sep	Mrs. Dane's Defence
1945	17-Sep	Flare Path	1946	16-Sep	While The Sun Shines
1945	24-Sep	Flare Path	1946	23-Sep	While The Sun Shines
1945	1-Oct	The Chinese Bungalow	1946	30-Sep	No Time For Comedy
1945	8-Oct	Sarah Simple	1946	7-Oct	Portrait In Black
1945	15-Oct	Manor House	1946	14-Oct	I'll See You Again
1945	22-Oct	Ten Little Niggers	1946	21-Oct	Fit For Heroes
1945	29-Oct	Ten Little Niggers	1946	28-Oct	The Silver Cord
1945	5-Nov	Quinneys	1946	4-Nov	The Lady From Edinburgh
1945	12-Nov	The Late Christopher Bean	1946	11-Nov	Granite
1945	19-Nov	Love In A Mist	1946	18-Nov	Frieda
1945	26-Nov	Uncle Harry	1946	25-Nov	George And Margaret
1945	3-Dec	Uncle Harry	1946	2-Dec	George And Margaret
1945	10-Dec	For The Love Of Mike	1946	9-Dec	The Young Mrs. Barrington
1945	17-Dec	A Doll's House	1946	16-Dec	Night Must Fall
1945	26-Dec	Housemaster	1946	26-Dec	Junior Miss
1945	31-Dec	Housemaster	1946	30-Dec	Junior Miss
1946	7-Jan	When We Are Married	1947	6-Jan	The Lady From Edinburgh
1946	14-Jan	Berkeley Square	1947	13-Jan	Tomorrow The World
1946	21-Jan	Love From A Stranger	1947	20-Jan	The Patsy
1946	28-Jan	Great Day	1947	27-Jan	The Hasty Heart
1946	4-Feb	Hay Fever	1947	3-Feb	The Years Between
1946	11-Feb	Othello	1947	10-Feb	The Years Between
1946	18-Feb	Othello	1947	17-Feb	The Hasty Heart
1946	25-Feb	His House In Order	1947	24-Feb	Green Waters
1946	4-Mar	Cock Robin	1947	3-Mar	Murder On The Nile
1946	11-Mar	Fresh Fields	1947	10-Mar	The Barton Mystery
1946	18-Mar	Ladies In Retirement	1947	17-Mar	No Medals
1946	25-Mar	The Marquise	1947	24-Mar	It Depends What You Mean
1946	1-Apr	Living Dangerously	1947	31-Mar	Thunder Rock
1946	8-Apr	Lady-Killer	1947	7-Apr	The Man In Possession
1946	15-Apr	The Widow's Cruise	1947	14-Apr	Anthony And Anna
1946	22-Apr	The Farmer's Wife	1947	21-Apr	The Door Opens
1946	29-Apr	French For Love	1947	28-Apr	Eden End
1946	6-May	Touch Wood	1947	5-May	We Proudly Present
1946	13-May	A Murder Has Been Arranged	1947	12-May	Whiteoaks
1946	20-May	Saint Joan	1947	19-May	To Have The Honour
1946	27-May	Saint Joan	1947	26-May	Barnet's Folly
1946	3-Jun	Murder Without Crime	1947	2-Jun	The Gleam
1946	10-Jun	Quiet Weekend	1947	9-Jun	Shadow And Substance
1946	17-Jun	The Two Mrs. Carrolls	1947	16-Jun	Wuthering Heights
1946	24-Jun	Are You A Mason?	1947	23-Jun	The Family Upstairs
1946	1-Jul	Duet For Two Hands	1947	30-Jun	Dr. Brent's Household
1946	8-Jul	The First Mrs. Fraser	1947	7-Jul	Mr. Bolfry
1946	15-Jul	Lovers Leap	1947	14-Jul	The Torch Bearers

YEAR	DATE	PLAY TITLE	YEAR	DATE	PLAY TITLE
1947	28-Jul	Young Woodley	1948	12-Jul	A Man About The House
1947	4-Aug	Full House	1948	19-Jul	Fifty Fifty
1947	11-Aug	To What Red Hell	1948	26-Jul	To Have And To Hold
1947	18-Aug	Robert's Wife	1948	2-Aug	The Man In Half Moon Street
1947	25-Aug	Fools Rush In	1948	9-Aug	The Distaff Side
1947	1-Sep	French Without Tears	1948	16-Aug	The Last Of Mrs. Cheyney
1947	8-Sep	Power Without Glory	1948	23-Aug	Easy Virtue
1947	15-Sep	See How They Run	1948	30-Aug	And The Music Stopped
1947	22-Sep	See How They Run	1948	6-Sep	Lilies Of The Field
1947	29-Sep	The Sacred Flame	1948	13-Sep	Acacia Avenue
1947	6-Oct	Arsenic And Old Lace	1948	20-Sep	The Corn Is Green
1947	13-Oct	They Walk Alone	1948	27-Sep	Peace Comes To Peckham
1947	20-Oct	Grand National Night	1948	4-Oct	Green Laughter
1947	27-Oct	Arsenic And Old Lace	1948	11-Oct	Children To Bless You
1947	3-Nov	The Cure For Love	1948	18-Oct	To Kill A Cat
1947	10-Nov	The Rossiters	1948	25-Oct	Fly Away Peter
1947	17-Nov	The Poltergeist	1948	1-Nov	The Girl Who Couldn't Quite
1947	24-Nov	And No Birds Sing	1948	8-Nov	The Linden Tree
1947	1-Dec	Love In Idleness	1948	15-Nov	Artificial Silk
1947	8-Dec	Double Door	1948	22-Nov	Present Laughter
1947	15-Dec	Bird In Hand	1948	29-Nov	High Temperature
1947	26-Dec	Is Your Honeymoon Really Necessary?	1948	6-Dec	Craig's Wife
			1948	13-Dec	There's Always Juliet
1947	29-Dec	Is Your Honeymoon Really Necessary?	1948	20-Dec	THEATRE CLOSED ALL WEEK
			1948	27-Dec	Miranda
1948	5-Jan	The Man From The Ministry	1949	3-Jan	Deep Are The Roots
1948	12-Jan	The Winslow Boy	1949	10-Jan	Born Yesterday
1948	19-Jan	The Winslow Boy	1949	17-Jan	Dr. Angelus
1948	26-Jan	Message For Margaret	1949	24-Jan	Life With Father
1948	2-Feb	Laburnum Grove	1949	31-Jan	Old Acquaintance
1948	9-Feb	Dear Murderer	1949	7-Feb	The Paragon
1948	16-Feb	The Ghost Train	1949	14-Feb	Easy Money
1948	23-Feb	Jane	1949	21-Feb	Flat To Let
1948	1-Mar	The Guinea Pig	1949	28-Feb	Trespass
1948	8-Mar	Payment Deferred	1949	7-Mar	While Parents Sleep
1948	15-Mar	She Wanted A Cream Front Door	1949	14-Mar	Dark Summer
1948	22-Mar	The Wind And The Rain	1949	21-Mar	The Lovely Lady
1948	29-Mar	The Shop At Sly Corner	1949	28-Mar	The Governess
1948	5-Apr	The Shop At Sly Corner	1949	4-Apr	The Barking Dog
1948	12-Apr	An Inspector Calls	1949	11-Apr	I Have Been Here Before
1948	19-Apr	Spring Meeting	1949	18-Apr	Don't Listen Ladies
1948	26-Apr	Heaven And Charing Cross	1949	25-Apr	Rain On The Just
1948	3-May	Wishing Well	1949	2-May	Dear Enemy
1948	10-May	Quiet Wedding	1949	9-May	Ever Since Paradise
1948	17-May	Painted Sparrows	1949	16-May	Rebecca
1948	24-May	The Fourth Wall	1949	23-May	The Younger Generation
1948	31-May	To See Ourselves	1949	30-May	They Fly By Twilight
1948	7-Jun	A Play For Ronnie	1949	6-Jun	The Eagle Has Two Heads
1948	14-Jun	The Day Is Gone	1949	13-Jun	Sit Down A Minute Adrian
1948	21-Jun	All Rights Reserved	1949	20-Jun	Gaslight
1948	28-Jun	On Approval	1949	27-Jun	The Dominant Sex
1948	5-Jul	Distinguished Gathering	1949	4-Jul	Sixteen

YEAR	DATE	PLAY TITLE	YEAR	DATE	PLAY TITLE
1949	11-Jul	Nightmare	1950	19-Jun	Other Men's Wives
1949	18-Jul	Canaries Sometimes Sing	1950	26-Jun	Laura
1949	25-Jul	My Mother Said…	1950	3-Jul	School For Spinsters
1949	1-Aug	Little Lambs Eat Ivy	1950	10-Jul	Happy With Either
1949	9-Aug	Two Dozen Red Roses	1950	17-Jul	Anna Christie
1949	16-Aug	Point To Point	1950	24-Jul	Love's A Luxury
1949	22-Aug	Moonlight Is Silver	1950	31-Jul	Cry In The Night
1949	29-Aug	The Days Dividing	1950	7-Aug	On Monday Next
1949	5-Sep	Summer In December	1950	14-Aug	Sweethearts And Wives
1949	12-Sep	Playbill	1950	21-Aug	The Foolish Gentlewoman
1949	12-Sep	The Browning Version	1950	28-Aug	Queen Elizabeth Slept Here
1949	12-Sep	Harlequinade	1950	4-Sep	If This Be Error
1949	19-Sep	The Damask Cheek	1950	11-Sep	Mr. Gillie
1949	26-Sep	Champagne For Delilah	1950	18-Sep	The Third Visitor
1949	3-Oct	The Chiltern Hundreds	1950	25-Sep	A Poor Weak Woman
1949	10-Oct	The Gioconda Smile	1950	2-Oct	Private Lives
1949	17-Oct	Sugar Plum	1950	9-Oct	The School For Scandal
1949	24-Oct	Night Was Our Friend	1950	16-Oct	Background
1949	31-Oct	Jam Today	1950	23-Oct	Castle In The Air
1949	7-Nov	Miss Turner's Husband	1950	30-Oct	Black Chiffon
1949	14-Nov	Miss Mabel	1950	6-Nov	A Lady Mislaid
1949	21-Nov	Mountain Air	1950	13-Nov	By Candlelight
1949	28-Nov	The Voice Of The Turtle	1950	20-Nov	The Heiress
1949	5-Dec	Someone At The Door	1950	27-Nov	We Laugh And Live
1949	12-Dec	The Glass Menagerie	1950	4-Dec	Mrs. Inspector Jones
1949	19-Dec	The Dover Road	1950	11-Dec	Writ For Libel
1949	26-Dec	Off The Record	1950	11-Dec	Writ For Libel
			1950	18-Dec	The Astonished Ostrich
1950	2-Jan	The Happiest Days Of Your Life	1950	26-Dec	Traveller's Joy
1950	9-Jan	The Late Edwina Black	1951	1-Jan	Murder At The Vicarage
1950	16-Jan	Marriage Aforethought	1951	8-Jan	Treasure Hunt
1950	23-Jan	Ann Veronica	1951	15-Jan	Mrs. Warren's Profession
1950	30-Jan	Edward, My Son	1951	22-Jan	Fair Passenger
1950	6-Feb	September Tide	1951	29-Jan	Harvey
1950	13-Feb	Love In Albania	1951	5-Feb	It Won't Be A Stylish Marriage
1950	20-Feb	The Blonde Is Fair	1951	12-Feb	Jupiter Laughs
1950	27-Feb	Little Women	1951	19-Feb	The Constant Wife
1950	6-Mar	Before The Party	1951	26-Feb	Macbeth
1950	13-Mar	Master Of Arts	1951	5-Mar	Springtime For Henry
1950	20-Mar	The Return Of Peggy Atherton	1951	12-Mar	Random Harvest
1950	27-Mar	Wasn't It Odd?	1951	19-Mar	Holiday House
1950	3-Apr	The Mollusc	1951	26-Mar	Accolade
1950	10-Apr	Bright Shadow	1951	2-Apr	Bonaventure
1950	17-Apr	Flowers For the Living	1951	9-Apr	The Anonymous Lover
1950	24-Apr	The Blue Goose	1951	16-Apr	Home At Seven
1950	1-May	Behold We Live	1951	23-Apr	Home And Beauty
1950	8-May	The Perfect Woman	1951	30-Apr	Ten Minute Alibi
1950	15-May	Three Wise Fools	1951	7-May	The Importance Of Being Earnest
1950	22-May	The Light Of Heart	1951	14-May	One Wild Oat
1950	29-May	Black Limelight	1951	21-May	Party Manners
1950	5-Jun	Young Wives' Tale	1951	28-May	Keep It From Dad
1950	12-Jun	The Enchanted Cottage	1951	4-Jun	The Gathering Storm

YEAR	DATE	PLAY TITLE	YEAR	DATE	PLAY TITLE
1951	18-Jun	Cousin Muriel	1952	9-Jun	The Orange Orchard
1951	25-Jun	I'll Leave It To You	1952	16-Jun	Intimate Relations
1951	2-Jul	Cat's Cradle	1952	23-Jun	Who On Earth?
1951	9-Jul	The Long Mirror	1952	30-Jun	Beggar My Neighbour
1951	16-Jul	Why Not Tonight?	1952	7-Jul	THEATRE CLOSED
1951	23-Jul	Wife Of Thy Youth			(Hols. & Renovat.)
1951	30-Jul	Bed Of Roses	1952	14-Jul	TTHEATRE CLOSED
1951	6-Aug	Count Your Blessings			(Hols. & Renovat.)
1951	13-Aug	Actresses Will Happen	1952	21-Jul	THEATRE CLOSED
1951	20-Aug	The Man With A Load Of Mischief			(Hols. & Renovat.)
1951	27-Aug	Lace On Her Petticoat	1952	28-Jul	THEATRE CLOSED
1951	3-Sep	Charley's Aunt			(Hols. & Renovat.)
1951	10-Sep	The Holly And The Ivy	1952	4-Aug	The Hollow
1951	17-Sep	Come Live With Me	1952	11-Aug	The White Sheep Of The Family
1951	24-Sep	Who Is Sylvia?	1952	18-Aug	Intent To Murder
1951	1-Oct	Open Verdict	1952	25-Aug	Navy At Sea
1951	8-Oct	What Anne Brought Home	1952	1-Sep	Pick-Up Girl
1951	15-Oct	Fair And Warmer	1952	8-Sep	Red Letter Day
1951	22-Oct	The Good Young Man	1952	15-Sep	White Cargo
1951	29-Oct	The Seventh Veil	1952	22-Sep	Sweet Madness
1951	5-Nov	Here We Come A-Gathering	1952	29-Sep	Murder In Motley
1951	12-Nov	It's You I Want	1952	6-Oct	After My Fashion
1951	19-Nov	Romeo And Juliet	1952	13-Oct	Separate Rooms
1951	26-Nov	A Pig In A Poke	1952	20-Oct	Ten Men And A Miss
1951	3-Dec	Where Streets Narrow	1952	27-Oct	Madame Tic-Tac
1951	10-Dec	Peg O' My Heart	1952	3-Nov	Of Mice And Men
1951	17-Dec	The Fourposter	1952	10-Nov	Nothing But The Truth
1951	26-Dec	But Once A Year	1952	17-Nov	Alibi
1951	31-Dec	Will Any Gentleman?	1952	24-Nov	Worm's Eye View
			1952	1-Dec	Merely Murder
1952	7-Jan	Black Coffee	1952	8-Dec	Maiden Ladies
1952	14-Jan	The Cocktail Party	1952	15-Dec	Laurey Puppet Company
1952	21-Jan	A Guardsman's Cup Of Tea	1952	15-Dec	The Magic Cupboard
1952	28-Jan	Waggonload Of Monkeys	1952	26-Dec	Rookery Nook
1952	4-Feb	His Excellency	1952	29-Dec	Rookery Nook
1952	11-Feb	The Case Of The Frightened Lady			
			1953	5-Jan	Piccadilly Alibi
1952	18-Feb	To Dorothy, A Son	1953	12-Jan	My Wife's Lodger
1952	25-Feb	A Streetcar Named Desire	1953	19-Jan	Peril At End House
1952	3-Mar	Who Goes There?	1953	26-Jan	Winter Journey
1952	10-Mar	A Priest In The Family	1953	2-Feb	Interference
1952	17-Mar	A Spot Of Bother	1953	9-Feb	Thark
1952	24-Mar	Johnny Belinda	1953	16-Feb	Dead Secret
1952	31-Mar	He Walked In Her Sleep	1953	23-Feb	I'll Paint A Gallows
1952	7-Apr	A Call On The Widow	1953	2-Mar	Twenty To One
1952	14-Apr	Just Married	1953	9-Mar	The Cat And The Canary
1952	21-Apr	The Biggest Thief In Town	1953	16-Mar	The First Year
1952	28-Apr	The Green Pack	1953	23-Mar	Dark Victory
1952	5-May	The Day's Mischief	1953	30-Mar	Sleeping Out
1952	12-May	Caste	1953	6-Apr	Bed, Board And Romance
1952	19-May	Master Crook	1953	13-Apr	The Man
1952	26-May	Smilin' Through	1953	20-Apr	The Man In Grey
1952	2-Jun	On The Spot	1953	27-Apr	The River Line

YEAR	DATE	PLAY TITLE	YEAR	DATE	PLAY TITLE
1953	4-May	The Gift	1954	29-Mar	Chance Of Happiness
1953	11-May	Busman's Honeymoon	1954	5-Apr	Murder Out Of Tune
1953	18-May	A Little Bit Of Fluff	1954	12-Apr	Shadow Of A Man
1953	25-May	The Teddy Bear	1954	19-Apr	Can This Be Love?
1953	1-Jun	Friendly Relations	1954	26-Apr	Trial And Error
1953	8-Jun	Doctor Morelle	1954	3-May	Job For The Boy
1953	15-Jun	Almost A Honeymoon	1954	10-May	Week-End At Woodcote
1953	22-Jun	Petticoat Influence	1954	17-May	The Poor Shadow
1953	29-Jun	TTHEATRE CLOSED (Hols. & Renovat.)	1954	24-May	The Gay Bachelor
			1954	31-May	My Son's Wife
1953	6-Jul	THEATRE CLOSED (Hols. & Renovat.)	1954	7-Jun	The Loving Elms
			1954	14-Jun	Double Event
1953	13-Jul	THEATRE CLOSED (Hols. & Renovat.)	1954	21-Jun	The Dixon Family
			1954	28-Jun	THEATRE CLOSED (Hols. & Renovat.)
1953	20-Jul	THEATRE CLOSED (Hols. & Renovat.)			
			1954	5-Jul	THEATRE CLOSED (Hols. & Renovat.)
1953	27-Jul	THEATRE CLOSED (Hols. & Renovat.)			
			1954	12-Jul	THEATRE CLOSED (Hols. & Renovat.)
1953	3-Aug	Murder Mistaken			
1953	10-Aug	The Deep Blue Sea	1954	19-Jul	THEATRE CLOSED (Hols. & Renovat.)
1953	17-Aug	Wild Horses			
1953	24-Aug	Relative Values	1954	26-Jul	THEATRE CLOSED (Hols. & Renovat.)
1953	31-Aug	Jane Eyre			
1953	7-Sep	Waters Of The Moon	1954	2-Aug	Someone Waiting
1953	14-Sep	Claudia	1954	9-Aug	Dial "M" For Murder
1953	21-Sep	The Happy Prisoner	1954	16-Aug	Royal Enclosure
1953	28-Sep	The Uninvited Guest	1954	23-Aug	Angels In Love
1953	5-Oct	Wuthering Heights	1954	30-Aug	For Better, For Worse
1953	12-Oct	Murder At The Ministry	1954	6-Sep	A Question Of Fact
1953	19-Oct	To Christabel	1954	13-Sep	Escapade
1953	26-Oct	Life Begins At Fifty	1954	20-Sep	Portrait Of A Gentleman
1953	2-Nov	The Haxtons	1954	27-Sep	Birthday Honours
1953	9-Nov	The Mannion Mystery	1954	4-Oct	Dear Charles
1953	16-Nov	Glad Tidings	1954	11-Oct	Recipe For Murder
1953	23-Nov	The Bad Samaritan	1954	18-Oct	Affairs Of State
1953	30-Nov	Crime Don't Pay	1954	25-Oct	The Confidential Clerk
1953	7-Dec	Women Of Twilight	1954	1-Nov	Whiteoaks
1953	14-Dec	Turtle In The Soup	1954	8-Nov	The Merchant Of Venice
1953	26-Dec	Madame Louise	1954	15-Nov	The Sport Of Kings
1953	28-Dec	Madame Louise	1954	22-Nov	We Must Kill Toni
			1954	29-Nov	The Living Room
1954	4-Jan	Trouble At No. 13	1954	6-Dec	The Jovial Parasite
1954	11-Jan	Once A Gentleman	1954	13-Dec	The Circle
1954	18-Jan	Come Back Peter	1954	20-Dec	THEATRE CLOSED (Hols. & Renovat.)
1954	25-Jan	Meet Mr. Callaghan			
1954	1-Feb	The Orchard Walls	1954	27-Dec	As Long As They're Happy
1954	8-Feb	Appointment With Death			
1954	15-Feb	Four Winds	1955	3-Jan	A Day By The Sea
1954	22-Feb	The Gay Dog	1955	10-Jan	Larger Than Life
1954	1-Mar	Tommy	1955	17-Jan	The Archers
1954	8-Mar	Immortal Garden	1955	24-Jan	It's Never Too Late
1954	15-Mar	Full Circle	1955	31-Jan	No Escape
1954	22-Mar	Down Came A Blackbird	1955	7-Feb	I Capture The Castle

YEAR	DATE	PLAY TITLE	YEAR	DATE	PLAY TITLE
1955	14-Feb	Keep In A Cool Place	1956	2-Jan	The Desperate Hours
1955	21-Feb	The Return	1956	9-Jan	No Time For Comedy
1955	28-Feb	The Secret Tent	1956	16-Jan	Double Door
1955	7-Mar	The Eleventh Hour	1956	23-Jan	The Shining Hour
1955	14-Mar	This Was A Woman	1956	30-Jan	My Three Angels
1955	21-Mar	The Pet Shop	1956	6-Feb	Dangerous Corner
1955	28-Mar	Family Affairs	1956	13-Feb	That Woman
1955	4-Apr	Meeting At Night	1956	20-Feb	The Imperfect Gentleman
1955	11-Apr	Seagulls Over Sorrento	1956	27-Feb	The Fourth Wall
1955	18-Apr	Suspended Sentence	1956	5-Mar	Young Mrs. Barrington
1955	25-Apr	Suspect	1956	12-Mar	Murder On The Nile
1955	2-May	It's A Boy	1956	19-Mar	The Sacred Flame
1955	9-May	The Little Foxes	1956	26-Mar	Duet For Two Hands
1955	16-May	The Manor Of Northstead	1956	2-Apr	Reluctant Heroes
1955	23-May	Pitfall	1956	9-Apr	Payment Deferred
1955	30-May	Both Ends Meet	1956	16-Apr	Dead On Nine
1955	6-Jun	The Barton Mystery	1956	23-Apr	Wanted: One Body
1955	13-Jun	The Family Upstairs	1956	30-Apr	Bell, Book And Candle
1955	20-Jun	Grand National Night	1956	7-May	Unseen Among Us
1955	27-Jun	THEATRE CLOSED	1956	14-May	The Shadow Of Doubt
		(Hols. & Renovat.)	1956	21-May	Lucky Strike
1955	4-Jul	THEATRE CLOSED	1956	28-May	Dr. Brent's Household
		(Hols. & Renovat.)	1956	4-Jun	Robert's Wife
1955	11-Jul	THEATRE CLOSED	1956	11-Jun	Tabitha
		(Hols. & Renovat.)	1956	18-Jun	Festival Of Drama
1955	18-Jul	THEATRE CLOSED	1956	18-Jun	Postman's Knock
		(Hols. & Renovat.)	1956	20-Jun	Fresh Fields
1955	25-Jul	THEATRE CLOSED	1956	22-Jun	Anastasia
		(Hols. & Renovat.)	1956	25-Jun	THEATRE CLOSED
1955	1-Aug	Witness For The Prosecution			(Hols. & Renovat.)
1955	8-Aug	Book Of The Month	1956	2-Jul	THEATRE CLOSED
1955	15-Aug	Sabrina Fair			(Hols. & Renovat.)
1955	22-Aug	The Little Hut	1956	9-Jul	THEATRE CLOSED
1955	29-Aug	The Seven Year Itch			(Hols. & Renovat.)
1955	5-Sep	Mother Of Men	1956	16-Jul	THEATRE CLOSED
1955	12-Sep	Beside The Seaside			(Hols. & Renovat.)
1955	19-Sep	Ten Little Niggers	1956	23-Jul	THEATRE CLOSED
1955	26-Sep	Simon And Laura			(Hols. & Renovat.)
1955	3-Oct	The Moon Is Blue	1956	30-Jul	THEATRE CLOSED
1955	10-Oct	The Love Match			(Hols. & Renovat.)
1955	17-Oct	The Dashing White Sergeant	1956	6-Aug	Mrs. Willie
1955	24-Oct	Serious Charge	1956	13-Aug	Ring For Catty
1955	31-Oct	Off The Deep End	1956	20-Aug	Doctor Jo
1955	7-Nov	I Killed The Count	1956	27-Aug	Mr. Kettle And Mrs. Moon
1955	14-Nov	The Bad Seed	1956	3-Sep	Fools Rush In
1955	21-Nov	French For Love	1956	10-Sep	The Happy Marriage
1955	28-Nov	Uncertain Joy	1956	17-Sep	Love From A Stranger
1955	5-Dec	Nest Of Robins	1956	24-Sep	The Lady From Edinburgh
1955	12-Dec	A Dash Of Bitters	1956	1-Oct	Murder When Necessary
1955	19-Dec	THEATRE CLOSED	1956	8-Oct	The Silver Cord
		(Hols. & Renovat.)	1956	15-Oct	Separate Tables
1955	26-Dec	All For Mary	1956	22-Oct	Indoor Fireworks
			1956	29-Oct	Pink String And Sealing Wax

YEAR	DATE	PLAY TITLE	YEAR	DATE	PLAY TITLE
1956	5-Nov	If Four Walls Told	1957	16-Sep	The Rainmaker
1956	12-Nov	The Hypnotist	1957	23-Sep	The Day Nursery
1956	19-Nov	Sweet Aloes	1957	30-Sep	Mrs. Gibbons' Boys
1956	26-Nov	Ladies In Retirement	1957	7-Oct	The Iron Duchess
1956	3-Dec	The Long Echo	1957	14-Oct	Sauce For The Goose
1956	10-Dec	The Green Letter	1957	21-Oct	The Telescope
1956	17-Dec	Message For Margaret	1957	28-Oct	Love On The Never Never
1956	26-Dec	Doctor In The House	1957	4-Nov	The Widower
1956	31-Dec	Doctor In The House	1957	11-Nov	Spring At Marino
			1957	18-Nov	A Murder Has Been Arranged
1957	7-Jan	Granite	1957	25-Nov	The Greatest Ornament
1957	14-Jan	A Yank In Lancashire	1957	2-Dec	They Walk Alone
1957	21-Jan	Night Of The Fourth	1957	9-Dec	Love In Idleness
1957	28-Jan	Fit For Heroes	1957	16-Dec	Murder Without Crime
1957	4-Feb	Lovers Leap	1957	26-Dec	Worm's Eye View
1957	11-Feb	A Likely Tale	1957	30-Dec	Worm's Eye View
1957	18-Feb	Without The Prince			
1957	25-Feb	Meet The Wife	1958	6-Jan	Subway In The Sky
1957	4-Mar	Design For Murder	1958	13-Jan	After October
1957	11-Mar	The Late Christopher Bean	1958	20-Jan	To Settle For Murder
1957	18-Mar	Touch Of Fear	1958	27-Jan	Silver Wedding
1957	25-Mar	South Sea Bubble	1958	3-Feb	Square Pegs
1957	1-Apr	Rebecca	1958	10-Feb	Black Chiffon
1957	8-Apr	The Whole Truth	1958	17-Feb	An Inspector Calls
1957	15-Apr	Who Cares?	1958	24-Feb	House By The Lake
1957	22-Apr	This Happy Home	1958	3-Mar	The Happy Man
1957	29-Apr	Cloud Across The Moon	1958	10-Mar	Summer Of The Seventeenth Doll
1957	6-May	Checkmate	1958	17-Mar	The Vanity Case
1957	13-May	For Pete's Sake	1958	24-Mar	Look Back In Anger
1957	20-May	Double Image	1958	31-Mar	Canaries Sometimes Sing
1957	27-May	Love In A Mist	1958	7-Apr	Towards Zero
1957	3-Jun	Each Wind That Blows	1958	14-Apr	Nude With Violin
1957	10-Jun	Mate In Three	1958	21-Apr	The Late Edwina Black
1957	17-Jun	The Linden Tree	1958	28-Apr	Old Acquaintance
1957	24-Jun	Night Must Fall	1958	5-May	While The Sun Shines
1957	1-Jul	Southgate Theatre Week	1958	12-May	I Have Been Here Before
1957	1-Jul	Little Lambs Eat Ivy	1958	19-May	As It Happened
1957	3-Jul	A Doll's House	1958	26-May	Odd Man In
1957	5-Jul	The Deep Blue Sea	1958	2-Jun	Mr. And Mrs. Bluebeard
1957	8-Jul	TTHEATRE CLOSED	1958	9-Jun	Portrait In Black
		(Hols. & Renovat.)	1958	16-Jun	Private Lives
1957	15-Jul	THEATRE CLOSED	1958	23-Jun	There's Always Juliet
		(Hols. & Renovat.)	1958	30-Jun	Southgate Theatre Week
1957	22-Jul	THEATRE CLOSED	1958	30-Jun	Queen Elizabeth Slept Here
		(Hols. & Renovat.)	1958	2-Jul	The Glass Menagerie
1957	29-Jul	THEATRE CLOSED	1958	4-Jul	Full House
		(Hols. & Renovat.)	1958	7-Jul	THEATRE CLOSED
1957	5-Aug	Spider's Web			(Hols. & Renovat.)
1957	12-Aug	Plaintiff In A Pretty Hat	1958	14-Jul	THEATRE CLOSED
1957	19-Aug	Blind Alley			(Hols. & Renovat.)
1957	26-Aug	The Reluctant Debutante	1958	21-Jul	THEATRE CLOSED
1957	2-Sep	It's The Geography That Counts			(Hols. & Renovat.)
1957	9-Sep	Mona Lisa Smith			

YEAR	DATE	PLAY TITLE	YEAR	DATE	PLAY TITLE
1958	28-Jul	THEATRE CLOSED (Hols. & Renovat.)	1959	13-Jul	THEATRE CLOSED (Hols. & Renovat.)
1958	4-Aug	Dry Rot	1959	20-Jul	THEATRE CLOSED (Hols. & Renovat.)
1958	11-Aug	The Chalk Garden	1959	27-Jul	THEATRE CLOSED (Hols. & Renovat.)
1958	18-Aug	September Tide			
1958	25-Aug	The Waltz Of the Toreadors	1959	3-Aug	Breath Of Spring
1958	1-Sep	Something To Hide	1959	10-Aug	The Unwary
1958	8-Sep	The Bride And The Bachelor	1959	17-Aug	Laura
1958	15-Sep	The Key Of The Door	1959	24-Aug	All My Sons
1958	22-Sep	Saturday Night At The Crown	1959	31-Aug	Murder On Arrival
1958	29-Sep	Laburnum Grove	1959	7-Sep	The Greater Sin
1958	6-Oct	Dear Delinquent	1959	14-Sep	Wolf's Clothing
1958	13-Oct	Yes And No	1959	21-Sep	Hatful Of Rain
1958	20-Oct	Verdict	1959	28-Sep	Fog
1958	27-Oct	The Patsy	1959	5-Oct	To Dorothy, A Son
1958	3-Nov	An Air For Murder	1959	12-Oct	The Long, The Short And The Tall
1958	10-Nov	Variation On A Theme	1959	19-Oct	Friends And Neighbours
1958	17-Nov	Person Unknown	1959	26-Oct	Search By Night
1958	24-Nov	Hippo Dancing	1959	2-Nov	Lace On Her Petticoat
1958	1-Dec	Late Love	1959	9-Nov	Gilt And Gingerbread
1958	8-Dec	They Fly By Twilight	1959	16-Nov	Not In The Book
1958	15-Dec	Springtime For Henry	1959	23-Nov	Prelude To Fury
1958	26-Dec	Sailor Beware	1959	30-Nov	This Modern Generation
1958	29-Dec	Sailor Beware	1959	7-Dec	Love's A Luxury
			1959	14-Dec	The Anonymous Lover
1959	5-Jan	A Touch Of The Sun	1959	26-Dec	Murder At The Vicarage
1959	12-Jan	By A Hand Unknown	1959	28-Dec	Murder At The Vicarage
1959	19-Jan	Harvest In Spring			
1959	26-Jan	The Glass Cage	1960	4-Jan	The French Mistress
1959	2-Feb	Champagne For Breakfast	1960	11-Jan	Out Of Thin Air
1959	9-Feb	A Lady Mislaid	1960	18-Jan	Come Live With Me
1959	16-Feb	The School For Husbands	1960	25-Jan	The Shadow Witness
1959	23-Feb	The Cat's Cradle	1960	1-Feb	By Candlelight
1959	2-Mar	Speaking Of Murder	1960	8-Feb	Home And Away
1959	9-Mar	Plan For A Hostess	1960	15-Feb	Black Coffee
1959	16-Mar	Dear Murderer	1960	22-Feb	Breakout
1959	23-Mar	On Approval	1960	29-Feb	Claudia
1959	30-Mar	Three Way Switch	1960	7-Mar	And This Was Odd
1959	6-Apr	Eden End	1960	14-Mar	The Man
1959	13-Apr	The Governess	1960	21-Mar	Your Obedient Servant
1959	20-Apr	Blithe Spirit	1960	28-Mar	The Sound Of Murder
1959	27-Apr	Gigi	1960	4-Apr	Aunt Edwina
1959	4-May	Indoor Sport	1960	11-Apr	To See Ourselves
1959	11-May	A View From the Bridge	1960	18-Apr	Seagulls Over Sorrento
1959	18-May	The Lovebirds	1960	25-Apr	The Last Word
1959	25-May	The Tunnel Of Love	1960	2-May	The Pleasure Of His Company
1959	1-Jun	The Flowering Cherry	1960	9-May	Fool's Paradise
1959	8-Jun	Man For The Job	1960	16-May	Love Everlasting
1959	15-Jun	The Third Visitor	1960	23-May	Get Away With Murder
1959	22-Jun	Why Not Tonight?	1960	30-May	The Gardener's Cottage
1959	29-Jun	Serious Charge	1960	6-Jun	The Grass Is Greener
1959	6-Jul	THEATRE CLOSED (Hols. & Renovat.)	1960	13-Jun	Guests In The House

YEAR	DATE	PLAY TITLE	YEAR	DATE	PLAY TITLE
1960	20-Jun	The Voice Of The Turtle	1961	22-May	Jane
1960	27-Jun	Madam Tic-Tac	1961	29-May	Unseen Among Us
1960	4-Jul	THEATRE CLOSED	1961	5-Jun	Me And My Girl
		(Hols. & Renovat.)	1961	12-Jun	One More For Dinner
1960	11-Jul	THEATRE CLOSED	1961	19-Jun	Murder Delayed
		(Hols. & Renovat.)	1961	26-Jun	Trial And Error
1960	18-Jul	THEATRE CLOSED	1961	3-Jul	The Corn Is Green
		(Hols. & Renovat.)	1961	10-Jul	THEATRE CLOSED
1960	25-Jul	THEATRE CLOSED			(Hols. & Renovat.)
		(Hols. & Renovat.)	1961	17-Jul	THEATRE CLOSED
1960	1-Aug	The Unexpected Guest			(Hols. & Renovat.)
1960	8-Aug	Roar Like A Dove	1961	24-Jul	THEATRE CLOSED
1960	15-Aug	The Housemaster			(Hols. & Renovat.)
1960	22-Aug	Five-Finger Exercise	1961	31-Jul	THEATRE CLOSED
1960	29-Aug	And Suddenly It's Spring			(Hols. & Renovat.)
1960	5-Sep	Murder At Midnight	1961	7-Aug	Pools Paradise
1960	12-Sep	The More The Merrier	1961	14-Aug	The Bargain
1960	19-Sep	A Clean Kill	1961	21-Aug	Settled Out Of Court
1960	26-Sep	A Shred Of Evidence	1961	28-Aug	Time To Kill
1960	3-Oct	This Thing Called Love	1961	4-Sep	The Nest Egg
1960	10-Oct	The Aspern Papers	1961	11-Sep	Time And Yellow Roses
1960	17-Oct	Hot And Cold In All Rooms	1961	18-Sep	Waiting In The Wings
1960	24-Oct	The Tender Trap	1961	25-Sep	Murder At Quay Cottage
1960	31-Oct	The Ticking Clock	1961	2-Oct	Jane Eyre
1960	7-Nov	Monkey Business	1961	9-Oct	Separate Rooms
1960	14-Nov	Welcome Little Stranger	1961	16-Oct	The Tiger And The Horse
1960	21-Nov	Hot And Cold In All Rooms	1961	23-Oct	The Hollow
1960	28-Nov	Week-End At Woodcote	1961	30-Oct	Come Back Peter
1960	5-Dec	Pot Luck	1961	6-Nov	The Closing Net
1960	12-Dec	The Paper Chain	1961	13-Nov	It Won't Be A Stylish Marriage
1960	19-Dec	Four In Hand	1961	20-Nov	Black Limelight
1960	26-Dec	Six Of The Best	1961	27-Nov	Wuthering Heights
			1961	4-Dec	The Chinese Bungalow
1961	2-Jan	Go Back For Murder	1961	11-Dec	The Astonished Ostrich
1961	9-Jan	A Taste Of Honey	1961	18-Dec	Cup And Saucer
1961	16-Jan	Keeping Up With The Joneses	1961	26-Dec	Simple Spymen
1961	23-Jan	This House Is Dark			
1961	30-Jan	Honey Pot	1962	1-Jan	Witness For The Prosecution
1961	6-Feb	Hot And Cold In All Rooms	1962	8-Jan	Watch It Sailor
1961	13-Feb	Bus Stop	1962	15-Jan	Murder To Boot
1961	20-Feb	Over The Odds	1962	22-Jan	My Wife's Lodger
1961	27-Feb	Ten Minute Alibi	1962	29-Jan	The Marriage Go Round
1961	6-Mar	Mice Will Play	1962	5-Feb	While Parents Sleep
1961	13-Mar	Sailor Beware	1962	12-Feb	The T.V. Murders
1961	20-Mar	Cousin Muriel	1962	19-Feb	Little Women
1961	27-Mar	Dead Secret	1962	26-Feb	Larger Than Life
1961	3-Apr	Love On The Never Never	1962	5-Mar	Two Faces Of Murder
1961	10-Apr	S' For Scandal	1962	12-Mar	Hot Summer Night
1961	17-Apr	I Met Murder	1962	19-Mar	Someone Waiting
1961	24-Apr	Gigi	1962	26-Mar	Jane Steps Out
1961	1-May	Power Without Glory	1962	2-Apr	Green Solitaire
1961	8-May	The Geese Are Getting Fat	1962	9-Apr	Billy Liar
1961	15-May	The Reluctant Debutante	1962	16-Apr	Odd Man In

YEAR	DATE	PLAY TITLE	YEAR	DATE	PLAY TITLE
1962	23-Apr	Towards Zero	1963	18-Feb	Distinguished Gathering
1962	30-Apr	The Irregular Verb To Love	1963	25-Feb	Young Wives' Tale
1962	7-May	Don't Tell Father	1963	4-Mar	Kill Two Birds
1962	14-May	Off The Camden Road	1963	11-Mar	Plaintiff In A Pretty Hat
1962	21-May	After My Fashion	1963	18-Mar	Roar Like A Dove
1962	28-May	A Shadow Of Doubt	1963	25-Mar	Miss Pell Is Missing
1962	4-Jun	The Caretaker	1963	1-Apr	Hot And Cold In All Rooms
1962	11-Jun	The Gazebo	1963	8-Apr	Message For Margaret
1962	18-Jun	Casanova's Pyjamas	1963	15-Apr	Policy For Murder
1962	25-Jun	Dead On Time	1963	22-Apr	Dear Delinquent
1962	2-Jul	Ladies In Retirement	1963	29-Apr	The Uninvited Guest
1962	9-Jul	THEATRE CLOSED	1963	6-May	The Final Twist
		(Hols. & Renovat.)	1963	13-May	Down Came A Blackbird
1962	16-Jul	TTHEATRE CLOSED	1963	20-May	Semi-Detached
		(Hols. & Renovat.)	1963	27-May	The Good Young Man
1962	23-Jul	THEATRE CLOSED	1963	3-Jun	Muder On The Nile
		(Hols. & Renovat.)	1963	10-Jun	Sauce For The Goose
1962	30-Jul	THEATRE CLOSED	1963	17-Jun	A Call On The Widow
		(Hols. & Renovat.)	1963	24-Jun	All My Sons
1962	6-Aug	The Amorous Prawn	1963	1-Jul	The Sleeping Prince
1962	13-Aug	Doctor At Sea	1963	8-Jul	THEATRE CLOSED
1962	20-Aug	The Big Killing			(Hols. & Renovat.)
1962	27-Aug	Dr. Brent's Household	1963	15-Jul	THEATRE CLOSED
1962	3-Sep	Guilty Party			(Hols. & Renovat.)
1962	10-Sep	Port In A Storm	1963	22-Jul	THEATRE CLOSED
1962	17-Sep	Ma's Bit Of Brass			(Hols. & Renovat.)
1962	24-Sep	Payment Deferred	1963	29-Jul	THEATRE CLOSED
1962	1-Oct	The Brontes Of Haworth			(Hols. & Renovat.)
		Parsonage	1963	5-Aug	Signpost To Murder
1962	9-Oct	Fallen Angels	1963	12-Aug	Goodnight Mrs. Puffin
1962	15-Oct	Write Me A Murder	1963	19-Aug	Shot In The Dark
1962	22-Oct	The Light Of Heart	1963	26-Aug	A Grave Situation
1962	29-Oct	Two Stars For Comfort	1963	2-Sep	The Bride Comes Back
1962	5-Nov	The Proof Of The Poison	1963	9-Sep	Trap For A Lonely Man
1962	12-Nov	The Family Upstairs	1963	16-Sep	My Wife's Uncle
1962	19-Nov	Matilda Shouted Fire	1963	23-Sep	Spider's Web
1962	26-Nov	Happy The Bride	1963	30-Sep	Both Ends Meet
1962	3-Dec	Don't Listen Ladies	1963	7-Oct	The Late Edwina Black
1962	10-Dec	The Magic Cupboard	1963	14-Oct	How Are You Johnnie?
1962	17-Dec	Chin-Chin	1963	21-Oct	Craig's Wife
1962	26-Dec	Rock-A-Bye Sailor	1963	28-Oct	Smilin' Through
1962	31-Dec	Love From A Stranger	1963	4-Nov	The Shot In Question
			1963	11-Nov	The Private Ear & The Public Eye
1963	7-Jan	Joy Of Living	1963	18-Nov	The House By The Lake
1963	14-Jan	Murder By All Means	1963	25-Nov	Affairs Of State
1963	21-Jan	All For Mary	1963	2-Dec	Pitfall
1963	28-Jan	THEATRE CLOSED	1963	9-Dec	Bell, Book And Candle
		(Bad Weather)	1963	16-Dec	We Must Kill Toni
1963	4-Feb	THEATRE CLOSED	1963	26-Dec	Murder At The Vicarage
		(Bad Weather)	1963	30-Dec	Rattle Of A Simple Man
1963	11-Feb	TTHEATRE CLOSED			
		(Bad Weather)	1964	6-Jan	Suspect
			1964	13-Jan	Birthday Honours

182

YEAR	DATE	PLAY TITLE	YEAR	DATE	PLAY TITLE
1964	20-Jan	He Who Murders	1964	28-Dec	One For The Pot
1964	27-Jan	Fools Rush In			
1964	3-Feb	Double Trouble	1965	4-Jan	To Kill A Cat
1964	10-Feb	Portrait Of Murder	1965	11-Jan	Ring For Catty
1964	17-Feb	Cornelia	1965	18-Jan	The Willing Horse
1964	24-Feb	House On the Cliff	1965	25-Jan	Nightmare
1964	2-Mar	The Boundary	1965	1-Feb	Olde Tyme Music Hall
1964	9-Mar	Key Witness	1965	8-Feb	Ordeal By Fire
1964	16-Mar	Who Goes There?	1965	15-Feb	Dodo In Love
1964	23-Mar	Four In Hand	1965	22-Feb	I Am A Camera
1964	30-Mar	No Time For Love	1965	1-Mar	Caroline
1964	6-Apr	Verdict	1965	8-Mar	Month Of Sundays
1964	13-Apr	Come Blow Your Horn	1965	15-Mar	Something To Hide
1964	20-Apr	The Guilty One	1965	22-Mar	The Intimate Revue
1964	27-Apr	Make It A Party	1965	29-Mar	Murder On Arrival
1964	4-May	Mary, Mary	1965	5-Apr	Springtime For Henry
1964	11-May	See How They Run	1965	12-Apr	The Sable Coat
1964	18-May	This Happy Home	1965	19-Apr	And Sat Down Beside Her
1964	25-May	Time To Speak	1965	26-Apr	A Man About The House
1964	1-Jun	Six Of The Best	1965	3-May	Dead On Nine
1964	8-Jun	Private Lives	1965	10-May	To Have And To Hold
1964	15-Jun	Lovers Leap	1965	17-May	To Settle For Murder
1964	22-Jun	The Heiress	1965	24-May	Old Time Music Hall
1964	29-Jun	Simon And Laura	1965	31-May	Return Ticket
1964	6-Jul	THEATRE CLOSED	1965	7-Jun	Love Locked Out
		(Hols. & Renovat.)	1965	14-Jun	Murder Without Crime
1964	13-Jul	THEATRE CLOSED	1965	21-Jun	Stranger In My Bed
		(Hols. & Renovat.)	1965	28-Jun	The Happiest Days Of
1964	20-Jul	THEATRE CLOSED			Your Life
		(Hols. & Renovat.)	1965	5-Jul	The Big Knife
1964	27-Jul	THEATRE CLOSED	1965	8-Jul	A Letter from the General
		(Hols. & Renovat.)	1965	12-Jul	THEATRE CLOSED
1964	3-Aug	The Unexpected Guest			(Hols. & Renovat.)
1964	10-Aug	Two Dozen Red Roses	1965	19-Jul	THEATRE CLOSED
1964	17-Aug	By Who's Hand?			(Hols. & Renovat.)
1964	24-Aug	Dear Charles	1965	26-Jul	THEATRE CLOSED
1964	31-Aug	Amber For Anna			(Hols. & Renovat.)
1964	7-Sep	Woman In A Dressing Gown	1965	2-Aug	THEATRE CLOSED
1964	14-Sep	Open To Murder			(Hols. & Renovat.)
1964	21-Sep	The Lodger	1965	9-Aug	Busybody
1964	28-Sep	The Fifty Mark	1965	16-Aug	The Reluctant Peer
1964	5-Oct	Make Me A Widow	1965	23-Aug	Person Unknown
1964	12-Oct	Foursome Reel	1965	30-Aug	A Public Mischief
1964	19-Oct	The Wings Of the Dove	1965	6-Sep	The Coburn Affair
1964	26-Oct	The Hot Tiara	1965	13-Sep	It's A Wise Child
1964	2-Nov	The Secret Tent	1965	20-Sep	Old Time Music Hall
1964	9-Nov	Never Too Late	1965	27-Sep	Old Time Music Hall
1964	16-Nov	Peril At End House	1965	4-Oct	Deadly Record
1964	23-Nov	Brush With A Body	1965	11-Oct	Haul For The Shore
1964	30-Nov	Night Was Our Friend	1965	18-Oct	The Late Christopher Bean
1964	7-Dec	Half Seas Over	1965	25-Oct	Counterfeit Murder
1964	14-Dec	Middle Of The Night	1965	1-Nov	I Found April
1964	26-Dec	One For The Pot	1965	8-Nov	Crime At 'The Donkey'

YEAR	DATE	PLAY TITLE	YEAR	DATE	PLAY TITLE
1965	22-Nov	Inquest On A Lady	1966	17-Oct	A Song At Twilight
1965	29-Nov	Stop The World - I Want	1966	24-Oct	The Music Hall
		To Get Off	1966	31-Oct	The Boy Friend
1965	6-Dec	Norman	1966	7-Nov	The Boy Friend
1965	13-Dec	Investigation	1966	14-Nov	A Man For All Seasons
1965	20-Dec	Cinderella	1966	21-Nov	The Man Outside
1965	27-Dec	Cinderella	1966	28-Nov	A Friend Indeed
			1966	5-Dec	The Rape Of the Belt
1966	3-Jan	Cinderella	1966	12-Dec	The Snow Queen
1966	10-Jan	The Long Weekend	1966	19-Dec	THEATRE CLOSED
1966	17-Jan	A Basinful Of The Briny	1966	26-Dec	Dick Whittington
1966	24-Jan	You Touched Me			
1966	31-Jan	Green Waters	1967	2-Jan	Dick Whittington
1966	7-Feb	A Whiskey Business	1967	9-Jan	Dick Whittington
1966	14-Feb	The Man With Red Hair	1967	16-Jan	Ask Me Tomorrow
1966	21-Feb	The Poker Session	1967	23-Jan	Black Coffee
1966	28-Feb	So Many Children	1967	30-Jan	Barefoot In The Park
1966	7-Mar	Pillar To Post	1967	6-Feb	Jane Eyre
1966	14-Mar	The Good Die Young	1967	13-Feb	Loving Uncle
1966	21-Mar	Cabinet Shuffle	1967	20-Feb	Intimate Theatre Music Hall
1966	28-Mar	Twinkling Of An Eye	1967	27-Feb	The Anniversary
1966	4-Apr	A Woman's Place	1967	6-Mar	The Importance Of
1966	11-Apr	Pyjama Tops			Being Earnest
1966	18-Apr	Old Time Variety	1967	13-Mar	The Home Front
1966	25-Apr	Just The Ticket	1967	20-Mar	The Killing Of Sister George
1966	2-May	Murder For The Asking	1967	27-Mar	Chase Me, Comrade
1966	9-May	The Paper Hat	1967	3-Apr	How's The World Treating You?
1966	16-May	Good Old Summertime	1967	10-Apr	A Sense Of Guilt
1966	23-May	The Heat Of The Moment	1967	17-Apr	Salad Days
1966	30-May	Alibi	1967	24-Apr	Salad Days
1966	6-Jun	Pinch And Run	1967	1-May	Salad Days
1966	13-Jun	The Touch Of Fear	1967	9-May	Boeing-Boeing
1966	20-Jun	This Year, Next Year	1967	15-May	Boeing-Boeing
1966	27-Jun	Out Of The Crocodile	1967	22-May	Boeing-Boeing
1966	4-Jul	The Waltz Of The Toreadors	1967	30-May	Outward Bound
1966	11-Jul	Pink String And Sealing Wax	1967	5-Jun	Outward Bound
1966	18-Jul	THEATRE CLOSED	1967	12-Jun	Outward Bound
		(Hols. & Renovat.)	1967	19-Jun	THEATRE CLOSED
1966	25-Jul	THEATRE CLOSED			(Hols. & Renovat.)
		(Hols. & Renovat.)	1967	26-Jun	THEATRE CLOSED
1966	1-Aug	THEATRE CLOSED			(Hols. & Renovat.)
		(Hols. & Renovat.)	1967	3-Jul	THEATRE CLOSED
1966	8-Aug	Old Time Music Hall			(Hols. & Renovat.)
1966	15-Aug	Murder After Hours	1967	10-Jul	THEATRE CLOSED
1966	22-Aug	Breakfast In Bed			(Hols. & Renovat.)
1966	29-Aug	The Right Honourable Gentleman	1967	17-Jul	THEATRE CLOSED
1966	5-Sep	The Peacocks Must Go			(Hols. & Renovat.)
1966	12-Sep	The Case Against Mrs. Dane	1967	24-Jul	THEATRE CLOSED
1966	19-Sep	The First Mrs. Fraser			(Hols. & Renovat.)
1966	26-Sep	The Lady's Not For Burning	1967	31-Jul	THEATRE CLOSED
1966	3-Oct	Shadows Of The Evening			(Hols. & Renovat.)
1966	3-Oct	Come Into The Garden, Maud	1967	7-Aug	THEATRE CLOSED
1966	10-Oct	Arms And The Man			(Hols. & Renovat.)

YEAR	DATE	PLAY TITLE	YEAR	DATE	PLAY TITLE
1967	14-Aug	THEATRE CLOSED (Hols. & Renovat.)	1968	15-Jul	THEATRE CLOSED (Hols. & Renovat.)
1967	26-Aug	A Midsummer Night's Dream	1968	22-Jul	THEATRE CLOSED (Hols. & Renovat.)
1967	28-Aug	A Midsummer Night's Dream	1968	29-Jul	THEATRE CLOSED (Hols. & Renovat.)
1967	4-Sep	A Midsummer Night's Dream			
1967	12-Sep	Candida	1968	5-Aug	THEATRE CLOSED (Hols. & Renovat.)
1967	18-Sep	Candida			
1967	26-Sep	Lord Arthur Savile's Crime	1968	14-Aug	Man With A Load Of Mischief
1967	2-Oct	Lord Arthur Savile's Crime	1968	19-Aug	Man With A Load Of Mischief
1967	10-Oct	Odd Man In	1968	26-Aug	Man With A Load Of Mischief
1967	16-Oct	Odd Man In	1968	2-Sep	Man With A Load Of Mischief
1967	24-Oct	Gaslight	1968	10-Sep	Relatively Speaking
1967	30-Oct	Gaslight	1968	16-Sep	Relatively Speaking
1967	7-Nov	The Ghost Train	1968	24-Sep	Out Of Order
1967	13-Nov	The Ghost Train	1968	30-Sep	Out Of Order
1967	21-Nov	Wuthering Heights	1968	8-Oct	Wait Until Dark
1967	27-Nov	Wuthering Heights	1968	14-Oct	Wait Until Dark
1967	5-Dec	Dial M For Muder	1968	22-Oct	Ten Little Niggers
1967	11-Dec	Dial M For Muder	1968	28-Oct	Ten Little Niggers
1967	18-Dec	Old Time Music Hall	1968	5-Nov	Upper Crust
1967	26-Dec	Mother Goose	1968	11-Nov	Upper Crust
			1968	18-Nov	Upper Crust
1968	1-Jan	Mother Goose	1968	26-Nov	Alfie
1968	9-Jan	Beyond The Fringe	1968	2-Dec	Alfie
1968	15-Jan	Beyond The Fringe	1968	10-Dec	Angie And Ernie
1968	23-Jan	Tons Of Money	1968	16-Dec	Angie And Ernie
1968	29-Jan	Tons Of Money	1968	24-Dec	Where The Rainbow Ends
1968	6-Feb	The Lodger	1968	30-Dec	Where The Rainbow Ends
1968	12-Feb	The Lodger			
1968	20-Feb	Emma	1969	6-Jan	Where The Rainbow Ends
1968	26-Feb	Emma	1969	13-Jan	Where The Rainbow Ends
1968	5-Mar	The Amazing Fogel	1969	20-Jan	Where The Rainbow Ends
1968	11-Mar	The Amazing Fogel	1969	28-Jan	Together We Did It!
1968	18-Mar	Southgate Drama Festival	1969	3-Feb	Together We Did It!
1968	26-Mar	Pierrot In Turquoise	1969	11-Feb	Faithful In My Fashion
1968	1-Apr	Say Who You Are	1969	17-Feb	Faithful In My Fashion
1968	8-Apr	Love In A Mist	1969	25-Feb	Collapse Of Stout Party
1968	15-Apr	Up The Garden Path	1969	3-Mar	Collapse Of Stout Party
1968	22-Apr	Old Time Music Hall	1969	10-Mar	Southgate Drama Festival
1968	29-Apr	Get Away With Murder	1969	18-Mar	Music Hall At The Intimate
1968	6-May	The Devil Was Sick	1969	24-Mar	Music Hall At The Intimate
1968	13-May	Minor Murder	1969	3-Apr	Brer Rabbit And Uncle Remus
1968	20-May	Nude With Violin	1969	7-Apr	Brer Rabbit And Uncle Remus
1968	23-May	Doctor In The House	1969	14-Apr	Brer Rabbit And Uncle Remus
1968	27-May	The Odd Couple	1969	22-Apr	Absente Rea
1968	3-Jun	Go Back For Murder	1969	22-Apr	A Game Of Chess
1968	10-Jun	Hot And Cold In All Rooms	1969	29-Apr	Forever April
1968	17-Jun	Let's All Go Down The Strand	1969	5-May	Forever April
1968	24-Jun	The Seventh Veil	1969	13-May	Hugo
1968	1-Jul	THEATRE CLOSED (Hols. & Renovat.)	1969	19-May	Hugo
1968	8-Jul	THEATRE CLOSED (Hols. & Renovat.)	1969	26-May	Arsenic And Old Lace
			1969	2-Jun	See How They Run

YEAR	DATE	PLAY TITLE	YEAR	DATE	PLAY TITLE
1969	9-Jun	Spider's Web	1974	21-Dec	Cinderella
1969	16-Jun	Palace Of Varieties	1974	23-Dec	Cinderella
1969	23-Jun	Palace Of Varieties	1974	30-Dec	Cinderella
1969	30-Jun	THEATRE CLOSED			
1969	7-Jul	The Anniversary	1975	6-Jan	Cinderella
1969	10-Jul	Intent To Murder	1975	6-Jan	Palace of Varieties
1969	17-Jul	Pygmalion	1975	20-Dec	Snow White And The Seven Dwarfs
1969	21-Jul	THEATRE CLOSED			
1969	28-Jul	THEATRE CLOSED	1975	22-Dec	Snow White And The Seven Dwarfs
1969	4-Aug	THEATRE CLOSED			
1969	11-Aug	THEATRE CLOSED	1975	29-Dec	Snow White And The Seven Dwarfs
1969	18-Aug	THEATRE CLOSED			
1969	25-Aug	THEATRE CLOSED			
1969	1-Sep	THEATRE CLOSED	1976	5-Jan	Snow White And The Seven Dwarfs
1969	8-Sep	THEATRE CLOSED			
1969	15-Sep	THEATRE CLOSED	1976	20-Dec	Jack And The Beanstalk
1969	22-Sep	THEATRE CLOSED	1976	21-Dec	An Evening Of Memories
1969	29-Sep	THEATRE CLOSED	1976	27-Dec	Jack And The Beanstalk
1969	6-Oct	THEATRE CLOSED	1976	27-Dec	An Evening Of Memories
1969	13-Oct	THEATRE CLOSED			
1969	20-Oct	THEATRE CLOSED	1977	3-Jan	Jack And The Beanstalk
1969	27-Oct	THEATRE CLOSED	1977	10-Jan	Jack And The Beanstalk
1969	3-Nov	THEATRE CLOSED	1977	21-Dec	Cinderella
1969	10-Nov	THEATRE CLOSED	1977	26-Dec	Cinderella
1969	17-Nov	THEATRE CLOSED			
1969	24-Nov	THEATRE CLOSED	1978	2-Jan	Cinderella
1969	1-Dec	THEATRE CLOSED	1978	9-Jan	Cinderella
1969	8-Dec	THEATRE CLOSED	1978	16-Jan	Cinderella
1969	15-Dec	THEATRE CLOSED	1978	21-Dec	Humpty Dumpty
1969	24-Dec	Cinderella	1978	26-Dec	Humpty Dumpty
1969	29-Dec	Cinderella			
			1979	1-Jan	Humpty Dumpty
1970	5-Jan	Cinderella	1979	8-Jan	Humpty Dumpty
1970	12-Jan	Cinderella	1979	15-Jan	Humpty Dumpty
1970	24-Dec	Mother Goose	1979	12-Nov	A Christmas Carol
1970	28-Dec	Mother Goose	1979	20-Dec	Robinson Crusoe
			1979	24-Dec	Robinson Crusoe
1971	4-Jan	Mother Goose	1979	31-Dec	Robinson Crusoe
1971	3-Jun	Olde Tyme Music Hall	1979	7-Jan	Robinson Crusoe
1971	2-Sep	Olde Tyme Music Hall	1979	14-Jan	Robinson Crusoe
1971	26-Dec	Babes In The Wood			
1971	2-Jan	Babes In The Wood	1980	22-Dec	Mother Goose
1971	9-Jan	Babes In The Wood	1980	29-Dec	Mother Goose
1972	7-Sep	Olde Tyme Music Hall	1981	5-Jan	Mother Goose
1972	26-Dec	Aladdin	1981	12-Jan	Mother Goose
			1981	16-Jun	In The Palm Of her Hand
1973	1-Jan	Aladdin	1981	22-Jun	In The Palm Of her Hand
1973	8-Jan	Aladdin	1981	30-Jun	Double Exposure
1973	6-Sep	Old Tyme Music Hall	1981	6-Jul	Double Exposure
1973	26-Dec	Dick Whittington	1981	22-Sep	The Taming Of The Shrew
1973	31-Dec	Dick Whittington	1981	28-Sep	The Taming Of The Shrew
1974	7-Jan	Dick Whittington	1981	21-Dec	Dick Whittington

YEAR	DATE	PLAY TITLE	YEAR	DATE	PLAY TITLE
1981	28-Dec	Dick Whittington	1984	31-Dec	Aladdin
1981	4-Jan	Dick Whittington			
1981	11-Jan	Dick Whittington	1985	7-Jan	Aladdin
			1985	6-Feb	Let's All Go To The Music Hall
1982	29-Mar	Public Relations	1985	18-Feb	Murder By The Book
1982	5-Apr	Public Relations	1985	27-Feb	The Pilgrim's Progress
1982	17-May	Private Lives	1985	19-Dec	Snow White And The Seven Dwarfs
1982	24-May	Private Lives			
1982	28-Jun	Wait Until Dark	1985	23-Dec	Snow White And The Seven Dwarfs
1982	5-Jul	Echo Of Murder			
1982	20-Dec	Jack And The Beanstalk	1985	30-Dec	Snow White And The Seven Dwarfs
1982	27-Dec	Jack And The Beanstalk			
			1986	6-Jan	Snow White And The Seven Dwarfs
1983	3-Jan	Jack And The Beanstalk			
1983	10-Jan	Jack And The Beanstalk	1986	13-Jan	Snow White And The Seven Dwarfs
1983	14-Feb	Gaslight			
1983	28-Feb	Don't Start Without Me	1986	27-Nov	Comedy Break
1983	19-Dec	Cinderella	1986	18-Dec	Cinderella
1983	26-Dec	Cinderella	1986	22-Dec	Cinderella
			1986	29-Dec	Cinderella
1984	2-Jan	Cinderella			
1984	9-Jan	Cinderella	1987	5-Jan	Cinderella
1984	10-Jul	Murder Is Child's Play	1987	12-Jan	Cinderella
1984	17-Jul	Hoagy Carmichael & The Songwriters	1987	17-Dec	Jack And The Beanstalk
			1987	21-Dec	Jack And The Beanstalk
1984	24-Jul	Champagne Charlie: George Leybourne	1987	28-Dec	Jack And The Beanstalk
1984	3-Sep	Leonardo: The Musical	1988	4-Jan	Jack And The Beanstalk
1984	10-Sep	Leonardo: The Musical	1988	11-Jan	Jack And The Beanstalk
1984	17-Dec	Aladdin			
1984	24-Dec	Aladdin			

INDEX

Pages shown in **_bold italics_** indicates an illustration

Also published by The Badger Press

"No Sails on Huttoft Mill" by J. O. Blake (out of print)
"A Glossary of Terms used in Variety, Vaudeville and Pantomime" by Valantyne Napier
"Laughter in the Roar" by Brian O'Gorman (available from the author)
"The Lost Theatres of Dublin" by Philip B. Ryan
"Bristol's Forgotten Empire" by Terry Hallett
"Coventry's Forgotten Theatre" (The Theatre Royal & Empire) by Ted Bottle

In preparation:
"Variety at Night is Good for You" by J. O. Blake
  One hundred London Variety Theatres remembered by a compulsive theatre-goer;
  profusely illustrated in line-and-wash by Nicholas Charlesworth, together with bills and
  programmes from each theatre. Edited by David F. Cheshire

Publishers of Theatrical Postcards, Books, Greeting Cards and Notelets

Lists sent on request

THE BADGER PRESS
Westbury, Wiltshire BA13 4DU
www.vaudeville-postcards.com
email: nc@vaudeville-postcards.com